PEOPLE OF COLOUR AND THE ROYALS

LADY COLIN CAMPBELL

Dynasty
Press

Dynasty Press

Dynasty Press Limited
36 Ravensdon Street
London SE11 4AR
www.dynastypress.co.uk

First published in this version by Dynasty Press Ltd.

ISBN: 978-1-9161317-0-5

Typeset by Biddles Books Ltd., Castle House, East Winch Road,
Blackborough End, King's Lynn, Norfolk PE32 1SF

Cover Design by Rupert Dixon

Printed and bound in the United Kingdom

Dedication

TO MY BELOVED SONS
Dima and Misha.

Contents

Chapter One

PEOPLE OF COLOUR and the royals might be a hot topic that is popularly believed to be a recent phenomenon because of Meghan Markle's inclusion in the British Royal Family, but any informed examination of the subject demonstrates that in fact the reality is far more nuanced than that. Without going into the numerous royal men who have married women of colour in the last quarter of the twentieth century, there were previously women of colour who married into our Royal Family, as well as into some of the other European royal families, from which the British Royal Family descends or with which it is intermarried. Our royals therefore have a rather more mixed heritage than is popularly supposed, and at the moment several members of the European royal families, including the British, have surprising dashes of colour. It would therefore be fair to say that the royals have kept pace, where exotic heritages are concerned, with the inclusiveness that has been demonstrated by the more liberal segments of the European population whose identity has undergone a sea change since the Sexual Revolution of the 1960s and the advent of Flower Power and Peace and Love. The purity of line of a significant percentage of European royals is therefore more illusory than real, and the presence of what used to be called 'a touch of the tar brush' makes them more representative of the multi-cultural, multi-racial world that Western Society has become than has hitherto been realised. That is truer of them than most aristocratic or middle class families, who are systematically less racially mixed.

In the world today, racial purity is fast becoming as much of an irrelevancy as it was in the centuries before racial prejudice gained the ascendancy it did in the nineteenth and twentieth centuries, for, make no mistake about it, the concept of racial purity, and its corollary, racial impurity, have, historically, been the oddities, while racial inclusiveness has been the hallmark of Western Civilisation for much of its existence. But for the limited span of a century, during which racial prejudice became an ascendant principle, and the half century either side of it where it gained and lost traction, racism has been an aberration rather than the rule, and it is interesting, as we re-enter a more enlightened period, to see how quickly Western Society has reverted to its unprejudiced acceptance of racial inclusiveness.

It is hardly surprising that racism gained the acceptance that it did. The role of race in Western Society is, and always was, a reflection of larger issues which were taking place in society as a whole at any one time. Racial prejudice did not spring out of nowhere. It came about as a result of the conflicts which were driving us from a non-racially prejudiced, feudal and agrarian society to a racially-prejudiced urban and industrialised society. The peak of prejudice can be fairly said to have taken place from the mid-nineteenth to the mid-twentieth centuries, with incremental periods of fifty or sixty years on either side.

The birth of racial prejudice coincided with the ascendancy of the sugar-producing West Indian colonies. Sugar was the gold of its day, to such an extent that when England lost the American War of Independence, Lord North, the Prime Minister, consoled himself and the king with the statement that it didn't matter so much, for they still had Jamaica. More valuable than the whole thirteen colonies of North America was little Jamaica, with its contribution to the British economy from sugar being some five times the value of the lost colonies. So rich was Jamaica and Jamaicans that Charlotte Bronte only had to describe mad Mrs Rochester in Jane Eyre as 'a Jamaican heiress' to conjure up an image of wealth beyond imagination. Jamaican planters were, at that time, the equivalent of what technological billionaires are to us and what the Maharajahs were to our grandparents. Unlike the Mark Zuckerbergs, Steve Jobses and Bill Gateses of today, however, with their deeply unglamorous, dressed down personae and their extravagant wealth hidden behind facades that are more evocative of hippies than potentates, Jamaican planters were like the Indian princes, residing in luxurious residences, travelling in magnificent carriages, arrayed in gorgeous raiments, with armies of servants and servitors in sumptuous livery. They were splendid creatures in a day and age when splendour was a bye-word for a world that only the privileged few could inhabit, when the poor could only gape at such wealth. No one in the eighteenth century hid their wealth or dressed down. Everything about the rich bespoke their wealth, just as how everything about the poor demonstrated their poverty.

The eighteenth century was not only a period of great and obvious disparities between the classes, but also the period when The Age of Reason came into being. The Enlightenment opened up many previously unconsidered vistas intellectually. For the first time in over a thousand years, educated people began to question the values and tenets not only of society generally, but the very basis upon which civilised societies rested. Was there a God? Was He a benevolent entity? What was the nature of the soul? As scientific knowledge and discoveries increased, the very role of Science versus Belief became an issue. What was the meaning of life?

Alongside this intellectual awakening was an appreciation of the pleasures of life. Art, music, history, interior decoration, good conversation, erudition, development of the person in ways and means that would have been unthinkable a hundred years previously, when knowledge was less treasured and soldiering was far more important than it was to the eighteenth century ruling classes, resulted in a flowering of civilisation that quickly became known as the Enlightenment. Good living had come into being in a way that had not been known since the Ancient Romans and the Byzantines had flourished. Status symbols, of course, had always existed, in their various forms depending upon which society one lived in, and exotica had always been highly prized, but now, these symbols of privilege, of civility, of enlightenment, increased along with an expanding and increasingly wealthy class.

One status symbol which proliferated amongst the upper reaches of society during the Age of Reason was the resident black. If you go to many of the stately homes of England and look at the portraits by the fashionable eighteenth century painters, you will often see a little black boy painted nearby the master or mistress of the house. There are just as many, if not more portraits depicting blacks than there are depicting the children of the house. This was because by this time blacks were regarded as exotic additions to a household. Where the average white servant had little or no advantages because of his race, blacks did, the exotic being desirable, the mundane not. Once they had grown up, these black children assimilated into local life, often marrying and producing children of their own who, often as not, would be mixed race, for interracial unions were common at a time when blacks were so rare in white communities that marriage between the races was inevitable.

One particularly famous picture, which inspired the 2013 film *Belle*, and highlights the eighteenth century phenomenon of blacks in England being incorporated into the households of the aristocracy, is the 1779 double portrait of Lady Elizabeth Murray and her mixed race cousin, Dido Elizabeth Belle. Once thought to be by the famous portraitist Johann Zoffany, but now attributed to David Martin, it was commissioned by their great-uncle, William Murray, 1st Earl of Mansfield, who as Lord Chief Justice presided over the two most important cases that would lead to the abolition of the slave trade, then of slavery itself, namely Somerset v Stewart (1772) and Gregson v Gilbert (1783), more popularly known as Somersett's Case and the Zong Massacre. Because of his importance to the cause, and his connection with Dido Elizabeth Belle, no examination of the abolition movement, or of the role people of colour played in eighteenth century England, would be complete without fully addressing that remarkable man and the unusual relationship he so proudly asserted in the exceptional painting.

The very existence of the portrait of Lady Elizabeth Murray and Dido Elizabeth Belle, and its quality, convey powerful messages. This was no ordinary representation of two beloved great-nieces, but a stunningly conceived and executed portrayal of two attractive young ladies of quality in whom Lord Mansfield took pride. It was displayed in Kenwood House, then the London home of the Mansfield family, until 1922. When the Lord Mansfield of the day was selling the house to the Guinness heir, the Earl of Iveagh, it was moved up to Scone Palace in Perthshire, the seat of the Earls of Mansfield. It depicts two young women richly attired in silk. One is titled and therefore of a higher rank than the other, and this is reflected in their clothing, as was the practice of the time. What makes this portrait truly exceptional is that one cousin is white, the other *café au lait*. She is unmistakeably what would then have been referred to as a *mulatto* or *mulatta*. She is equally unmistakeably a lady. While not as grand a lady as her cousin Lady Elizabeth, she being merely Miss, her clothing issues the clear message that she is nevertheless a gentlewoman.

Elizabeth and Dido (she was not called Belle, which was her surname, by her family, but Dido) were both brought up in the household of their childless great-uncle, the Honourable William Murray (1705-1793), Lord Mansfield from 1756 and the Earl of Mansfield from 1776, and his wife Lady Elizabeth Finch, daughter of the 2nd Earl of Nottingham. Both cousins were wards of William as a result of being motherless. Lady Elizabeth Murray's father was David Murray, son of William's eldest brother, also David, who succeeded to the Stormont title upon the death of their father in 1731. Upon the elder David's death in 1748, Elizabeth's father became Lord Stormont. An Ambassador, he would end up succeeding to William's title as well in 1793. It was while he was posted to Saxony that he met Elizabeth's mother, the Countess Henrietta von Bünau, but she died in 1766, when Elizabeth, their only child, was six years old. Elizabeth was duly shipped off to England to live with her father's Uncle William and Aunt Elizabeth, where she joined the Mansfields' other ward, Dido Elizabeth Belle.

Dido was one year younger than Elizabeth. Her grandmother was William's sister Amelia, their parents' seventh child and third daughter. Her father was (ultimately Rear Admiral Sir) John Lindsay, scion of another Scottish aristocratic house. A naval officer in the West Indies during the Seven Years War (1756-1763), the first global war involving Britain and all the European global powers which was in large measure played out on the Caribbean Sea, Lindsay appears to have encountered Dido's mother, a slave named Maria Bell (so the name is spelt on Dido's baptismal certificate), when he captured the Spanish vessel upon which she was being held. She became his concubine and produced their daughter in the West Indies in 1761. Because she was a slave, so too was Dido.

At the conclusion of the war, Lindsay returned to England and was knighted for valour on 10 February 1764. It is not certain exactly when he brought Dido to England, but she was baptised in 1765, by which time she had been left by her father in the care of his uncle William, who raised her as a member of the family and a freedwoman despite the fact that she technically remained a slave. Her status as a freedwoman would only be confirmed by Lord Mansfield in the will he made in 1783, but there is no doubt that she was well educated and intelligent. She acted as Lord Mansfield's secretary aside from managing the dairy and poultry yards at Kenwood, responsibilities that normally devolved upon the more capable females in gentle families.

Although there are few direct references to Dido in primary source material, she does appear in volume II of James Beattie's *Elements of Moral Science*. Beattie was a Scottish moralist and abolitionist who, in 1760, was appointed Professor of Moral Philosophy at Marischal College, later Aberdeen University. In his 1770 *Essay on the Nature and Immutability of Truth*, he argued against the institution of slavery on a variety of grounds, one of which was intellectual. By this time, the perception that the black race was intellectually inferior to the white was gaining ground, and in volume II of his 1790-93 *Elements of Moral Science* he used Dido as an example of the mental capacity of blacks, stating: 'my conjecture (was) established by a negro girl about ten years old, who had been six years in England, and not only spoke with the articulation and accent of a native, but repeated some pieces of poetry, with a degree of elegance, which would have been admired in any English child of her years.' He later confirmed her identity in a footnote, stating: 'She was in Lord Mansfield's family, and at his desire, and in his presence, repeated those pieces of poetry to me. She was called Dido, and I believe is still alive.'

Her place in the heart of the Mansfield family is also borne out by one of Mansfield's friends, the Loyalist former Governor of Massachusetts, Thomas Hutchinson. He wrote that Dido 'was called upon by my Lord every minute for this thing and that, and shewed the greatest attention to everything he said.' He noticed that she 'came in after dinner and sat with the ladies, and after coffee, walked with the company in the gardens, one of the young ladies having her arm within the other. She had a very high cap, and her wool was much frizzled in her neck, but not enough to answer the large curls now in fashion. I knew her history before, but my Lord mentioned it again. Sir Lindsay, having taken her mother prisoner in a Spanish vessel, brought her to England, where she delivered of this girl, of which she was then with child, and which was taken care of by

Lord M., and has been educated by his family. He calls her Dido, which I suppose is all the name she has. He knows he has been reproached for shewing a fondness for her – I dare say not criminal.'

What needs to be remembered is that, when Hutchinson was making these remarks, illegitimacy was a far greater stain than colour. Dido was not only what one writer called a *mulatta* but was also illegitimate. While the Mansfields incorporated her into their family and raised her as a gentlewoman, causing her to associate socially with the family and their friends, they also took care to draw a veil over her illegitimacy. This was of far greater importance than her colour, and places in its context the values of that time. It was this drawback, rather than her race, which ensured that her status was anomalous and at times second tier, for illegitimate progeny, whether incorporated under some fiction of being wards, or passed off with some other fictional fig leaf, were never quite the equals of their legitimate brethren. Indeed, the mere fact that Dido was living at all with the Mansfields, and was socialising with the family and their friends, conveys a degree of broadmindedness which was unusual for those times. The fate of most illegitimate progeny was to be farmed out to underlings or even discarded along with their mothers.

To further place Dido in her correct context, Lady Mansfield's sister Mary was married to the noted Whig politician Thomas, 1st Marquis of Rockingham, whose son would later become Prime Minister. Although the first marquis was a well-established politician, and would prove helpful in the furtherance of his brother-in-law William Murray's splendid career, the Murrays were a family whose history reflected the profound political schisms then prevalent in eighteenth century British society as a result of the unresolvable conflicts that surrounded the Crown, and had done so for a hundred years. These could easily have scuppered the brilliant legal and political career William would have, and William had had to work, as a young man, to negotiate his way round the dangerous shoals upon which his ship of ambition could easily have foundered.

While the young William was making his way in the world as a barrister, gaining a justified reputation as a brilliant orator with an incisive command of the law, he had to negotiate his way around a system whose conflicts went to the heart of the body politic. Nowadays it is only with difficulty that people remember that Britain was in political turmoil from the mid- seventeenth to the mid-eighteenth century. The English Civil War, which began in 1642, and culminated in the execution of King Charles I in 1649, was followed by the Commonwealth and Protectorate under Oliver Cromwell and, following his death in 1658, his son Richard, until the restoration of the monarchy under Charles II in 1660. The upheaval continued with a second revolution, the Glorious Revolution of 1688, which resulted in the exile in France of the rightful king, James II. This precipitated another half century of political instability, for Parliament took it upon itself to hand over the throne firstly to James II's elder daughter Mary and her husband, who was also his nephew William of Orange, then to his younger daughter Anne following Mary's death in 1694 and William's in 1702. When Anne died without issue in 1714, her half-brother, the legitimate king, was not recalled from exile. Rather, the crown passed to a distant cousin, Prince George, the Elector of Hanover.

At the time that William Murray was working his way up to becoming a Member of Parliament for Boroughbridge in 1742, colour was an absolute irrelevancy compared with who the legitimate king of England was, or indeed whether the Hanoverian dynasty would survive. In 1701, the deposed King James II had died in France. His heir, the legitimate Prince of Wales, had succeeded to his father's displaced throne and was recognised by legitimists throughout Europe and the British Isles as King James III of England and James VIII of Scotland. At that time, there was no Act of Union, so England and Scotland were two separate states fused under one crown, and there were many, in Scotland especially, who felt that no English Parliament had the right to give away the Scottish crown to a German princeling when the rightful King of Scotland was alive and well, living in France at the **Château** de Saint Germain-en-Laye outside Paris, under the protection of his first cousin-once-removed, Louis XIV.

Amongst those who regarded King James III of England and VIII of Scotland as the true king were William Murray's parents, the 5th Viscount Stormont and his wife, the former Marjory Scott. William was the fourth son of this openly Jacobite couple, who, despite being Protestant, firmly believed in the legitimacy of the Stuarts and the illegitimacy of the Hanoverians, to such an extent that they supported the

Jacobite Rebellion of 1715, which sought to expel George I and replace him with James III and VIII. Following the failure of this rebellion, Lord and Lady Stormont's second son James joined the Court of the Old Pretender, as James III and VIII came to be known to history, in Rome, where he had moved, under the protection of the Pope, following the Treaty of Utrecht in 1713 and the death of Louis XIV in 1715. For a while, William's brother James served as Secretary of State to the exiled king, who raised him to the peerage as the Earl of Dunbar, made him a Knight of the Thistle, Scotland's highest order of chivalry, and appointed him Governor and tutor to his heir, the exiled Charles Edward, Prince of Wales, better known to history as Bonnie Prince Charlie or the Young Pretender. Meanwhile, the other Prince of Wales, who would succeed to the throne as George II when his father George I died in 1727, lived between England and Hanover with little confidence that his dynasty would remain on the throne to which they had a far more tenuous claim than their cousins across the water.

It was against this backdrop of uncertainty arising from the existence of two kings, and the imposition of a new dynasty of appointed interlopers, that William Murray's life unfolded. Many well-established political figures worked the system in such a way that they could plead tacit support for whichever side prevailed. There was always the possibility that the Hanoverians would fall and the Stuarts be restored, so the interior decoration of many noble and political residences contained carefully coded symbols of support for the dynasty across the water, and indeed many an aristocrat and government functionary was known to toast the king across the water as well as the one in Whitehall.

Although William Murray's family were well-known Jacobite sympathisers, what hampered William from childhood, even more than his family's support for the Stuarts, was a lack of funds. Despite the splendour of Scone Palace, where the Stormont family resided, there was little money to spare for a fourth son, so William really had very few prospects. However, the boy turned out to be particularly bright, flourishing at the local grammar school in Perth, so he was sent south to Westminster School at the age of 13 in 1718, where he became a King's Scholar. He was given an allowance of £200 a year by a family friend,

Thomas, the 1st Lord Foley, which enabled him to study at Christ's Church, Oxford, and Lincoln's Inn, where he was called to the Bar on 23rd November 1730.

Three years earlier, William had made a clever move which was decisive in his later success. He entered and won a competition to write a poem in Latin entitled *The Death of the King*, to mark the passing of King George I on 11th June 1727. This demonstrated not only his intellectual abilities but also his support for the Hanoverian status quo over the exiled House of Stuart, and paved the way for the tremendously successful legal and political career he would thereafter have. It also paved the way for a rivalry he would have to endure with an entrant to the competition whom he beat: William Pitt the Elder, later Leader of the House of Commons, Lord Privy Seal, Prime Minister and 1st Earl of Chatham.

By the time Elizabeth and Belle came to live with William and his wife, he was already an established member of the judiciary who had managed to occupy all the most eminent legal posts in the land. He had been Solicitor-General for England and Wales from 15th December 1742 till 6th March 1754, Attorney-General for England and Wales from 6th March 1754 till 8th November 1756, and would remain Lord Chief Justice from 8th November 1756 till 4th June 1788. During his tenure as Lord Chief Justice, he also managed to be appointed Chancellor of the Exchequer in 1757 and Lord Speaker in 1783.

William's greatest contribution to the abolitionist movement occurred in 1772, when three people claiming to be godparents of a slave named James Somersett issued a writ of habeas corpus. Somersett had been brought to England from America by his master, a customs officer named Charles Stewart. Once ashore, he attempted to escape, but was caught and imprisoned on a ship named *Ann and Mary*, owned by Captain John Knowles and headed for Jamaica, where his owner intended to sell him. John Marlow, Thomas Walkin and Elizabeth Cade, however, applied to the Court of the King's Bench for an order for Somersett to be 'delivered up'. In his capacity as Lord Chief Justice of the King's Bench, Mansfield ordered a hearing for the 22nd January 1772, to determine the legality of the detention and imprisonment of Somersett. This hearing was adjourned until the 7th February 1772, when no fewer than five eminent barristers appeared on behalf of Somersett, who was backed by a wealthy abolitionist named Granville Sharp. They argued that while colonial law permitted slavery, English law did not, as neither English Common Law nor any Parliamentary Statute had ever recognised the existence of slavery in England, and therefore, in the absence of any such law, slavery as a legal entity did not exist in England. Somersett's owner Charles Stewart's two lawyers argued that as contracts for the sale of slaves were recognised in England, the existence of slaves must therefore be legally valid. Mansfield adjourned the case for consultation with the twelve judges of the King's Bench in May and gave his judgement on 22nd June 1772 when he stated: 'The state of slavery is of such a nature, that it is incapable of being introduced on any reasons, moral or political; but only by positive law, which preserves its force long after the reasons, occasion and time itself from whence it was created, is erased from memory: it is so odious, that nothing can be suffered to support it, but positive law. Whatever inconveniences, therefore, may follow from a decision, I cannot say this case is allowed or approved by the law of England; and therefore the black must be discharged.'

Mansfield's ruling was a masterpiece of the measured application of the law. Although many newspapers and a large proportion of the populace thought that he had actually freed slaves within England and Wales, his own comments, made during and after the trial, suggest that emancipation was not his objective. In a preliminary judgement, he said that 'the setting of 14,000 or 15,000 men at once free loose by a solemn opinion, is much disagreeable in the effect it threatens.' Some modern scholars think he feared the economic consequences of such a draconian judgement, not only for the owners of slaves, but for the slaves themselves, whose lives and welfare remained the responsibility of their owners only as long as they owned them. This was a dilemma which would time and again come back to haunt abolitionists, for while slavery was an iniquity, the sudden emancipation of slaves without a period of transition, which would protect their welfare as well as the economic welfare of their owners, invited calamity for everyone concerned.

Despite the limitations of the ruling, Mansfield had knocked the cornerstone out of the edifice of slavery, not only in England, but in the colonies as well. By granting rights to slaves in England, and doing so in such a moralistic manner, after 1772 there was a general awareness that slavery and the slave trade were existing on borrowed time, even in the West Indies. This gave the abolitionists a perch upon which to sling their arrows against the hated institution, and in 1783 Mansfield handed down the second of his decisions which would be so fateful to the continuance of slavery, when he found against the plaintiffs in the insurance claim arising out of the deaths of some 130 slaves being transported from Africa to Jamaica on board the slave ship *Zong*.

The *Zong* Massacre captured the public imagination in a way that was so striking that JMW Turner immortalised it in his 1840 seascape, *The Slave Ship*. The *Zong* was a slave ship owned by the Gregson slave-trading syndicate based in Liverpool. In keeping with standard practice at the time, the syndicate took out insurance on the lives of the slaves being transported as cargo. Slaves, it must be remembered, were valuable commodities, and any loss of life was a financial loss to their owners. Navigational errors in the crossing from Africa to Jamaica resulted in the ship running low on drinking water. The crew took the decision to throw some 130 slaves overboard, partly to ensure the survival of the remaining hands on board, and partly to ensure that the insurers would compensate the Gregson syndicate for the loss of the cargo, whose loss could not be claimed for if they died of thirst on board ship.

Beginning on 29th November 1781, the crew of the *Zong* began throwing the slaves overboard. When the ship reached Black River, Jamaica, the Gregson Syndicate made a claim for the loss of the 130 slaves. Gilbert the insurers refused to pay out on the claim, so the Gregson Syndicate sued them, arguing that the deliberate killing of slaves was legal in certain circumstances and therefore the insurers should compensate them for the loss of their cargo. The presiding judge, the Lord Chief Justice, Lord Mansfield, disagreed. Again, the ruling was on a narrow point, namely that, as the captain and crew were at fault for the lack of drinking water, they were liable for their loss, rather than the insurers, who had no liability to compensate them for their losses.

Granville Sharp, who had funded the Somersett case, tried to have the ship's crew prosecuted for murder. Although not successful in that endeavour, the Zong Massacre brought the horrors of the Middle Passage to the public's awareness in a way that nothing had before then. By 1787, the Society for Effecting the Abolition of the Slave Trade was up and running, and the following year Parliament passed the Slave Trade Act of 1788, which for the first time regulated the number of slaves a ship could take. This not-so-small step was followed in 1791 by Parliament prohibiting the insurance companies from compensating ship owners when slaves were thrown overboard, and in 1807 Parliament abolished the trade altogether when it passed The Slave Trade Act.

William Murray, Earl of Mansfield, is rightly regarded as being the judge who, more than any other, formulated the two decisions that provided the catalyst for ending the slave trade and slavery. Although his judgements were measured, they were undeniably successful in putting a spanner in the wheels of slavery and the trade without which it could not survive. William Leslie, as late as 1957, called him 'the legal genius of his generation', while Mansfield's contemporary Edward Foss, author of *Biographia Juridica*, stated that 'there has never been a judge more venerated by his contemporaries, nor whose memory is regarded with greater respect and affection.' He described him as 'the great oracle of the law'. His arch-rival, William Pitt, begged to differ, describing him as 'a very bad judge, proud, haughty to the Bar and hasty in his determinations.' History, however, favours the views of Foss and Leslie.

What no one can determine is: To what extent did Dido's existence influence her great-uncle's judgements? Speculation is pointless, but the evidence points to her very existence, and her undoubted intellectual ability, providing a living testament to the fact that blacks were not inferior to whites when given equal opportunities of education and nurturing, and therefore that the growing prejudice against blacks should not be countenanced to the exclusion of their rights and opportunities. In the very way he brought up Dido, Mansfield demonstrated unmistakably that he regarded his mixed-race great-niece as being every bit as fit for inclusion in his family life as his white great-niece. In so doing, he silently articulated a degree of inclusiveness that demonstrates a commendable lack of prejudice.

This begs the question: To what extent was racial prejudice prevalent in England in the eighteenth century? Was it as prevalent as is commonly supposed nowadays? Until the closing days of slavery, when the atrocities which had kept the sugar industry buoyant became known in England, the suffering caused by the practice had been kept well away from the general public in the Mother country. They therefore felt neither guilt nor concern. It would take such events as the Zong Massacre and, later on in America, the publication of Harriet Beecher Stowe's novel, *Uncle Tom's Cabin*, to wake up the citizenry to the horrors of slavery. Until then, they functioned in a bubble of ignorance, believing that the lot of the black man remained as it had been throughout the ages. There had been blacks in post-Renaissance England since the time of King Henry VII, and in the pre-Renaissance period since the time of the Ancient Romans. Those who put down roots in England assimilated into the local population, interbreeding and being accepted without prejudice or comment within the community. This was also true throughout Europe. One only needs to refer to Shakespeare's play *Othello* to see that the Moor was not a despised inferior, but a man of rank intermarried to the beautiful European native, Desdemona. Nowhere in the play is Othello's race a cause for prejudice or for him to be looked down upon by the Europeans surrounding him. Malice, not racial prejudice, is the theme of the play, with Iago being the culprit and Othello the victim. Had racial prejudice been at the root of the tale, Shakespeare would have written an entirely different play, and the fact that he did not, indicates that interracial unions were far more acceptable than we nowadays suppose.

Further proof of this theory is Alessandro de' Medici (1510-1537), who became Duke of Florence in 1532. The first Medici to rule Florence as a hereditary monarch, he was the acknowledged but illegitimate son of Lorenzo II de' Medici, grandson of Lorenzo il Magnifico, and an African former slave named Simonetta da Collevecchio. Although no one actually knows where in Africa she was from, African slaves were usually from territories like present-day Chad and Cameroon and were therefore categorised, then as now, as black. It is also worth noting that in Italy, especially in Papal families, there was a higher tolerance of illegitimacy than ever existed in England. There was therefore nothing unusual about Alesssandro's recognition of paternity, though it was rather less commonplace for an aristocrat to father a child with a slave, colour making little difference to the situation. Despite the Pope's acknowledgement of paternity, matters were further complicated by the possibility that Alessandro was actually sired by Lorenzo il Magnifico's nephew Giulio de' Medici, who became Pope Clement VII. (This, incidentally, is the pope who would deny Henry VIII his divorce from Katherine of Aragon.) *Il Moro*, as the biracial Alessandro was called in allusion to his dark skin and African features, was married off by the Emperor Charles V (nephew of Katherine of Aragon) to his natural daughter Margaret of Austria in 1536. To put matters in their proper context, Charles V was Europe's greatest monarch, the head of Europe's greatest House, the Hapsburgs, and ruler of the world's greatest empire, the Spanish and Austro-European Empire of the Hapsburgs, as well as the Holy Roman Empire. This marriage was therefore one of distinction and indicates that neither Alessandro's colour nor illegitimacy were held against him.

Although Alessandro would be assassinated the following year by his cousin Lorenzino de' Medici, and therefore had no lawful issue from Margaret, he fathered two children with his mistress, the former Marchesa Taddea Malaspina. She was from one of the most distinguished families in Italy, which further confirms how acceptable he was. Related to the late Pope Innocent VIII, she was the widow of Count Giambattista Boiardo di Scandiano, and younger daughter of the sovereign Marquis of Massa and Lucrezia d'Este, who was herself a member of the royal house which produced successive Dukes of Ferrara, Modena and Reggio, as well as being a member of the more senior royal house of Guelph, which produced the Dukes of Bavaria, Saxony, Brunswick and Lüneburg, who ultimately would sit upon the throne of England as the Hanoverians. The d'Este dynasty also features later in this work.

Following Alessandro's death, both his natural children with Taddea Malaspina were recognised by Cosimo I, Alessandro's successor as Duke of Florence. They were raised at Court as acknowledged members of the family. Giulio di Alessandro de' Medici became the First Knight of the Order of St. Stephen before being made Ambassador to Mantua and Rome, while Giulia Romala di Alessandro de' Medici had an even more illustrious life. First, she made an advantageous marriage at about fifteen years of age to the Duke of Popoli. The size of her dowry, some $8m in today's currency, indicates that neither her illegitimacy nor her African ancestry weighed against her desirability. When her first husband died, she remarried her cousin, Benedetto de' Medici, Cosimo I's first cousin. This is fulsome proof that the presence of colour which in later centuries would prevent marriages into well-known families, simply did not exist in those days. She and Benedetto ended up moving to Naples, where they successfully laid claim to the principality of Ottajano. Their descendant, Giuliano de' Medici di Toscana di Ottajano, is the current and 15th Prince of Ottajano and the 12th Duke of Sarno. The family is one of the most aristocratic in the world, their African ancestors never having been a preventative to their illustriousness.

These examples demonstrate that, in the sixteenth century, people of colour were simply not the targets for prejudice that they would later become. They were no threat, being few enough in number not to present a threatening power block. Racial purity as a political concept had not yet taken root, so, as and when people of colour appeared on the landscape, they were accepted and incorporated. This was as true in Europe as it was in the British Isles. In Spain and Portugal, there had been relatively large black populations, those countries having been occupied by the Moors for centuries. Although the Jews and European Iberians had been the administrators of the state during the years of Moorish ascendancy, the Moors were also a slave society, and most of their slaves originated in Africa. Again, there is no evidence that their dark complexions prevented freedmen and freedwomen from achieving their aspirations, while there is evidence that many dark-skinned people flourished as functionaries of and in the state.

The Spanish and Portuguese were also the great colonisers of the age. Not only did they capture and purchase slaves in Africa, they brought their slaves with them wherever they lived or traded. Their ships were often manned by slaves, and when these ran aground or were captured, the slaves were often as not survivors along with the sailors and passengers. According to Miranda Kaufmann, author of *Black Tudors: The Untold Story*, 'If you captured a Spanish ship, it would be likely to have some Africans on board. One prized ship brought into Bristol had 135. They got shipped back to Spain after being put up in a barn for a week. The authorities didn't quite know what to do with them.' Smaller numbers, however, had always been incorporated into the community, and would continue to be.

Kaufmann recounts how blacks were brought to England in a variety of ways. They came in the entourages of King Henry VII; Henry VIII's queen, Katherine of Aragon; and Mary I's husband, King Philip II of Spain (son of the Emperor Charles V and therefore brother-in-law to Alessandro de' Medici). They came as merchants, or were aristocrats who came to do business, and stayed for extended periods, sometimes permanently. There was the West African Dederi Jaquoah, who lived in England with a merchant for two years; Diego, a sailor enslaved by the Spanish in Panama and freed by Sir Francis Drake, with whom he circumnavigated the globe; Cattelena, who lived independently in Almondsbury and was prosperous enough to own a cow; the sailor John Anthony, who came to England on a pirate's boat; a salvage diver named Jacques Francis; and Reasonable Blackman, the Southwark silver weaver. According to Kaufmann, these were 'examples of people who are really valued for their skills. In a later age, you get these portraits of Africans sitting sycophantically in a corner looking up at the main character, but they're not just these domestic playthings for the aristocracy. They're working as a seamstress or for a brewer. Even in aristocratic households they are performing tasks – as a porter, like Edward Swarthye, or as a cook – they are doing useful things, they get wages.' John Blanke, for instance, was a royal trumpeter who earned twice the average wage of an agricultural labourer and three times that of a typical servant.

Kaufmann makes the point that black Tudors were no worse off than white ones. At a basic level, they were acknowledged as citizens rather than viewed as outcasts. 'It is enormously significant, given how important religion was, that Africans were being baptised and married and buried within church life. It's a really significant form of acceptance, particularly the baptismal ritual, which states that "through baptism you are grafted into the community of God's holy church", in which we are all one body.' They were not being beaten or put in chains or being bought and sold. They were not forbidden entry into the most important community of the day, namely the church, nor were they being denied its sacraments. They could and did marry in the church, often interracially. Their children were also welcomed into the community, hence why a compelling number of Britons, when they have their DNA tested, discover that they have a distant Sub-Saharan ancestor despite their purely Caucasian appearance.

This happy state of incorporation would continue with little or no change until the eighteenth century. There is little doubt though that, as that century progressed, prejudice against what was then called the Negro took increasing root. While in England such prejudice remained relatively marginal, in the West Indies it had become endemic. The cause appears to have been economic. By the eighteenth century, the West India Lobby had become one of the most powerful in Parliament. The reason was obvious. The sugar produced by the blacks was the most important product on the English market. It formed the basis of England's prosperity. Without the slaves, there could be no sugar industry. The stakes were high, and when the primary source of a nation's wealth is the issue, it should hardly be surprising that expediency blinds people to the rights of others. Had the black slaves of the West Indies been blue eyed blondes, Adonis himself would have been reviled.

It was after Jamaica and the other West Indian sugar-producing islands became such sources of wealth, and the demand in Britain for sugar became so overwhelming, that the planters were incentivised to exert maximum pressure upon their slaves to fill the demand, and the real trouble started. Life for the overworked slaves became unbearable, and, once this happened, everyone's way of life in the West Indies suffered. Where formerly a plantation owner had enjoyed a measure of security and comfort surrounded by peaceable slaves, the imminent threat of rebellion, of having one's throat slit in one's bed or cane field without warning, created a sense of insecurity that was tantamount to paranoia. Up to that point, there had been an uneasy but bearable truce between the enslaved and the enslavers. There was also much intermingling between white men and black slave women, and many an overseer or planter had his 'outside' family alongside his legitimate, white one. As the occupants of Auschwitz and Belsen proved during the Second World War, people try to make their peace with even the most appalling of living conditions.

This the displaced Africans had done in the West Indies. They had created new families, new communities, even farmed the plots of land their masters gave them, upon which to grow the produce that would feed them and their families. Some slave owners were undeniably cruel, but many were not, and many communities functioned peaceably until working conditions became so onerous that the slaves were goaded into rebelling.

Once rebellion had been introduced into the equation as a viable reaction to the status quo, the prospect of loss and the threat of violence led to a worsening of relations between enslaved and enslaver. All social groups have a tendency to reserve the most positive aspects of humanity for their own group, while attributing the less desirable traits proportionately to groups the further away they are from their own. This dehumanising mechanism is a phenomenon that is entirely natural. Versions of it are witnessed in the animal kingdom, demonstrating that *homo sapiens* is really no different from other animals when its welfare or survival is at stake. We are all programmed by nature to protect our own kind first of all, and, if necessary, to attack those who threaten us.

It was therefore inevitable that ever-increasing hostility would lead to increased dehumanisation, and this resulted in the white enslavers deciding that the black race was inferior. Some people even went so far as to question whether blacks had a soul, which just goes to show the extent to which the dehumanisation was taken, for prior to that, all human beings had been welcomed into the Body that was the Christian Church.

Jamaica, being the premier English colony, led the way, with slave rebellion after slave rebellion as the white overseers cracked the whip trying to force the blacks to optimal production. The blacks, no longer having anything to lose, started fighting back. Although superficially the fight seemed to be between white and black, the real struggle was not actually black against white, but slave against master. It just happened that the slaves were black and the masters white. Had they both been the same race, the struggle, which came to be viewed in racial terms, would have been clearly seen for what it truly was, which was the oppression of the enslaved by the enslavers. Race was merely the incidental by-product of a way of life that would have been unbearable whether the races were the same, different, or reversed. However, because the West Indian masters were white, and the slaves were black, and because oppressor and oppressed divided along racial lines, the difference in colour became a convenient peg upon which to hang ideas that actually owed more to the status of the enslaver and the enslaved than to race. This is borne out by the fact that freemen of colour, who owned slaves, would end up being lumped with their white counterparts by the blacks, who despised both equally and regarded them as being the same.

That statement is easy to make in writing in 2019, but in the heat of the moment, in eighteenth century Jamaica or Haiti or Barbados or Virginia, when the black man looked at his white oppressor, or the white slave owner looked at his agitating black slave, the first thing he saw was someone of a markedly different complexion. It was a short leap from that observation to the belief that the white man was an inhumane superior and the black man a trouble-making inferior. So began the racial prejudice which would blight the former imperial colonies for two centuries, distorting race relations in the most grotesque ways.

There were sound reasons why Jamaica led the way in slave rebellions, as indeed it would later lead the way in improved race relations. Traditionally, Jamaican slaves had always been the cream of the crop of imports from Africa. Because Jamaica was Britain's foremost sugar-producing colony, the biggest, strongest, and fittest men and women were saved for that island, where they achieved the highest price at the slave auctions. Slaves, it must be remembered, were not only human beings. They were also valuable commodities, human work machines and invaluable reproductive tools without which the liquid gold that was sugar could not flow. The reasoning was sound. Take the biggest, brawniest men, for working in the fields, and the strongest-looking women, for breeding purposes, combine the two, let nature takes its course, thereby enhancing not only an estate's productivity but also its value, as fit young men and women would inevitably procreate, and slaves being valuable commodities, the more progeny they produced, the greater an estate's value would be.

However, such hard-headed reasoning had an unintended effect. Pooling strong individuals together over a lengthy period of time created a population of blacks who were more robust and aggressive than they would otherwise have been, had they been left to reproduce in their native habitats, where weak and strong would have mixed in a more natural way than they did in this early experiment at producing a superior specimen. Strength in all its forms gradually became a characteristic of the Jamaican population, to include strength of character and strength of resistance.

Overwork having led to disaffection amongst the slaves, when it continued, the uprisings began. These coincided with a growing awareness in England of the evils of slavery, especially of the Middle Passage, where, following the widespread coverage of the Zong Massacre, people became aware of the unspeakable horrors that awaited the newly-captured slaves as they were being transported in shackles across the Atlantic from Africa to the West Indies.

Although slavery had never actually been a benevolent or desirable way of life, it is important at this juncture to remember that in the 18th century it was rife throughout the world, and had been for millennia. Nor was slavery limited to white enslavement of black people. Slavery flourished on all the inhabited continents. It is a misnomer for us to think that only in Western Europe and its colonies did slavery exist, or that only the black race was suppressed by the white. Oliver Cromwell sent out Irish dissidents to the West Indies as slaves. In Africa, slavery was rife amongst Africans. A disturbingly large percentage of Africans were captured and sold into slavery by their fellow Africans to European, and later, Arab, slave traders. Indeed, it would be fair to say that the slave trade could not have flourished the way it did between Africa and the West Indies had the Africans not been active partners in the profitable enterprise that slavery was. Discomfiting though it is, the reality is that slavery continued to flourish in Africa long after it had been abolished in Europe and the Americas. It was not until 1981 that Mauretania abolished slavery, and only in 2007 that the Mauretanian government passed a law, under international pressure, which allowed slaveholders to be prosecuted. Previous to that, there had been no laws on the statute books punishing the crime, with the result that the practice of *de facto* slavery continued for the thirty-six years between its abolition and its criminalisation.

Ironically, one of the first countries to abolish slavery was Russia. This Tsar Peter the Great did, in 1723. However, he converted the slaves into serfs, which was supposed to improve their position without ruining the slave owners economically. What this meant, in reality, was that they actually remained in a lifelong form of bondage, defeating the purpose of the abolition of slavery. It was not until 1861 that Tsar Alexander II, known as the Liberator, abolished serfdom with a stroke of the pen, thereby freeing tens of millions of souls from feudal ties to the land.

Although France became the second European power to free its slaves, during the Revolution in 1794, in 1802 Napoleon, then the First Consul of the French Republic, revoked the decree, thereby reinstituting slavery. It was only in 1848, when the monarchy of King Louis-Philippe fell and the Second Republic was instituted, that slavery was abolished again, this time permanently.

Britain therefore became the second major European power to abolish slavery, which it did by statute in 1834, though there was a four year transitional period and the slaves were not actually freed until 1838.

When I was a student in Jamaica in the 1960s, we were taught that one of the decisive factors in the abolition of slavery in the British colonies was the discovery of beet sugar. I gather that this is presently ignored as a driving force for abolition, now that Britain has positioned itself as spearheading the anti-racism movement in Europe, and revisionists would like to lay claim to having brought about the abolition of slavery on moral grounds. While it is true that a moral movement, originating with the Quakers, came about at the same time as the discovery of sugar beet in the mid-1700s, it is historically unsound to ignore the harsh economic factors, that were rightly acknowledged by the British educational system in the 1960s, as having played so crucial a part in the abolition of slavery. A fuller picture is always preferable to a narrower one, at least by those who seek the truth, so I propose to impart the multiplicity of reasons which I was taught were once accepted as helping to bring about the end of so important a way of life.

The discovery of beet sugar was one of the most fundamental and liberating discoveries of its time. In 1747, Andreas Sigismund Marggraf, Professor of Physics at the Academy of Science in Berlin, demonstrated that sugar, identical in taste and quality to that produced from sugarcane, could be extracted from the beetroot. The possibilities of this discovery were immediately apparent to the Prussian king, Frederick II, otherwise known as Frederick the Great. Beet could be cultivated, in vast quantities, on the Silesian plains of Prussia, meaning that a northern European power could share in the liquid gold that West Indian sugar was. Frederick therefore subsidised experiments for the production of sugar from various beets. The research was arduous and slow, but effective. Initial tests from Professor Marggraf resulted in only a 1.3 - 1.6% yield, but his student and successor, Franz Karl Achard, began the selective breeding of twenty-three varieties of mangelwurzel for sugar content in an attempt to increase yield. A local strain from Halberstadt in present-day Saxony-Anhalt was finally selected, which Moritz, Baron von Koppy and his son narrowed down even further to white, conical tubers, whose sugar content provided the vastly increased yields of 6%. It was this strain, the Altissima cultivar group of the *Beta vulgaris*, that would form the basis of all future sugar beet production.

In 1801, King Frederick William III decreed the first sugar beet factory open in Kunern, Silesia. Napoleon, getting wind of this venture, sent a commission of scientists to investigate. He ordered the opening of two factories, but the initial results were not impressive. However, he had a strong incentive to develop an alternative source of sugar which would preclude reliance on supplies from the West Indies. Firstly, the British blockade of France prevented the free flow of goods into France, and while the Treaty of Amiens ended hostilities in 1802, by 1803 Britain and France were once more at war. This resulted in a renewed naval blockade of France, which once more affected the flow of goods into France, especially from the French colonies, who themselves were a source of trouble. The downfall of France's leading sugar-producing colony, St. Domingue, and the creation of the black, Haitian state under Toussaint l'Overture, Jean-Jacques Dessalines, and Henri Christophe (who declared himself King), meant that West Indian sugar, even if obtainable, was no longer desirable. France would therefore be unable to meet its national need for sugar unless it could be produced locally. Necessity forced the pace, and Napoleon more than anyone else is responsible for the rapidity with which sugar beet production grew. He issued a decree appropriating

1 million francs for the establishment of schools specialising in beet sugar production, ordered the farmers to plant vast swathes of beet, and during the brief Peace of Amiens banned the importation of cane sugar from the West Indies.

Napoleon's success in meeting the French demand for sugar through beet was noticed and emulated by his neighbouring rulers. This, more than worthy moralising, signalled the death knell of the West Indian sugarcane industry and, along with it, slavery.

By 1837, France was the largest beet-sugar producing nation in the world, a position it held well into this millennium, though by 1880 Germany had become the largest producers of sugar from beet, as they processed much of the French produce as well as their own. Even Russia got in on the act, introducing subsidies similar to those introduced by the French and Germans, with the result that the bottom fell out of the sugarcane industry. There would be a limited revival after 1915 as a result of the destruction wreaked upon the beet lands of the various countries during the First World War, but the fact is, once Napoleon showed Europe that it could produce its own sugar, the claxon sounding the termination of the West Indian sugar industry could be heard worldwide.

Unsurprisingly, the West India Lobby did what it could to protect the interests of the West Indian planters. Compensation was paid by the government for the loss of property, which the slaves had been legally. There was by this time rampant prejudice throughout much of the Western World against 'the Negro', as the Africans and their descendants in the West continued to be called. The years of rebellion and agitation had poisoned the pond in which both European and African swam, and the prospect of living with a freed majority of the population who had previously been oppressed,   filled the West Indian planters with trepidation. The black man was truly feared. Nor was this fear limited to the Caribbean. In the United States of America, where slavery still flourished in the southern, cotton-producing states, which supplied the cotton mills of Manchester in England with a constant supply of the raw material necessary to manufacture the cotton fabric that was then sold throughout the British Empire, blacks were despised with a passion that the West Indian whites had never possessed.

When the American Civil War began, the British supported the Confederacy against the Unionists despite having freed their own slaves, and despite never having possessed the rabid contempt for blacks which Southern Americans possessed. British support, however, was based upon the need for Southern cotton to continue crossing the Atlantic, not upon a desire to emulate or perpetuate a system which the average Briton now regarded with distaste.

When the Civil War ended in 1865, and slavery throughout the United States was abolished, the South's whole way of life was 'gone with the wind', in Margaret Mitchell's memorable words. The lot of the blacks worsened, if such a thing were possible, but so too did the lot of the whites. Where previously the South had been a gracious civilisation, albeit one propped up by slavery, prosperity gave way to penury. There were myriad ways in which the blacks suffered, the advent of the Ku Klux Klan, an American white supremacist hate-group, being but one of them. The Jim Crow Laws, which rained down upon the blacks unfortunate enough to remain in the South, saw just about everything banned, from drinking water from the same fountain to sleeping with, or marrying, someone of a different race. Blacks were discriminated against in the legal system, which was notionally equal if separate, but in reality created a two tier system where whites were legally superior to blacks, where they could oppress blacks, and where the blacks would have no recourse to defend themselves against injustice and oppression. Nor was there any escape from the grinding poverty except by moving north or, later on, west. There was little or no work for anyone, black or white, and all classes and colours of the formerly prosperous South sank into penury.

As the nineteenth century gave way to the twentieth, and the lot of Southern whites improved marginally, that of the blacks did not. They could still not eat in the same restaurant, sit on the same seats on public transport or even on public benches, use the same lavatories, hotels, or general facilities as whites. This persisted into the 1960s. The consequences could be very unpleasant for not only those who had to endure it on a daily basis, but for those who experienced it on an ad hoc basis. I remember, as a teenager in the 1960s, going to Miami, where all Jamaicans of a certain class went to shop for just about everything. On one occasion when I was there with my parents, I ran into some friends from Jamaica on Flagler Street and suggested that they come back to the McAllister Hotel, where we were staying, for tea. My mother's cousin, who was with me and lived locally, was most insistent that we did not have the time, despite the fact that we had nothing to do but shop. It was only after she had killed my idea stone dead and they had left us that she said, 'You can't take coloured people into the McAllister. They wouldn't allow them.' Having been brought up in Jamaica – then regarded as one of the most racially progressive societies on earth – where people of all races mixed socially, class, not colour, being the deciding factor – I was shocked to my core to discover that such petty restrictions not only existed, but that they had the force of law.

Quite why the United States of America managed their post-slavery society more disastrously than any other, is open to interpretation. Whatever the reasons, the reality is that both America and South Africa, which was never a slave society, committed the cardinal error of legislatively raising racial prejudice to a statutory level, and in so doing, worsened race relations in a way that countries like Jamaica, and even Brazil, where slavery was abolished only towards the end of the nineteenth century, did not.

Ten years after America had abolished slavery, Brazil, with a population of 10 million, of which 15% were slaves, still had a large proportion of its population enslaved. Even though it had freed three quarters of its slaves by manumission, it was not until 1888 that that country became the last in the Americas to free all its slaves when Isabel, the Princess Imperial of Brazil, called "the Redemptress", freed the remaining slaves, an act that helped to cost her the throne when she was exiled the following year along with her father, the Emperor Pedro II 'the Magnanimous', whose magnanimity might have gained him the love of his people but who was nevertheless pushed out of power so that an ambitious clique of politicians could begin the slow dissolution of the prosperity which he had created during his 58 years on the throne.

As the nineteenth century drew to its close, racial prejudice against the blacks was at a height that would have been unimaginable even a century before, when slavery still flourished. This would allow the most dreadful atrocities to occur, none of which surpassed the horrors done to the Congolese people in the Congo Free State, a concession in central Africa which was not a colony of the Belgian nation, but a private possession of its king, Leopold II. A vast territory, some 1,000,000 square miles in size, it was the private fiefdom, and Hell on earth, between 1885, when the Berlin Conference confirmed Leopold's right to it, and 1908. As the Congo was bled for rubber, its people were annihilated in the most brutal manner, the hands of reluctant workers, even children, being cut off for the most minor of infractions. The whole state was turned into one huge concentration camp which made even the worst days of slavery in the West Indian and the American South seem benevolent by comparison. The world remained blissfully ignorant of the exploitation of a whole nation of people long after slavery had been abolished in other European possessions.

An international campaign against the abuses being perpetuated throughout Congo Free State began in 1890 and reached its zenith after 1900, under the leadership of the British activist E.M. Morel. Joseph Conrad's novel *Heart of Darkness*, published in 1899, brought the atrocities being committed against the Congolese people to the world's attention. Putting aside the mutilation of a large segment of the population, usually for the most minor of infractions, fifty per cent of the population was estimated to have perished, either directly or indirectly, as a result of the forced labour system then prevalent. The public outcry was so widespread that the British Consul, Sir Roger Casement, was instructed to compile a report which became known as the Casement Report. This led to the arrest and punishment of officials who had been responsible for killings during a rubber-collecting expedition in 1903 which was, unfortunately, only too typical of the plethora of rubber-collecting expeditions then in force throughout the massive state. Sir Arthur Conan Doyle, famous throughout the world as the author of the Sherlock Holmes mysteries, waded in with a damning indictment: his book entitled *The Crime of the Congo*. Finally, in 1908, international pressure resulted in the Belgian government taking over the administration of the Free State and converting it into a colony, the Belgian Congo, after which the worst of the atrocities were brought to a halt. Forced labour was phased out, but the territory had been so depopulated in the twenty years of its existence as an ironically named Free State, that the government had to not only import labour, but also mandated that residents were obliged to give a certain number of days to the creation of infrastructure.

The sheer scale of the crimes committed against the natives has gone down in history as one of the worst atrocities of all time. It is unlikely that such crimes could have been committed against any but the black race at the time they were being committed. A more damning indictment of the dehumanisation of a whole race of people by another race is hard to come by, but the atrocities committed against the slaves in the West Indies and America paved the way. In less than two centuries, an entire race that had once been incorporated willingly into European society was now denigrated so utterly that even the mutilation of children was possible.

Yet it would be unproductive for us, in the early twenty-first century, to take an anachronistic view of the institution of slavery and to condemn everyone who played a part in it, if only because that would mean that we would have to condemn virtually everyone who has lived in any society, whether civilised or semi-civilised, from the beginning of time until the latter part of the nineteenth century. It would be fair to say that it has only been since then that slavery, as a way of life, has become the exception rather than the rule, and while no conscionable person would seek to justify slavery's existence as a desirable form of labour, it is equally unrealistic to view it as having been something that was systematically harsh at all times.

Unless one wishes to indulge one's prejudices while benefitting from the sanctimonious delights of righteous indignation, one needs to take a dispassionate look at a system that undoubtedly left much to be desired, but was nevertheless the norm throughout much of the world for much of history. The sad but true fact is that slavery is as old as humankind. Moses, Jesus Christ, Mohammed and Buddha were all born into slave societies. Throughout the ages there had been good slave owners and bad slave owners, irrespective of whether slaves were of the same race as, or a different race from, their masters. The Roman philosopher Cicero, for instance, was a benevolent master, his slave then freedman, Marcus Tullius Tiro, becoming his secretary and the inventor of their earliest form of shorthand, who did all in his power after Cicero's tragic death to keep his master's work alive. Spartacus, also an ancient Roman slave like Tiro, was another Caucasian like his masters, yet he headed up the greatest slave rebellion of the ancient Roman Republic in the early 70s BC. According to Plutarch and Appian, he was killed in the final battle of the Third Servile War, though the latter author does make the telling observation that his body was never discovered and he might well have escaped the fate of his rebel army. Those who were not killed on the battlefield were captured by Crassus's legions, six thousand of them being crucified along the Appian Way between Capua and Rome as a warning to other slaves who might be tempted to rebel.

Plainly, whether slaves were the same race as their masters or of different races, the same variables dictated whether they received kind or cruel treatment, indeed whether they were viewed as work-fodder or human beings. A case in point is the relationship between Thomas Jefferson, signatory of the American Declaration of Independence and the third president of the United States of America, and his three-quarter white slave, Sarah 'Sally' Hemings (1773-1835). She was one of six children born to her mother Betty, a so-called '*mulatta*' whose mother was herself a slave owned by Jefferson's father-in-law John Wayles, but whose father was an English ship's captain named Hemings. There is a legend that Hemings wanted to buy his daughter and her mother from Wayles, but he refused to sell them. Instead, John Wayles started what was known as a 'shadow' family with Betty, while marrying three white women and fathering a series of children with the first two of his wives.

Shadow families were common in the West Indies and the Southern states of America. As long as they were not flaunted, and did not threaten the legitimate children's heritage, they were accepted as a valid if silent dimension to civilised life. More often than not, white men had their legitimate wives and children with white women who were their social and legal equals, while having alternate families with attractive slave women. Under the principle of *partus sequitur ventrum*, meaning 'that which is brought forth follows the womb', all children assumed the legal status of their mothers. The child of a freewoman was therefore free; that of a slave, a slave. The result was that many slave owners had their 'shadow' children functioning on their estates or properties in superior positions, whether as butlers, valets, carpenters or housemaids, while the harder work was done by the slaves who had no blood links to their owners. Sometimes, when there were no legitimate heirs, they were even freed and succeeded to their father's entire estate.

The year after Martha married her third cousin Thomas Jefferson in 1772, her father died and she inherited all eleven members of the Hemings family, along with 125 other slaves and 11,000 acres of land. She also inherited a sizeable debt of £4,000, which Jefferson and his father-in-law's other executors worked for years to clear, while her half-siblings took up residence at Monticello, the gracious Palladian residence located just outside of Charlottesville, Virginia, which Jefferson was in the process of constructing, and which is now a UNESCO World Heritage Site. Martha's half-sister Sally was an infant of about a year old when she moved from the Wayles plantation, The Forest in Charles City County, to Monticello, where she remained for most of the remainder of her life.

While baby Sally was growing up, her half-sister and owner Martha and her half-brother-in-law Thomas Jefferson were evidently a devoted couple. They produced six children together, but only their eldest child, Martha 'Patsy' Jefferson, would survive past the age of 26. Martha appears to have suffered from diabetes, and remained in delicate health throughout the eleven years of their marriage and the two years between 1779 and 1781 when Jefferson served as Governor of Virginia during the American War of Independence. Following her death in 1782, their daughter wrote that she was 'a solitary witness to many a violent burst of grief,' while her father himself stated that he finally emerged 'from that stupor of mind which had rendered me as dead to the world as was she whose loss occasioned it.'

Two years after his wife's death, Thomas Jefferson was appointed American envoy to France. He was accompanied by his eldest daughter Patsy and some of his slaves, including Sally Hemings's older brother James, who learnt French cuisine during his stay in France, was paid $4 per month by Jefferson, and would, upon his return to Pennsylvania, earn not only a wage for himself but also for Jefferson the reputation of having one of the finest tables in the country. In return for training his brother to replace him as chef, James was given his freedom in 1793, and when

Jefferson became president, he offered him the position of chef at the White House. In the interval, though, James had become an alcoholic, so he declined the offer of the post, and would later commit suicide aged 36.

By this time, Sally had become Jefferson's concubine. The relationship had started innocently enough. After his youngest daughter Lucy Elizabeth died in the United States, Jefferson had his surviving daughter, nine year old Polly (Maria Jefferson), sent over to France. She was supposed to 'be in the care of her nurse, a black woman, to whom she is confided with safety,' according to Jefferson's letter to Abigail Adams dated 21st December, 1786. However, according to Abigail Adams, in a letter dated 26th June 1787, 'The old Nurse whom you expected to have attended her, was sick and unable to come [to London, England, *en route* to France]. She has a Girl about 15 or 16 with her.' A day later Abigail Adams was writing to Jefferson stating: 'The Girl who is with Polly is quite a child, and Captain Ramsey is of opinion will be of so little Service that he had better carry her back with him. But of this you will be a judge. She seems fond of the child and appears good natured,' though within days she was adding, 'The Girl she has with her, wants more care than the child, and is wholly incapable of looking after her, without some superiour to direct her.'

Capable or not, Sally was 'light coloured and decidedly good looking,' according to Jefferson's legitimate grandson, Thomas Jefferson Randolph. She was paid $2 a month and, while there is no record of whether she lived with her brother James and Jefferson at the Hôtel de Langeac on the Champs-Élysées, or at the Abbaye de Penthemont convent with Patsy and Polly, who were boarded there and might well have had their own attendant, Jefferson bought her some fine clothing, which suggests that she accompanied Patsy as a lady's maid to social events. Since her relationship with him also developed into something more personal than master and slave at the same time, it also suggests that he had respect for her, for all women at that time understood that one of the surest ways of discerning whether a man valued them was whether he was prepared to spend money on them or not. Although the French Revolutionary government abolished slavery in France while Jefferson was in his post as envoy, James and Sally opted to return to the United States with him in 1789. Both appear to have had stronger ties with their family in Virginia than a desire for freedom, and there was definitely trust on both sides. Each of the siblings struck an agreement with Jefferson which was honoured: James would continue to receive his salary and be freed in 1793 after agreeing to train his younger brother as a chef in lieu of the cost Jefferson had incurred having him trained in Paris, while Sally, whose sexual relationship with Jefferson began while they were in Paris, became pregnant, and agreed to return as long as any children born of their union would be freed after they came of age. According to the memoirs of Sally's younger son with Jefferson, Madison Hemings (1805-1877), Sally's first child with Jefferson died soon after her return from Paris, but between 1795 and 1808 they had a further six children together. Of the four who survived past childhood, all were freed in accordance with the terms of the agreement struck in Paris. Beverley was the first, running away at the age of 24 from Monticello, to be followed shortly afterwards by his sister Harriet, aged 21. According to the Monticello overseer Edmund Bacon, she was 'near white and very beautiful', and he gave her $50 (over $1,000 in today's money) and put her on a stagecoach to the North. She evidently joined her brother in Washington, D.C., where they entered white society and both made good marriages, according to the memoirs of their brother Madison. He was freed, along with his brother Eston Hemings, in their father's will, as neither child had yet achieved his majority. Jefferson also petitioned the Virginia legislature to allow them to stay in the state.

Jefferson did not free Sally in his will, however. The likely reason is that he did not wish to create more talk than already existed about their relationship. Bacon recounts in his memoirs, published posthumously, how there was talk when Beverley and Harriet left Monticello, that Jefferson had freed them because they were his children. By then he was a huge national figure, and any indiscretion could and most likely would have been seized upon by his political enemies. This could have resulted not only in a diminution of his reputation but also of his family's prominence, so the matter of Sally's freedom was handled with the decorum that one would expect from honourable and civilised people. Sally was given 'time' by Jefferson's heiress, his daughter Martha 'Patsy' Jefferson Randolph, who of course was also Sally's niece. She lived out

the remaining nine years of her life with her two youngest sons in Charlottesville.

After her death, Eston would move West, changing his name from
Hemings to Jefferson. His two sons, John Wayles Jefferson and Beverley
Jefferson, entered the Union Army as white men. It was his second son's
descendant, John Weeks Jefferson, who provided the DNA sample that
matched up his Y chromosome to the rare haplotype of the Thomas
Jefferson male line, conclusively proving that Jefferson or one of his close
male relations, none of whom had a relationship with Sally, had indeed
enjoyed the long and faithful relationship which not only produced seven
children, but also endured for the remainder of the former president's
life. Nor did Sally Hemings have another relationship with any other
man after Jefferson's death, which provides further evidence that their
relationship not only had durability, but also affection, depth, trust and
honour. They were indeed a couple, albeit a shadow one.

During his lifetime, Jefferson's lifestyle was not only elegant and
tasteful, but also in keeping with his importance as one of America's
leading statesmen. Having to maintain a way of life in keeping with his
eminent position meant that he was seldom, if ever, out of debt. This
was in part due to the debts Martha had inherited from her and Sally
Hemings's father John Wayles, but the necessity to maintain a gracious
existence beyond his means meant that, by the end of his life, he was
virtually bankrupt. His entire estate had to be sold. House, land, slaves,
everything, went. Fortunately, he had given his children their freedom
otherwise they too would have been put up for sale. His penury might
well have had an unforeseen effect which would ultimately benefit the
American people, for, by passing out of his family's hands, Monticello
was preserved intact for the nation in a way it might well not have been,
had it remained a possession of his heirs. In so doing, the way of life of
the third President of the United States, including the role of his shadow
family and slaves, has been, so to speak, set in stone. Recent excavations
confirm that Sally's bedroom was even more accessible to Jefferson's than
had been previously thought. But this in itself should come as no surprise
to anyone knowledgeable about the way of life of those times, for there
was far more mixture between black and white, slave and master, than is

often presumed today, when the prism of racism and racist misconceptions have distorted so many perceptions of what truly took place in the final centuries of slavery.

Undesirable though slavery as a way of life was, in the beginning of the eighteenth century it was not as unbearable as it became towards the end of that century or the beginning of the nineteenth. That was when racial prejudice really intensified, the relict of which society dealt with throughout the twentieth century. Nor was the rampant racism that ended up characterising relations between blacks and whites in the Southern states of America ever experienced in the West Indies, whether British or French. A case in point is St. Domingue, the leading French colony which would, during the French Revolution, become Haiti. St. Domingue was as valuable to the French as Jamaica was to the British. Yet the racial prejudice that took hold in Britain never did so to the same extent in France, which demonstrates that there were degrees of prejudice against the blacks depending on whether the territories were American, British, or French. A case in point is the French author, Alexandre Dumas *père*. Born Dumas Davy de la Pailleterie, he was the grandson of a French aristocrat named Alexandre Antoine, Marquis Davy de la Pailleterie, who fathered a child with a slave of African descent, Marie-Cessette Dumas. The product of that union became a famous general in France whose reputation was so august that Napoleon felt threatened by his existence and blocked him from further progress: something which had everything to do with ability and nothing to do with colour. Dumas *père*'s novel, *The Count of Monte Cristo*, was, and remains, one of the most widely read books of all time. If his so-called '*mulatto*' father's eminence is not convincing enough, the very place in which he began his career is all the testament that is needed that the presence of black blood was not a preventative to a good situation in life in France, for Alexandre Dumas started out in the office of Louis-Philippe, Duke of Orleans and, after 1830, King of the French. While Dumas *père* encountered occasional racial prejudice – he once told a man who alluded to his African ancestry, 'My father was a mulatto, my grandfather was a Negro, and my great-grandfather was a monkey. You see, Sir, my family starts where yours ends' - he was nevertheless accepted throughout all the Courts of Europe, especially after he became a well-known author. At various times, he resided in Belgium,

Russia, and Italy, where he was warmly received by the monarchs and aristocracy. He made a respectable marriage, had at least forty mistresses, and not only earned, but spent, a vast fortune living the lavish life of a well-heeled aristocrat.

People who are ignorant of history are often ignorant of the tolerance which was once shown to people from different races. Only by recognising, and understanding, why racial prejudice became the potent and destructive force that it did for a two hundred year period, can we begin to place race relations in their proper context, and to appreciate that racism has, historically, been the exception, rather than the rule.

Chapter Two

THE MULTIFARIOUS EFFECTS of slavery in the West Indies and American South not only resulted in the tremendous increase in racial prejudice against people who originated in Sub-Saharan Africa, but even distorted the very meaning of the word race. The changes in the meaning of 'race' eloquently tell the story of how people of colour moved from being acceptable albeit different, to exotic, then to different and unacceptable, before becoming suspected, reviled, denigrated and held to be inferior.

The wheel has fortunately begun to turn back to what it was five hundred years ago, when people were accepted with their differences, and such differences were not regarded as a mark of inferiority but a reflection of originating history.

It might be useful, before proceeding further, if we actually define what the word race used to mean. Race has meant different things at different times. In Tudor times, race had little to do with colour the way it often does nowadays. There was the human race and all within it were souls who shared a common humanity. Within that one species, there were obvious differences, some visible, some auditory, others cultural. Society had not yet come up with the concept of humanity consisting of different races, of what in reality would be sub-groups of the human race which would become racial entities separate from each other. Obviously, there were differences between people from different territories. The Chinese, Indians, Mongolians, Moors, Sub-Saharan Africans and Europeans were all known to one another by Tudor times. Each looked, spoke, acted and dressed differently from the other. Within the European population, there appeared to be an even greater degree of divergence between the citizens of the various Germanic, Italian, French and Iberian states than appeared to be the case amongst the non-European. In other words, everyone was different, some more so than others, but all were fundamentally offshoots of the same core group: humanity.

In some ways, that time's concept of race was both inclusive and contradictory, for the word not only meant people from the same species of being, but could also be used interchangeably with nationality. It therefore did not refer to colour or hue, but to humanity or nationality. For instance, people from the Italian state of Padua in Italy were usually duskier than those from Saxony in Germany, but all were recognised as being members of the same race though, contrarily, Paduans were acknowledged to be of a different race from the Genoese, despite both being Italian. This differentiation applied across the board in a day and age when similarities were as much treasured as differences, with the result that the English race was accepted as being different from the Welsh, the Welsh from the Scottish, the Scottish from the Irish, notwithstanding all of them being Celtic.

As society evolved and people travelled more and more, the idea that people were both the same while being different underwent subtle changes, with the similarities being ignored and the differences brought to the fore. Books not only reflect ideas that are prevalent, but help to crystallise, and sometimes distort, them. The first attempt to classify the differences that were becoming more and more evident the more and more people interacted with others from different nationalities, was François Bernier's 'Nouvelle division de la terre, par les différentes espèces ou races d'homme qui l'habitent' (*New division of Earth by the different species or races which inhabit it*), published in 1684. The work was not an attempt to create racial divisions, but to demonstrate the multiplicity of cultures which existed throughout the relatively-newly discovered (by Europeans) lands of Asia, Africa, and the Indies. Bernier was a world-traveller in an age when few people travelled, and his work was intended to enlighten the patrons of the great literary salons of France run by such intellectuals as Jean de La Fontaine and Ninon de Lenclos with regard to the wide disparity of the many different peoples populating the various cultures worldwide. Bernier divided the world into four quarters and labelled the occupants European, Far Eastern, Negro and Lapp.

To put the publication in its proper historical context, and demonstrate how late an arrival the first definition of racial distinctions was to Western civilisation, South America, Central America, and large swatches of North America had been Spanish or Portuguese colonies for nearly two hundred years. The English Civil War had been fought and won by the Roundheads, who had decapitated Charles I a quarter century previously. Charles II was sitting on the English throne which would be wrested from his brother James II four years later in the Glorious Revolution. In France, Louis XIV had abandoned the royal palace of the Louvre in preference for the Château de Versailles, while across the Atlantic Ocean, Virginia had been a British colony for three quarters of a century, Barbados for a half a century, and Jamaica had been captured from the Spanish nineteen years before. It was therefore not news to any educated person that there were different looking people in different countries on different continents all over the world. What was new, however, was trying to define and describe them to those who had never seen them and had no real knowledge of them. Today, we have photographs and film to capture visually what Bernier was trying to convey verbally. A picture is worth a thousand words, especially when trying to evoke images of people and places that have never been seen before.

This straightforward attempt to categorise the various groups of people that Bernier had come across in his travels might now seem inadequate, but it was an honest attempt to enlighten. By existing, however, it also had the effect of becoming a reference point for those who later wished to twist his definitions so that innocent differences could be made into something more ominous.

By the eighteenth century, 'race' was being splintered so that it no longer had the dual meaning of 'same but varied', as in human beings being the same species despite being of various nationalities. The concept that some humans were superior to others by virtue of being of different races (as in colour) was taking root. Scientific knowledge now found itself being hijacked in the interests of justifying the slave trade, slavery, the profitability of the sugar industry and the economic desirability of explaining away the increasing atrocities being perpetrated upon the human beings who produced this magical substance. Ironically, it was the publication in the Netherlands in 1735 of *Systema Naturae*, the first edition of the ground-breaking work by the father of modern taxonomy and one of the founders of the ecological movement, the great Swedish botanist, zoologist, and physician, Carl Linnaeus (1707-1778), that was alighted upon by racists to further their prejudices.

Systema Naturae was the first comprehensive scientific classification of animals and plants. By the time he had published the 10th edition of his masterpiece in 1758, Linnaeus had classified 4,400 species of animals and 7,700 species of animals. He was truly one of the great men of his time, renowned for his brilliance. For instance, when, in 1760, the 12th edition needed a more efficient way of classifying and codifying his material than hitherto existed, he invented the index card.

In his very first edition, Linnaeus caused an enormous hue and cry when he classified humanity and monkeys under the same category: Anthropomorpha. The objections were two-fold. The Bible stated that man had been made in God's image, yet here was a scientist stating that essentially man and monkey were more or less the same. Moreover, humanity was assumed to be the most evolved being on earth, uniquely in possession of a soul, yet Linnaeus had classified him with a being without a soul. Linnaeus, however, refused to budge, at least at first, regarding it as quite likely that other living beings also had souls, though in 10th edition he would take the religious sting out of his scientific tale by introducing the terms Mammalia and Primates, the latter replacing Anthropomorpha, and in so doing provide the palliative of giving only humans the full binomial *homo sapiens*. The controversy surrounding his assertion that man was a type of animal would nevertheless rumble on for another hundred years until 1859, when his hypothesis was overtaken by the still-ongoing controversy surrounding Charles Darwin's *On the Origin of the Species*.

Linnaeus's unintentional contribution to the advancement of racism was his scientific sub-division of the human species into four categories based upon continent and predominant skin tone. In the first edition of *Systema Naturae*, which was published (as were all works of that kind at that time) in Latin, he broke down the races into *Europaeus albus* (white European), *Americanus rubescens* (red American), *Asiaticus fuscus* (brown Asian) and *Africanus niger* (black African). In the tenth edition, he included the Asian description of *Asiaticus luridus* (yellow Asian). Andrew

Dickson White observed in *A History of the Warfare of Science with Theology in Christendom* in 1896 that Linnaeus 'was the most eminent naturalist of his time, a wide observer, a close thinker' and that he 'advanced the hypothesis that all the species of one genus constituted at the creation one species.' In other words, humanity being the same species, all the races within humanity were simply variations of the same entity.

Linnaeus needs to be placed in his proper historical context. Not only was he working at a time when theology was a far greater factor than it is nowadays, he was also the very first scientist to classify both the animal and plant kingdoms. His work strove to be neutral, and two of the great philosophers, who were his contemporaries, both appreciated his contribution to society. Jean-Jacques Rousseau said, 'I know of no greater man on earth,' while Johann Wolfgang von Goethe wrote, 'With the exception of Shakespeare and Spinoza, I know no one among the no longer living who has influenced me more strongly.' Nor has his reputation withered on the vine. The mathematical algorithm, applied to 24 multilingual Wikipedia editions in 2014 which was published in PLOS ONE in 2015, placed Carl Linnaeus as the top historical figure of all time, above Jesus, Aristotle and Napoleon.

If someone of his merit can have had his well-intentioned, neutral, scientific work seized upon to advance racist theories which were based upon economic aggrandisement, how much more understandable is it that lesser minds have found their contributions trampled in the dust of prejudice? For what the racists did was alight upon the categorisations so neutrally and innocently adopted by Linnaeus, to advance the notion that the white man was superior to the brown and yellow, both of whom were superior to the black.

Yet civilisation itself teaches us that the human being is inclined to invest the most importance in those who are closest to him. Ancient civilisations from Rome to China placed more importance on familial or tribal links than they did on an individual's physical attributes. Notwithstanding that fact, those societies were inclined to link physical characteristics such as hair or eye colour with psychological and moral attributes, ascribing superiority to the features which were similar to theirs, with the inevitable corollary of inferiority going to those whose physical features differed more pointedly from their own. Thomas F. Gossett, in the Oxford University Press 1997 edition of *Race: The History of an Idea in America*, describes how a historian of the 3rd century Han Dynasty in modern-day China described Barbarians with blond hair and green eyes as resembling 'the monkeys from which they are descended.'

Yet physical differences did not inevitably result in exclusion, especially not in the ancient Greek and Roman civilisations. Although someone who was not a Greek or a Roman was regarded as a barbarian, this was so whether or not they looked like a Greek or Roman. Moreover, barbarians were not condemned to perpetual exclusion from either Greek or Roman society. If they became Greek or Roman citizens, they ceased to be barbarian. They were then fully accepted as if they were genetically Greek or Roman. Indeed, several Emperors of Rome were of non-Roman stock. Septimus Severus, although partly Roman on his father's side, was from Leptis Magna, present day Libya, on his mother's. This mixture did not militate against him ascending to the throne. Nor did the fact that his wife, Julia Domna, was an Emesan Syrian whose father, Julius Bassianus, descended from the royal house of Samsigeramus and Sohaemus. Their two sons, Lucius Septimus Bassianus, known to history as Caracalla, and Publius Septimus Geta, succeeded to the throne as Emperors without any difficulty. Their grandson Elagabalus would be assassinated, but that was not because of his non-Roman heritage, but because of his scandalous conduct. This included being the possibly first openly trans ruler of any state, and moreover, the greatest military state of all time, where masculinity was treasured above all else, and women were judged to be incapable of ruling, irrespective of whether they were born female or were what we would now refer to as self-identifying.

There were other noted Emperors whose bloodlines contained no Roman blood. The first purely Syrian Emperor of Rome was Philip I, called 'Philip The Arab', Following him was a Moorish Emperor, Aemilianus, whose wife Cornelia Supera was of African origin, meaning, in the vernacular of the time, that she was a negress.

The story of Western Civilisation is one long saga of people of different races melding with the natives of the more fertile lands of the Mediterranean, thereby forming the basis of our civilisation. It was the

Eastern civilisations of China and the Indies that maintained their racial purity to a far greater extent than the European civilisations. The cradle of Western civilisation is Mediterranean, and we had a series of invasions and migrations, from the East, South and North, each bringing waves of people who would ultimately be absorbed. Genghis Khan's soldiers, for instance, not only colonised the western lands they occupied, but also spread their seed far and wide. Admittedly, Alexander the Great tried to do the same in reverse, ordering the 'mingling' of his Greeks with the Persians, Egyptians, Syrians and everyone else he conquered, but his empire fell apart soon after his death, and such absorption within the occupied races was of a short enough duration to make little difference to their cultural identity. Under the Roman Empire, however, Romans mixed happily with Thracians and Nubians, Numidians with Egyptians, and the many other nationalities which made up the ancient Roman Empire, until everyone who was a citizen of Rome had a common identity.

It is that commonality of identity which has begun to emerge once again in Western society, as colour prejudice lessens and there is a greater intermingling of the races.

Fifty years ago, it was relatively common to hear Britons state that '*wogs* start at Calais'. The Italians were often called '*dagos*', and other Mediterraneans '*wops*'. This is now regarded as racist, but the language of the day also told a tale, no matter how unintentionally. The fact of the matter is that there was much racial intermingling during the ancient Roman Empire, and their descendants to this day carry the exotic blood lines of their ancestors. While the British seemed oblivious of the degree of intermingling that had taken place in their own country, they had nevertheless alighted upon a truth, namely that most of the citizens of the Mediterranean basin do indeed have strains of alien cultures. The simplest trace of the cross-migration that took place explains why so many of the French, Italians, Greeks, and Iberians have crinkly hair and olive skins. Nor are the Northern Europeans impervious to the consequences of migrating cultures. Russia is a rich amalgam of cultures which blended with each other, hence the presence of the slanted eyes of so many blue-eyed, blonde Russians, betraying the presence of a long-lost Tartar or Mongolian ancestor. Moreover, this phenomenon is not the exclusive province of the masses. The Youssoupov family, who married into the Imperial Family at the beginning of the twentieth century, was well known to have Tartar blood.

Nowadays, with access to genetics which were not previously available to scientists, the study of populations has become an illuminating science. According to the eminent population geneticist, Luigi Luca Cavalli-Sforza (1922-2018), 'From a scientific point of view, the concept of race has failed to obtain any consensus; none is likely, given the gradual variation in existence. It may be objected that the racial stereotypes have a consistency that allows even the layman to classify individuals. However, the major stereotypes, all based on skin colour, hair colour and form, and facial traits, reflect superficial differences that are not confirmed by deeper analysis with more reliable genetic traits and whose origin dates from recent evolution mostly under the effect of climate and perhaps sexual selection.'

These findings confirmed the ideas of the 'Father of American Anthropology', Franz Uri Boas (1858-1942), whose research on the skeletal anatomy of various human beings showed that cranial shape and size were determined not by race, but by environmental factors such as health and nutrition. Until then, racial anthropologists had believed that head shape was a stable racial trait, meaning that each race was limited by fixed physiognomy. Boas was able to demonstrate, at a time when racial discrimination was at its peak in the United States of America and laws prevented the various races from embarking on perfectly normal activities, that differences in human behaviour were not primarily determined by innate biological factors, but were mostly the result of cultural differences acquired through social experiences. In so doing, Boas introduced the concept of culture being the primary determining factor of the differences between various people. Taken to its logical conclusion, his findings explain why a Barack Obama has the elegance and patrician manner of an ancient Greek orator, but Adolf Hitler was the rabble-rousing demagogue that he was.

At the time that Boas was making his contribution to the constructive progress of American society, the 'one drop rule' prevailed in the United States. This meant that anyone who had 'one drop' of 'negro' blood should be categorised as black. This therefore means that, if you go back far enough, every human being should be categorised as black. According to the British anthropologist Dr. Christopher Stringer, FRS (1947-), who is one of the chief proponents of the 'Out of Africa' theory, all modern human beings originated in Africa, replacing the archaic forms of humanity such as Neanderthals and *Homo floresiensis* prior to migrating across Africa and into the non-African world between 50,000 and 100,000 years ago.

The 'one drop rule' was the most extreme form of racial prejudice ever known to man, an even more extreme application of racism than the Nazis applied to Jewishness. Under the Nuremberg Race Laws of 1935, anyone with three or more Jewish grandparents was a Jew, irrespective of whether they were practising Jews, converts, or atheists. Jews were excluded from possessing Reich citizenship, from marrying or having sexual relations with persons of 'German or related blood', and under ancillary laws, from owning businesses, attending universities, and ultimately from existing at all. Yet someone who was one eighth Jewish was not regarded as Jewish and did not fall prey to the draconian race laws the way Americans categorised as 'coloured' did. It is worth noting that the Jim Crow laws in America remained in force not only while the Nuremberg Laws were in force in Nazi territory, but both before and after.

Racism is racism, irrespective of whether it is a Nazi believing in the superiority of the Aryan race (which incidentally wasn't German all, but Iranian) and in so doing, depriving half Germans of their rights because they were also half Jewish, or a Southern racist from Alabama circa 1957 beating the one drop drum and decreeing that people who were fifteen-sixteenths white and one sixteenth Sub-Saharan African in origin should be categorised as black. There can be few more explicit affirmations of racism than ignoring one part of an individual's heritage at the expense of another, which is why the recent fashion for categorising mixed race people as being exclusively of the darker race is so dangerous.

To someone like me, whose great-grandmother was Jewish and who would not actually have existed at all had Hitler won the war, and who was also born and brought up in racially inclusive Jamaica, it is absolutely horrifying that there is a modern trend, now that anti-Jewishness is reviled, to extend the 'one drop rule', which was the ultimate in racism, and to present it as being anything but racism of the highest order. There has been a disturbing trend in recent years by the right-on lobby, to hijack the various gradations of colour that exist in mixed race communities, to expunge the differences, and to pretend that the only racial group worthy of recognition is the black. This is both factually inaccurate and racist. Of course, many people who fall into the trap of using the 'right-on' lingo do not actually intend to be racist. Indeed, I would go as far as saying that a good proportion of them actually think they are being politically correct and therefore the antithesis of racist. Yet political correctness has fallen into the trap dug for mixed race people by the 'one drop' lobby, of describing them in the identical way that racist Southerners used in the bad old days of Jim Crow.

A case in point is a most unfortunate incident that happened with the broadcaster Piers Morgan. Last year October, after Meghan Markle's pregnancy was announced, I was invited to go onto the *Good Morning Britain* TV show, which he hosts, to discuss the impending birth. Now, I declare an interest: I like and admire Piers Morgan. I know he is not everyone's cup of tea, but then neither am I. Nor indeed is anyone else with any character. He is straightforward and actually has principles, which he sticks to, whether they accord with popular opinion or not. I'd go as far as saying that a few more Piers Morgans are needed in the media at any time, whether today or in Germany in the mid-1930s, for it's people like him who defuse fashionable stupidities and would have reined in the Nazis if only more like him had existed. His championing of the rights of prisoners of war in Iraq at the turn of the century and of gun control laws in the United States more recently demonstrate unmistakably that, whether one agrees with him or not, he stands up for what he believes in, even to the extent of it costing him the editorship of a British national newspaper or a popular American television show. He is also a big enough man to allow others to disagree with him, which is why I alighted upon the erroneous description that his writers used in describing Meghan Markle and Prince Harry's baby as black. I had, and still have, no doubt that everyone at ITV thought that they were being very politically correct when they employed such an erroneous description. Yet Meghan herself has been, quite rightly, at pains, over the years, to describe herself as being bi-racial, not black or white. So I made the point that a child, who is three quarters or seven eighths white and only fractionally black, cannot be accurately described as being black. Piers very responsibly questioned me as to my premise, and I alluded to how similar such prevailing descriptions were to the categorisation of partly Jewish people under the Nazis, as they were being de-Germanised and shoved into gas ovens. He nodded, I blew him a kiss, and could not have been more astonished later on to read on the internet that one or two viewers seemed to think that I was accusing Piers of being racist, which I most certainly was not.

This incident highlighted, however, how, despite the progress made in Britain and America in dismantling the laws, customs and habits that so distorted race relations for so many years, our society needs to agree upon new definitions of race. Some of the prevailing ones are not only inaccurate, but verge on neo-racist. When they are employed in all innocence, as they were on the *Good Morning Britain* show, they highlight the need for accuracy, and for people everywhere, including the political-ly-correct, to use terms that do not unintentionally coincide with such odious concepts as the 'one drop' rule.

The irony is that many of the older descriptions and categorisations of race, and of racial gradations, which we as a society have been assiduously avoiding recently, are more factually accurate than some of the more fashionable terms employed today. No one would wish to return to the descriptions of the past, but even so, some of the current descriptions could do with some fine-tuning. I agree with Meghan Markle. Someone who has a Caucasian father and an Afro-American mother is not black or white, but bi-racial. By extension, no child of hers with Harry can be accurately categorised as black. The old description of coloured, which at least had the merit of acknowledging the duality of its heritage, is no longer regarded as being desirable, but even more offensive to the many white ancestors of the child would be their erasure if it were categorised as black.

Looking back on the descriptions used to categorise the different races, it becomes apparent that, prior to the massive immigration that took place worldwide in the second half of the twentieth Century, there was a degree of coincidence between colour and continent. Europeans were categorised as white. That applied whether they were olive-skinned Italians from Calabria, fair-skinned blondes from the Baltic region or swarthy Caucasians from the Caucasus.

The categorisation of whites as Caucasian was in itself telling. The Caucasians are a people whose territory borders that of Persia, Turkey and Russia. They are on the whole neither blue eyed nor blonde, nor even particularly fair-skinned. Caucasians as a racial group run the gamut from being dark-eyed, dark-haired and olive-complexioned to blue-eyed, fair-haired and fair-skinned, depending on where in Europe they originated.

Though Linnaeus's categorisation of the various races on continental grounds provided fodder for racists, and his description of Europeans as white and Africans as black caught on, the terms used by George Cuvier, the 'Founding Father of Palaeontology', to describe the various races were what entered the popular vocabulary. He categorised as Mongoloids not only the Red Americans and Brown Asians, but enlarged the spectrum to include the peoples indigenous to North Asia, East Asia, Central Asia, South East Asia, South Asia, and South America. This could include the indigenous peoples of the Arctic, North America, Central America, the Incas of Peru, New Zealand, Micronesia, and Polynesia. He also used the Spanish word for black, which the Spanish had used to describe the indigenous peoples of Sub-Saharan African: *negro*. This too caught on. The Spaniards having been the first importers of African blacks into their New World colonies to replace the indigenous Arawak, Carib and other Indians who died out shortly after Columbus discovered the West Indies, there was a degree of justice in their language being used to describe the people they had transplanted from one continent to another. It should be remembered, however, that the word *negro* in Spanish has no pejorative overtones. It means black, pure and simple.

For hundreds of years thereafter, people divided the world's population into three races: the Caucasian or white, the Negro or black, and the Mongoloid, or pretty much everything Asiatic or Asiatic looking.

If you were partly Indian and partly British, you were an Anglo-Indian. If you were partly Chinese or Japanese and partly Caucasian, you were

Eurasian. Because the most prevalent mixtures were between the whites and blacks, if you were half European and half Sub-Saharan African, you were a *mulatto/a*. If you were three quarters European and one quarter Sub-Saharan African, you were a *quadroon*, and if it was one eighth, you were an *octoroon*. While it is understandable that such terms as *mulatto* or *octoroon* fell out of use for the good reason that they were evocative of a time when racism was more acceptable than it should have been, unless they are replaced with equally accurate descriptions, or the terms bi-racial or/or multi-racial where appropriate are used as catch-alls to describe anyone who is to any degree interracial (which in itself suggests a discomfiting awareness of race), the drift towards mislabelling people might well continue. And it really should not. No child born to the Duke and Duchess of Sussex, or anyone else of such a heritage, can be truthfully described as being black, for since when did Caucasian blood become so deserving of neglect that a child whose ancestors are mostly white, and whose racial configuration is decidedly not black, should be described by the smallest percentage of its heritage at the expense of the largest part?

In fact, as racial melding continues and the old concept that one race was inferior to another disappears, the likely outcome is that the aggressiveness which previously characterised racial awareness will lessen. Already, one can see the progress made over the last fifty years, from racist separatism and racial supremacy to racial inclusiveness and its by-product, inter-racial unions. As a society, we are well on the way towards reverting to the acceptance of people from different racial backgrounds as being worthy of inclusion, not only in our world but also in our families. This was the attitude which was prevalent in the sixteenth and seventeenth centuries in Europe, and in the centuries before.

Long may it continue.

Chapter Three

THERE ARE UNDOUBTEDLY several people of colour in the present-day European royal families, but the first Queen of England, who is alleged to have been partly black, might – but equally might not – have been. Her name is Philippa of Hainault and she was the consort of King Edward III. Born at Valenciennes in the county of Hainault in the Low Countries (present day Belgium) circa 1313, she was the second daughter and fourth child of William I, Count of Hainault, and Joan of Valois, daughter of King Philip III of France and sister of the future King Philip IV. To say that she was well-connected would be an understatement. Her elder sister Margaret married the Wittelsbach prince Louis IV, who was King of the Romans from 1314, King of Italy from 1327, and Holy Roman Emperor from 1328. Margaret became Countess of Hainault in her own right following the death of their brother, William II, in battle in 1345. By then, Philippa had been married for some years to Edward III, whose father, Edward II, had sent Bishop Stapledon to Flanders in 1322 to inspect the Count's daughters with the idea of marrying one of them to his heir in the interest of securing an alliance with that strategically important territory. The bishop sent back a detailed account of Philippa:

> 'The lady whom we saw has not uncomely hair, betwixt blue-black and brown. Her head is clean-shaped, her forehead high and broad, and standing somewhat forward. Her face narrows between the eyes, and the lower part of her face is still more narrow and slender than her forehead. Her eyes are blackish-brown and deep. Her nose is fairly smooth and even, save that it is somewhat broad at the tip and also flattened, and yet it is no snub-nose. Her nostrils are also broad, her mouth fairly wide. Her lips somewhat full, and especially the lower lip. Her teeth which have fallen and grown are white enough, but the rest are not so white. The lower teeth project a little beyond the upper;

49

yet this is but little seen. Her ears and chin are comely enough. Her neck, shoulders and all her body are well set and unmaimed; and nought is amiss so far as a man may see. Moreover, she is brown of skin all over, and much like her father; and in all things she is pleasant enough, as it seems to us. And the damsel will be of the age of nine years on St. John's day next to come, as her saint saith. She is neither too tall nor too short for such an age; she is of fair carriage, and well taught in all that becometh her rank, and highly esteemed and well beloved of her father and mother and of all her meinie, in so far as we could inquire and learn the truth.'

Depending on their sympathies, historians are inclined to believe or discount the fact that Philippa might have had what used to be called a '*touch of the tar brush*.' Historians who accept that she did indeed have a black ancestor are inclined to the view that she was a '*throwback*', again another term from the past which is seldom used nowadays but seems appropriately descriptive in these circumstances, no other word existing to describe the presence of her dark complexion and the suggested Sub-Saharan cast of her facial features. There are no known contemporaneous portraits of her, so it is impossible to tell whether the bishop's description was accurate. It seems likely that it was, however, for Stapledon had been charged by Edward II with the specific purpose of inspecting her as a possible bride for his son, and it would make no sense to invent a misleading description when his sovereign was relying upon him to convey accurate information.

The British Crown in the early fourteenth century was not only French in lineage, as a result of being descended from the Duke of Normandy, who conquered England in 1066 and became King William I, but was also French in attitude, and indeed would soon claim the crown of France as being rightfully theirs. The Norman conquest of England was one of the greatest upheavals in history. Not only did the English people find themselves occupied by a strange race, but one which was oppressive, spoke another language, had alien customs, was physically different, and set about imposing its will upon its captive subjects.

Up to the Norman Conquest, the English were primarily a mixture of Briton and Anglo-Saxon. They were relatively fair skinned and light-haired. The French, on the other hand, had a far greater range in skin and hair colour. They went from fair to dark. Although the tendency was for the northern French to be fairer and the southern French darker, there were exceptions within those rules. Yet the average Occitan was appreciably darker than the average Parisian, with the peoples from the southern territories of France being swarthy, indicating that the Romans and Moors, and their slaves from Africa, had left their mark in more than merely cultural ways.

Bishop Stapledon made the point that Philippa was very much like her father, the Count of Hainault. It is therefore likely that she was not a '*throwback*' and that she inherited not only her features and complexion from him, but like him resembled the ancestor who introduced the strain of darkness together with features with a hint of Africa about them. Such a lineage was neither a consideration nor a preventative in marital terms in the early 1300s. Position and class were infinitely more important than the colour of one's skin or the cast of one's features. This would remain true in royal circles, even during the two hundred years while anti-black prejudice was playing out throughout the Western world and its colonies. As we will see, time and again women of colour would marry into Caucasian royal families. Whenever there was opposition to the marriage, the primary objection would not be on the grounds of colour, but on the disparity of rank. This mattered far more than the tint of the skin.

Whether Philippa was simply a dark-complexioned Caucasian with an African cast to her features, or had African blood, is unverifiable several centuries after the fact, but what is indisputable is that King Edward II of England regarded her as sufficiently desirable a bride for his son and heir Edward, Prince of Wales, to commit to a marriage taking place within two years of an offer being made for her hand.

Four years later, young Edward's mother travelled to Hainault with her son in tow to seek the Count of Hainault's assistance in deposing her husband. If the Count of Hainault helped, which he did, his daughter Philippa would become Queen of England. In keeping with the code of honour then prevailing, Edward II's assurance of a marriage taking place within two years of a formal agreement remained one of the conditions for its taking place, even though the king's deposition was central to it.

Edward II's queen, Isabella of France (1295-1358), was a formidable woman. Her role was pivotal to her son becoming King Edward III years before his time, and central to Philippa becoming his Queen Consort. For those reasons alone, a detailed examination of the part she played would be desirable. What makes such an examination crucial, however, is how her character and antecedents changed the course of the English state. It is fair to say that, without Queen Isabella, events in England and on the Continent would have taken an entirely different route. She was truly what nowadays would be called a 'game-changer'.

She was the first cousin of Philippa of Hainault's mother, Joan of Valois, both women being granddaughters of King Philip III of France through an elder and a younger brother. Known to history as the 'She-Wolf of France', she was the youngest surviving child and only surviving daughter of King Philip IV of France and the Queen Regnant of Navarre, Joan I. Isabella had arrived in England aged 12 to marry the fourth and eldest surviving son of King Edward 1, who created his heir the first Prince of Wales in 1301, following the execution of the last Welsh prince of Wales, Dafydd ap Gruffydd, on 3rd October 1283. Edward II was approximately eleven years Isabella's senior and had been king for a year before their marriage in 1308. She arrived during a period of growing dissension between the king and his barons owing to Edward II's excessive devotion to his favourite, Piers Gaveston. According to Medieval chroniclers, Edward had a taste for sodomy and his favourite was his lover. The very mention of this fact signified significantly more than people today might appreciate. In that rigidly Christian, anti-homosexual age, sodomy was viewed with horror and revulsion, so for a king to have such a reputation was akin to a ruler today being known as a flagrant paedophile, or something equally antipathetic to contemporary values.

The king's lover himself deserves examination, for without him the world into which Isabella married would have been less threatening, and the whole course of her life, and that of her son Edward III and his consort, Philippa, would have been more predictable and conventional. Gaveston was the son of a Gascon knight and had made such a favourable impression upon Edward I, as a result of his chivalrous conduct and martial skills, that in 1300 the king had appointed him to the household of his heir, the younger Edward, then known as 'Edward of Carnarvon'. This appointment was one which the king would come to rue, but not before he had appointed Gaveston as Guardian to the 3rd Lord Mortimer, Roger, 1st Earl of March (1287-1330), at young Edward's request - an appointment which would also have a knock-on effect in the later lives of the She-Wolf, her son and daughter-in-law, as we will soon see. It sharpened Gaveston's taste for preferment, for the Guardian of a rich young man could cream off sizeable amounts from his charge's estate. As Gaveston flourished, so too did his relationship with the Heir to the Throne. So close did the two men become that it caused a series of scandals. Gaveston was exceedingly greedy, the young prince generous to the point of entrancement. So obviously was he beguiled by Gaveston that onlookers came to an inevitable, and for the time, odious, indeed dangerous and ultimately disastrous, conclusion that they were homosexual lovers.

One scandal involved the Treasurer of England, Walter Langton, Bishop of Coventry and Lichfield. This resulted in the king banning his heir from Court and banishing Gaveston from the royal household because of pecuniary excesses. No sooner was that matter resolved than there was another scandal, when Gaveston deserted a Scottish campaign to attend a tournament. According to *The Chronicle of Walter of Guisborough*, the final straw for Edward I was when the Prince of Wales appeared before him requesting that his County of Ponthieu be gazetted to Gaveston. Gaveston had only been pardoned the month before, and the king was so furious that his heir not only wanted to surrender valuable Crown territory to his 'friend' but was prepared to put this friend's financial interests above the good of the Crown, that he ripped handfuls out of his son's hair, threw him out of his apartments, and ordered Gaveston to leave the Realm after 30th April 1307.

Gaveston's departure was as much a commentary on the extent of young Edward's captivation as it was upon the relish with which his supposed lover accepted his prince's largesse. It also places in disturbing context the full extent of the triangularity of the marital bed that Isabella would be occupying when she married Edward II. Before that, however, Edward II ensured that he thwarted his father's punishment of his lover by sending him into exile equipped with richly caparisoned horses, fine clothing, and the then vast sum of £260 in cash, causing further consternation in the land.

However, Gaveston was not away for long. By early July, Edward I lay dying at Burgh by Sands in Carlisle, near the Scottish border. The king beseeched his most trusted advisors, Guy de Beauchamp, Earl of Warwick; Henry de Lacy, Earl of Lincoln; and Aymer de Valence, 2nd Earl of Pembroke, to keep Gaveston away from young Edward. This, however, proved impossible. No sooner was Edward II king than he recalled Gaveston from exile. He arrived within a month.

Edward II was remarkably injudicious in showering his favourite not only with riches but honours. On the 6th August, 1307, one day short of a calendar month after succeeding to the throne, he named Gaveston 1st Earl of Cornwall in the fifth creation of the title. This caused a sensation in the kingdom, for the young man was of relatively humble stock. Yet here was the captivated king raising an obscure Gascon knight's son to the then highest levels of the peerage. Until then, the Earls of Cornwall had been connections of the Royal Family. For instance, William the Conqueror's half-brother Robert, Count of Mortain, had been the Earl of Cornwall of the second creation, and the previous earl had been Richard, King of the Romans, second son of King John of England.

Nor was the earldom of Cornwall an empty title. It came with vast land holdings bringing in an income of £4,000 per annum, a sum in excess of the annual budget of many small states. These holdings included most of Cornwall, large swathes of Devonshire, Berkshire, Oxfordshire and Lincolnshire, as well as parts of Yorkshire and sundry other more minor properties. To add insult to injury, Edward II arranged a marriage between his beloved Gaveston and his niece, Lady Margaret de Clare, daughter of the 7th Earl of Gloucester, 6th Earl of Hertford, and 9th Lord de Clare etc. etc. and his wife, Joan of Acre, a granddaughter of King Edward I, and the second eldest of Edward II's sisters.

Kings were founts of honour and wealth, and anyone who became a favourite of the monarch had access to them. Responsibility, however, required both monarch and favourite to demonstrate sufficient restraint in order that the gush of privilege would not douse one individual so utterly that everyone else was left parched with resentment and envy. To raise one relatively humbly-born favourite to such heights, as Edward II did, not only antagonised the other magnates, but also raised questions as to the capability of the monarch to rule wisely.

Although Edward II enjoyed the goodwill of the people at the time of his accession, he quickly alienated his barons with his promotion of the newly minted Earl of Cornwall. Edward then compounded the offence by appointing Gaveston Regent when he left his kingdom to marry Isabella, which he did on 25th January 1308 at Boulogne-sur-Mer. Edward II plainly believed that his match with the French princess was a royal union which would reflect well upon him and bring him worldly advantage. What he cannot have realised was that he was also marrying into one of the most terrifyingly competent political institutions in the world, the result of which would be his ultimate destruction. His bride would prove to be his undoing, replacing him with his namesake son and heir, whom she would marry off to her cousin, whose parents would assist her to seize the throne and elevate their daughter to the premature majesty of a queen before her time.

The French chronicler Geoffrey of Paris described Isabella as being 'the beauty of beauties….in the kingdom if not all Europe.' So far, so good. Good looks ran in the French royal family, if not the Navarrese. Philip IV was known as '*Philippe le Bel*', 'Philip the Fair', not because of his colouring but for his striking good looks. On the other hand, Isabella's mother Joan of Navarre was described contemporaneously as being plump and plain. Nevertheless, she had a far more attractive character than her husband, being enterprising, bold and courageous, in contrast to Philip, who was obsessed with material possessions, rigid, inflexible, and so cold that the Bishop of Pamiers said, 'He is neither man nor beast. He is a statue.' Despite this, Henry and Joan were a loving and devoted couple, so Isabella had first-hand insight into what a good marriage was all about. However, Joan died in 1305 in childbirth. One contemporary chronicler asserted that Philip killed Joan, but this seems unlikely, though there was a financial benefit to her death. Not only had she been, in her own right, Queen of Navarre, but she had also been Countess of Champagne, a rich province. Henry was chronically short of money, not only because of the wars he waged, but also because of his extravagant lifestyle. With Joan dead, his influence over her territories became unchecked.

Following the victorious conclusion of his Flemish War during the same year as Joan's death, Henry found a novel way of making money which destroyed his reputation for all time and showed that he was as much a wolf as his daughter would later be credited as being. He shamelessly decreed that the silver coinage which had lost its purchasing power through his fecklessness should return to its 1285 level of 3.96 grammes of silver per *livre*, and that the old and new currencies should be harmonised by devaluing the debased coinage of 1303 by two-thirds. This destroyed the debtors of France, who were obliged to repay their old-value loans at the new-value rates. Philip then cynically sequestered the silver of the money-lenders, who were usually Jewish, by expelling the Jews on the 22nd July 1306. He confiscated their property a month later, in the hope that this would result in the books being balanced and the coinage restored. But the Jews had been fair dealers while Philip's collectors were rapacious, and riots ensued. On 30th December 1306, Philip was forced to seek refuge in the Temple (where Louis XVI and Marie Antoinette would centuries later be imprisoned prior to their execution), the Paris headquarters of the Knights Templar, the monastic military order which, by that time, had surrendered their traditional role of being protectors of Christian pilgrims in preference for banking and other commercial enterprises. They were one of Philip's main creditors, and within ten months of giving the king refuge, he turned on them the way he had turned on the Jews. On Friday, 13th October 1307, hundreds of Knights Templar all over France were simultaneously arrested and accused of simony, usury, sodomy, blasphemy, financial corruption and fraud amongst other charges. Their properties were seized, their bank confiscated, and they were tortured into making false confessions. Despite being answerable only to the Pope, they were condemned to death and burnt at the stake after Philip forced the Holy Father to disband the organisation.

Philip IV was a brilliant tactician who not only destroyed the Jews of France and the Knights Templar, but also subverted the Papacy itself. Isabella, being his daughter, would have been privy to enough of what was going on to sharpen her political perceptiveness as she witnessed her father devouring his adversaries and creating power blocs in his favour. Pope Clement V was a Frenchman, the former Raymond Bertrand de

Goth. He had succeeded to the Papal Throne in 1305 following a year's interregnum while the French and Italian cardinals struggled to find a successor to Benedict XI. Although his election was an attempt to neutralise the various factions, it had the effect of converting the Papacy into a French pawn. When Clement moved the seat of the Papacy from Rome to Avignon, the rout of the Italians was complete, and would remain so for the next seven Papal reigns. During that time, all the Popes were French. It was only in 1377, when Gregory XI returned the Papal Court to Rome, that the French stranglehold on the Papacy ended, since when there has never been another French Pope.

It was into this powerful, ruthless and politically effective institution that Edward II was marrying and which his children would be products of. His bride Isabella was not only a ravishing beauty with the brains and character to become the power she ultimately would, but she was also the sole surviving daughter of the three girls born to her parents. She had four brothers, a younger one who died in childhood, and three elder ones who all lived to become kings of France in adulthood. Only girls in families of boys are often made to feel special, and Isabella was no exception to that rule. Her father struck a hard bargain, both on her own behalf and on behalf of the French Crown, for the hand of his daughter. Edward II was forced to concede administrative aspects of his lands in France to the French Crown, and to pay homage to Henry IV as his liege in his capacity as Duke of Aquitaine. Isabella also enjoyed the benefit of enhanced dower rights, while Edward II had to concede further to a commission to implement the Treaty of Paris of 1303, which had not only confirmed that Isabella would marry Edward but had returned Gascony to English ownership, thereby setting the stage for the 'Hundred Years' War' which raged from 1337 to 1453.

Being only twelve years old at the time of her marriage, there was never much prospect of Isabella sharing Edward II's bed during the first years of their marriage, had he even been inclined to do so, but Edward's tastes ran to men, if his contemporaries are to be believed.

The newlyweds returned to England the month after their wedding. Edward II had ordered the Palace of Westminster to be sumptuously restored in preparation for their coronation and wedding feast. There were specially constructed marble tables, a fountain which produced wine and the spiced medieval drink pimento, as well as lavish hangings and other symbols of wealth typical of the period. The event itself became the source of yet more scandal and consternation, neither of which enhanced the security or stability of the Nation and Institution into which Isabella was marrying.

It comes as some surprise to discover, therefore, that Isabella seems to have had a tolerably civil relationship with Gaveston, at least at first. Nevertheless, his role at the celebrations, following his regency, caused disquiet. Notwithstanding the fact that Gaveston had actually acquitted himself responsibly during the regency, there were rumours that he had purloined royal funds as well as Isabella's wedding presents. His excessive influence over Edward II and royal policy led one chronicler to observe that 'two kings reigned in the kingdom, the one in name and the other in deed.' Neither Edward II nor Gaveston had learnt that flaunting the closeness of their bond, and the influence that the latter had over the former, was neither clever nor judicious.

Both young men seemed to exult in overt displays of their intimacy. During the coronation and wedding feast Edward ostentatiously hurled the centrality of Gaveston's role in his life in the faces of the onlookers. Using the occasion to affirm the power of one and the affection of the other was neither tactful nor wise. Isabella's uncles Louis, Count of Evreux, and Charles, Count of Valois (whose daughter Joan, Countess of Hainault would later on play a crucial part in dethroning the wayward bridegroom) were but two of the many onlookers in both the English and French contingent who were outraged by Gaveston's precedence, first at the coronation ceremony and then at the wedding feast. As they took in the unmissable splendour of the upstart's raiments, as they observed the king ignoring his queen, seated by herself while Edward sat with Gaveston, to whom he was plainly in thrall, as they witnessed the two young men chatting, giggling, and cavorting while ignoring Isabella's presence, Edward II was fanning the flames that would scorch both his reputation and Gaveston's. The result of such a flagrant display was fury throughout the ruling classes of the land, and consternation in France when Philip heard of his son-in-law's disrespectfulness and mistreatment of his daughter.

Both king and favourite, who should have learnt from their previous errors, which had resulted in Gaveston's previous exiles, soon learnt that, yet again, their conduct had political consequences. The Parliament which met shortly after the coronation and wedding feast refused to discuss government business until the issue of Gaveston had been resolved to their satisfaction. Although the Earl of Lincoln convinced the barons to back down, the succeeding Parliament once more raised the problem of Gaveston and demanded his exile. This time they refused to budge. Their position was strengthened when Isabella and her father supported the motion in the first display of their wiliness. Outmanoeuvred, Edward II acquiesced to the demands and agreed to exile Gaveston to his duchy of Aquitaine. When the time came, however, he changed his mind, and rather than sending him into a distant exile, appointed his nephew-by-marriage and flagrant favourite Lord Lieutenant of Ireland.

During the next three years, Gaveston's fortunes ebbed and flowed along with the king's as a power struggle involving Parliament and the barons ensued. One of the main planks of Edward's policy was continuing the war with Scotland which his father had started. Both kings were determined that the Scots acknowledge the English king as their overlord. This required funds, which meant that Edward II needed Parliament. Throughout this time, Isabella maintained a good working relationship with her husband's favourite. After further exiles and recalls involving Gaveston, during which Edward II made concessions to Parliament known as the Ordinances of 1311, the business of governing the country appeared to be on track. However, tensions remained high between the barons and Edward II, who then revoked the Ordinances and recalled Gaveston from his latest exile in 1312. The two men, with Isabella in tow pregnant with her first child, travelled together, before Gaveston separated from the royal couple, remaining at Scarborough while they continued on to York. Gaveston was then entrapped by his enemies. When he surrendered, he had in his possession a vast horde of gold, silver and gems, which appeared to be part of the royal treasury. He would later be accused of stealing it from Edward, though it is far more likely that he was entrusted with it by the king himself. Gaveston was nevertheless tried under the Ordinances which Edward II had revoked but which the barons, under the leadership of Edward's cousin Thomas, Earl of Lancaster, now brought back into being. On the grounds of being a traitor, Gaveston was executed at Blacklow Hill on 19th June 1312.

Edward II was not only grief-stricken but furious, but there was nothing he could do to bring Gaveston back to life. Nevertheless, it looked as if civil war would break out. It was narrowly averted when the Earl of Pembroke negotiated a peace treaty between the opposing factions, with the king pardoning the barons for Gaveston's murder while Parliament supported the king's campaign against the Scots.

With Gaveston dead and Edward II and Isabella the proud parents of a baby boy, the future Edward III, the way was paved for a rapprochement with Philip IV. He agreed generous terms for resolving his differences with his son-in-law over Gascony when Edward II and Isabella went to Paris in June 1313. There were sumptuous banquets, heraldic occasions and spectacular ceremonies, such as the knighting of Isabella's brothers and some 200 other men at Notre Dame Cathedral, with both kings and their respective daughter and wife agreeing to embark upon a crusade to the Levant.

Upon his return to England, Edward II discovered that there were benefits to the loss of his favourite. For the first time since his accession, peaceable relations with his barons and prosperity became the order of the day. Parliament had agreed to the raising of taxes, the Pope had loaned him £25,000, Philip a further £33,000, and there were further loans from the Italian banker, Antonio Pessagno, who had replaced the Frescobaldis, to whom Edward II had been so deeply in debt that he had found it more convenient to break off relations with them than to continue the relationship.

Within a year, the oasis of peace and prosperity was revealed to be a mirage when King Robert the Bruce of Scotland thrashed Edward II's army in the Battle of Bannockburn. This misfortune was followed by an even greater one: the Great Famine of 1315-17. During it, Isabella gave birth to her second son, John, at Eltham Palace on 15th August 1316. Two years later, she would produce her first daughter, Eleanor, followed three years after that by Joan. Known to history as 'Joan of the Tower' as a result of being born in the Tower of London on 5th July 1321, she became Queen Consort of Scotland when she married King David II. In a day and age when annual babies were the rule rather than the exception, even when couples had little or no love for each other, the gaps between the four children suggested that there might well have been a reluctance on Edward II's part to fulfil his conjugal duties. Be that as it may, Joan of the Tower's birth coincided with the beginning of the long-threatened Civil War, which began as a result of her father's fateful propensity towards male favourites. It also signalled the end of her parents' marriage in all but name, giving Isabella further opportunity to earn the sobriquet of She-Wolf for the skilful way in which she protected her own interests and those of her children.

After Gaveston's execution, Edward II had quickly replaced his late favourite with a new one: Roger D'Amory, the younger son of Sir Robert D'Amory. Lord D'Amory, as he soon became, was not as avaricious as his predecessor, nor did he seek to flaunt the advantages his patron heaped upon him, with the result that his existence did not antagonise the barons in the way that Gaveston's had done. In 1317 Edward II endowed him with the ultimate accolade, when he arranged a marital alliance between his favourite and his niece. D'Amory became the third husband of Lady Elizabeth de Clare, youngest daughter of the Earl of Gloucester and Edward's sister Joan of Acre. Her elder sister Margaret had been married to Gaveston, and her younger, Eleanor, had been the wife of Hugh Despenser the Younger (1286-1326) since 1306.

The husbands of all three women are accepted as being the king's lovers, leading to the conclusion that Edward had found a way of rewarding them for services rendered in the bedroom while tying them to him maritally.

The Despenser family in particular was an interesting one and they played a huge and catastrophic role in English politics. Their connection with the king would force Isabella's hand, ultimately leading to Edward's, and their own, destruction, bringing about the elevation of Isabella's son and daughter-in-law Philippa as well as her lover and causing their own and the king's downfall. There were two Hugh Despensers, father and son, known as the Elder and the Younger. Hugh Despenser the Elder had originally been a minor nobleman whose family had been loyal supporters of the monarchy, resulting in his advancement to a position of pre-eminence. His wife was Lady Isabella de Beauchamp, daughter of the 9th Earl of Warwick, a powerful magnate. He had loyally served King Edward I on the battlefield and as a diplomat, being rewarded with a barony in 1295. Edward I, who was perpetually short of money, had owed him 2,000 marks, but this debt was expunged by the marriage of Hugh Despenser the Younger to the king's granddaughter, Lady Eleanor. Both Hugh Despensers were loyal to both Edwards. Following the death of Edward I, Hugh the Elder and the Younger remained supportive of the king throughout his travails arising out of his devotion to Gaveston. The Elder was one of the few powerful barons to openly stand by Edward II and was rewarded for his efforts by being made Chief Administrator. His corruption and avariciousness were so flagrant, however, that he rapidly lost support nationwide, though he retained the confidence of the king.

Throughout the first eight years of his marriage to Edward II's niece Eleanor, Despenser the Younger remained a relatively impecunious knight. Then his wife's only brother Gilbert, 8th Earl of Gloucester, was killed at the Battle of Bannockburn. Eleanor became joint heiress, along with her sisters Elizabeth and Margaret, to the enormous wealth of the earldom of Gloucester. Eleanor alone inherited vast swathes of Glamorgan, which Despenser expanded with such ruthlessness that it led to a rebellion in the Welsh Marches. He cheated his sister-in-law Elizabeth out of Gower and Usk in Wales, and forced Alice de Lacy, who was Countess of Salisbury and Lincoln in her own right, to turn over lands to him that were rightfully hers. He murdered Llywelyn Bren, known in England as 'Llewellyn of the Woods', who had led a revolt against the king two years before, despite the Welsh nobleman being Despenser's hostage and therefore assured of safety under the codes of honourable conduct then prevailing. This act alone would go some way towards losing Edward II support, and would hasten his and both Despenser's deaths. According to W. Childs, in *Vita Edwardi Secundi* (2005: New York, Oxford University Press), Despenser the Younger was such an unscrupulous and lawless character that he had even, for a while, been a pirate in the English Channel, 'a sea monster, lying in wait for merchants as they crossed the sea.'

Edward II would have been well advised to have remained with his favourite Lord D'Amory. Had he done so he would have kept his throne, his wife and his life. None of the barons had any complaints against D'Amory, who was one of their own and reassuringly not avaricious. However, in 1318 the king appointed Despenser the Younger as Chamberlain. A ruggedly attractive man who was as wily as he was energetic and resourceful, he used his position at Court to inveigle the King away from his favourite. According to the 14th century Court historian Jean Froissart, 'he was a sodomite' who used his sexual prowess to seduce and entrance the king. This was an accusation which would be repeated from the pulpit by the Bishop of Winchester, Adam Orleton, in 1326, when 'the king and his husband' fled to Wales. Being the son of Hugh Despenser the Elder, who by this time was an important member of Edward II's inner circle and whose faithful support of the king against his political opponents, the followers of the Earl of Lancaster and their allies, the lords in the Welsh Marches, Despenser the Younger rapidly became all-powerful once he was Edward II's latest favourite.

Trouble began as soon as Despenser the Younger supplanted D'Amory. He was even more avaricious than his notoriously greedy father, who had faced widespread condemnation for his practice of trumping up charges to steal or extort land and money. But this was of scant import beside the self-aggrandisement and corruption wielded by the new royal favourite, who was soon regarded as worse than Gaveston. Within three years of his appointment as Chamberlain, the Younger was not only loathed by all strata of society, but feared by them as well. Chief amongst these was the queen herself, who had been able to come to a *modus vivendi* with Gaveston which had permitted them to work together, but she was unable to find common ground with Despenser the Younger. As he gained power and caught up her friends and supporters in the 'sweeping revenge' which was meted out to anyone who crossed him or had supported the execution of Gaveston, Despenser the Younger went so far as to refuse to return money owed to the Queen and refused to return to her the Castles of Marlborough and Devizes which he and his father had seized from her. Edward also began to treat Isabella more meanly than he had hitherto done, refusing to include her in any of the spoils of battle following the Battle of Boroughbridge which resulted in the execution of his enemy/

cousin, the Earl of Lancaster.

Worse, however, was to come. Isabella was nearly captured by the Scots when Edward left her in a vulnerable position then, when capture seemed imminent, offered to send Despenser troops to her aid. This she refused, stating that she preferred friendly troops, and, when these were not forthcoming, her knights commandeered a ship which she used to escape capture, though not before two of her ladies-in-waiting were killed. Furious with her husband for abandoning her to the Scots, and with the Despensers for advising him to retreat rather than help her, Isabella hereafter unofficially separated herself from her husband, leaving him to live with Despenser the Younger, for whom she had developed a frank loathing. Successive authors, including the respected historical novelist Alison Weir, have speculated that he either tried to assault her, or succeeding in doing so. Whether this was so or not, the fact is, Isabella was subjected to a degree of provocation that would have created hatred in even the most benign personality. Then she refused to take an oath of loyalty to the Despensers, which resulted in her being stripped of her right to grant royal patronages. All her lands were then confiscated, her household staff detained, and her younger children removed from her custody and placed in the care of the Despensers. Assault or no assault, she would have had to be made of stone not to have ended up reviling Despenser the Younger. This she now did, ultimately becoming the focal point of opposition to him.

This was a dangerous position for the king to be in. Wives who are mothers of the heirs to the throne as well as rallying points of opposition, and whose existence is endangered by the presence of a loathsome favourite, are a threat. But when that threat is exacerbated by the presence of a fourth side to what was previously a triangle, trouble is bound to loom. This came in the form of Roger Mortimer, 3rd Baron Mortimer and 1st Earl of March (1287-1330), who had once been Gaveston's ward. His grandfather had killed Despenser the Younger's. Now that the Younger had power, he let it be known that he intended to settle scores by eliminating Mortimer. This was quite possibly blunderbuss talk, intended to justify his rapacious acquisition of lands belonging to the Mortimers. Mortimer, however, was a rich and powerful noble, Lord Lieutenant of

Ireland and the husband of Joan de Geneville, 2nd Lady Geneville in her own right as well as heiress to many estates in the Welsh Marches. After Edward II granted Despenser the Younger lands in the Marches belonging to Mortimer, and bearing in mind the Younger's threats to his life, Mortimer joined the growing opposition to the king and the Despensers. He and the other Marcher lords, whose land had been diverted to the favourite, embarked upon devastating raids on Despenser lands in Wales. When Mortimer was summoned, along with the 4th Earl of Hereford, to appear before Edward II in 1321, he refused to do so while 'the younger Despenser was in the King's train.' He then marched his uniformed troops to London, besieging the capital when they were prevented from entering it.

This insurrection caused the Lords Ordainers, led by Edward's first cousin, the 2nd Earl of Lancaster, to demand the banishment of both Hugh Despenser the Elder and the Younger. Edward II's half-brother Edmund of Woodstock, Earl of Kent, replaced the Elder as Lord Warden of the Cinque Ports, while father and son sailed into exile. It was not to be for long, however. The following year, with the Mortimers distracted in Wales putting down uprisings in their lands, Edward II felt able to recall the two Hugh Despensers. He elevated the Elder to Earl of Winchester while the younger was the 1st Lord Despenser.

By now, the king and queen were on opposite sides of the struggle, though Edward II did not yet realise it. Isabella, however, had gradually come to the understanding that there was not room enough in her kingdom for both her and her husband's favourite. She appreciated that the only way she could survive and have a tolerable life would be if Despenser the Younger and her husband were overthrown. Getting rid of the lover wasn't enough. What might happen in the event that the Younger was got rid of, and Edward II found another favourite who might be as bad or worse than this one had proven to be? No. There was only one solution: eradication.

Moreover, Isabella now had her equivalent to Edward's Despenser. At which point Mortimer had become her lover is not known to scholars, but most modern historians believe that they became romantically involved while they were both in England during these struggles. It was not merely a case of my enemy's enemy is my friend, for contemporary depictions of Mortimer indicate that he was a potently attractive man. There is therefore every reason to believe that the relationship that developed between them owed as much to genuine attraction as to expediency and a desire to survive against the odds.

With the Despensers back in England, Mortimer and another Marcher lord, Humphrey de Bohun, led the rebellion against them which became known as the Despenser War of 1321-1322. Throughout this, Isabella had to play a canny hand, and she did, never letting slip that she wished to see her husband overthrown and his favourite dead.

In January 1322, Mortimer put Bridgnorth to flames, but when he attacked Shrewsbury, being outnumbered, he was defeated by Edward II. This was the beginning of the end of the Despenser War, which came with the Battle of Boroughbridge, north-west of York. Mortimer and the king's cousin Thomas, Earl of Lancaster, were captured and both condemned to death, and the Lancastrian prince executed while Mortimer's sentence was commuted to life imprisonment and he was taken to the Tower of London. The Despenser War was now at an end, but, by allowing Mortimer to live, its objective, the removal of Despenser the Younger, remained very much alive. In the Tower, Mortimer entered into a plot with Gerald de Alspaye, the sub-lieutenant of the Tower's Constable, to drug the warders during a feast, thereby enabling him to escape. After he escaped and failed to capture Windsor and Wallingford Castles, warrants were issued for Mortimer's capture dead or alive, but he fled to France.

Isabella, meanwhile, was desperate to escape from her husband and the influence wielded by the hated younger Despenser. She seized her opportunity when a territorial conflict known as the 'War of Saint-Sardos' between her husband and her brother King Charles IV of France, , gave her good cause to travel to her native country to negotiate a peace settlement between them. She was helped in this by the Pope, who had suggested her as an intermediary. It is likely that Pope John XXII appreciated Isabella's predicament, and understood the need for finding a means of her departing from the kingdom without arousing the suspicion of her husband or his putative lover. The condition of England, with its turbulence, instability, and unpredictability, was of grave concern, not only to the Pontiff, but to other foreign powers. Since Isabella had proven herself to be politically adept throughout the years of strife, while Edward II had shown himself to be the antithesis, there is every reason to suppose that the momentous journey she embarked on was no coincidence, but a created opportunity.

In France, Isabella was greeted with all due pomp by her brother. Relatively benevolent terms for peace were agreed, which also suggests that the Pope and French King were in cahoots to prop up the English queen's position. If that is so, Edward II fell into the trap laid by them. He now made the ultimately fatal error of creating his son and heir Duke of Aquitaine in his stead, to avoid leaving the kingdom to pay homage to Charles. By sending the future Edward III to France to pay the homage that he, the English king, would not, Edward II had exposed himself to replacement in a hitherto unthinkable way.

Isabella took full advantage of her husband's error. Now that she and her son were safely out of the kingdom, she refused to return to England, forcing Edward II to send increasingly urgent messages to the Pope and Charles IV requiring his wife and son's return. John XXII and Charles IV both stonewalled the king. The French king responded to his brother-in-law stating that the 'queen has come of her own free will and may freely return if she wishes. But if she prefers to remain here, she is my sister and I refuse to expel her.' Charles IV then double-crossed Edward II, refusing to return the lands in Aquitaine which he had previously promised to, resulting in a new provisional agreement whereby Edward would resume administration of the unoccupied territories while France would continue to remain in those already under occupation.

Worse was to follow. Isabella refused to receive her husband's emissary, Walter Stapledon, Bishop of Exeter. She began dressing as a widow, stating that Despenser had ruined her marriage. More ominously, she now emerged as the rallying point for opposition to her husband's regime. Amongst those who joined her in France were two members of the English Royal Family, men who until recently had been numbered amongst Edward II's most loyal supporters: his half-brother Edmund of Woodstock, 1st Earl of Kent, sixth son of their father and of Margaret of France, sister of Isabella's father; and John of Brittany, 4ᵗʰ Earl of Richmond, a grandson of Edward I.

Also in France was Mortimer, who had ended up there after his escape from the Tower of London. While both he and Isabella were in Paris, they re-met through her cousin Joan, Countess of Hainault. They now began an open affair. This was particularly daring, for adultery was a serious crime for all women, but especially so for the wives of kings and princes. It was also treason for a man to sleep with a queen; the penalty was death by drawing and quartering. Moreover, Isabella herself had been responsible for the imprisonment of the wives of her three brothers during the 'Tour de Nesle Affair' of 1314, when she had accused them of adultery. The consequences to her three sisters-in-law could not have been more serious. At the time that Isabella began conducting her affair with Mortimer with almost as much flagrance as Edward II had been conducting his with Despenser the Younger, her youngest brother Charles IV was king. Blanche of Burgundy, his first wife, had recently died, after years of imprisonment followed by banishment to a nunnery when she became Queen of France, while her sister-in-law, Margaret of Burgundy, had been confined to a dungeon at the Château Gaillard during the year she was queen, before dying of pneumonia. Both their lovers were executed. Only Blanche's sister Joan had escaped a long imprisonment, partly because her husband, who became King Philip V of France from 1316-1322, refused to repudiate her, and she was finally cleared of wrongdoing by the Parlement of Paris.

The Tour de Nesle Affair created a huge scandal which would have a knock-on effect on the French monarchy for the remainder of its existence, the questionable paternity of potential rulers of France thereafter resulting in a strict application of Salic Law, which prevented any female from acceding to the throne of France. Yet there was Isabella, openly flouting her affair with Mortimer, while they plotted how to overthrow her husband and seize his throne with themselves in the seats of power.

Helping them was Isabella's immensely rich cousin, Joan of Hainault. She now proposed a match, suggested previously by Edward II through Stapledon, the same bishop Isabella now refused to receive, between her daughter Philippa and Edward, Prince of Wales. There is little doubt that

Joan's aim was the crown of England for her daughter, and not the crown some time in the distant future either, but here, and now. She promised a substantial dowry as well as troops and ships which could be used to invade England and place Philippa's husband-to-be Edward III on his father's throne.

In the summer of 1326, Isabella, her son Edward and her lover Mortimer headed north to the Hainault court. Once there, Edward was betrothed to Philippa. The wedding would take place within the time previously stipulated by Stapledon. With that agreed, Isabella and Mortimer, William I of Hainault and his wife Joan knuckled down to raising an army with which to invade England and hopefully depose Edward II. To prevent Edward II from learning of their activities, William detained the king's envoys, while his queen, Isabella, used the proceeds of their son's dowry, together with a loan from her brother Charles, to raise an army of mercenaries. This consisted of a small detachment of Hainault troops provided by William I and Joan, together with a supplement of men ferreted out by scouring the countryside of Brabant. There are also indications that Isabella secretly sent emissaries to the Scottish king, Robert the Bruce, asking for his co-operation with the promise of ending the war against Scotland if her plan succeeded, if she became regent, and if Edward II were removed from the throne. This was a clever move at a propitious moment. Two years before, Pope John XXII had recognised Robert as the rightful King of Scotland following the Scottish nobility's submission of the 'Declaration of Arbroath', thereby depriving Edward II of just cause to continue the war under the pretext that he was Scotland's overlord. In obtaining the acquiescence of the Scots with the promise of peace, which would be enshrined in the Treaty of Edinburgh-Northampton two years later, when Edward III refuted the right to make any future claims to the throne of Scotland for himself or his heirs, Isabella had not only outflanked her husband, but effectively brought a long and costly war to a close.

Before doing so, however, she had to invade England and supplant her husband with their son. Edward II suspected that an invasion was imminent, so sent out the fleet to intercept it. Isabella and Mortimer, who had set out on 22nd September 1326, managed to evade it, landing by the Orwell River on the eastern coast. Theirs was a small army. Estimates range from 500 to 2,000, with a mean figure of 1,200 being likely. Whatever its size, Isabella's invading force had justice and the people on its side. All the local levies, which had been mobilised to stop them, joined forces with them. As they cut a swathe through Bury St. Edmunds, then Cambridge, supporters from all classes joined them. These included yet more English royals: Thomas of Brotherton, 1st Earl of Norfolk, fifth son of King Edward I and therefore half-brother of Edward II, as well as being full elder brother of Edmund of Woodstock, Earl of Kent who had joined Isabella in France; and another first cousin Henry, Earl of Leicester, whose brother was the attainted Thomas, Earl of Lancaster, executed and stripped of his lands and title, though these would be restored to Henry following the accession of Edward III. Both these men were also cousins of Isabella, their mothers being French princesses, Isabella's aunt Margaret of France and cousin Blanche of Artois.

Within three days of the invasion, news of it had reached Edward II and the Despensers in London. Local unrest made the capital unsafe for them, so they prepared to leave for Wales. Edward II ordered the local sheriffs, along whichever route the invaders took, to detain them, but rather than doing so, the sheriffs greeted them as liberators. Isabella had effectively brought all of Edward II's opponents into a single coalition, and when she marched in pursuit of her husband and his lover, through London, which was in the hands of rioters who were supporters of her cause, she found that the government's authority no longer existed. One consequence was that Bishop Stapledon, who had tried to apply his authority to protect his property from the rioters, was killed by the mob, and his head sent to Isabella as a mark of its support for her.

By then, Isabella, Mortimer and their ever-swelling troops were in hot pursuit of Edward II and his 'husband', as Adam Orleton, Bishop of Hereford, who had come out of hiding to support the queen, had so colourfully described the pair. Hugh Despenser the Elder was the first to fall. Besieging Bristol until he surrendered, Isabella was able to recover custody of her two daughters, Eleanor and Joan. Although the queen argued for sparing Despenser the Elder's life, Mortimer and Henry, hereafter called Earl of Lancaster, demanded that he be tried and executed following the precedent which he, his son and Edward II had established when they had executed Henry's captured elder brother Thomas, 2nd Earl of Lancaster after the Battle of Boroughbridge. He was duly tried and summarily hanged in his armour on 27th October 1326. This method of execution indicated a degree of bitterness that conveyed how unpopular he was. Aristocrats were normally beheaded. Only common criminals were hanged. So widespread had the Elder's criminality been, so accepted was it that he had headed up a kleptocracy whose dishonesty was exceeded only by his avaricious son's, that he was not even permitted the dignity of a gentleman's execution. After his death his head was hacked off, sent for display to Winchester, a city which had supported the king, while his body was cut into pieces and fed to the local dogs. Pardons were then issued to the thousands of people who had been falsely accused by him over the years, an action which was popular as well as just.

By this time, support for Edward II and Despenser the Younger had sloughed off like the skin of a moulting python. Moving her headquarters to the Welsh border town of Hereford, Isabella ordered Henry, soon to be restored by Parliament to the earldom of Lancaster for which he is better known, to locate and capture her husband and Despenser the Younger. After a fortnight, they were found in South Wales near Llantrisant, on the 16th November 1326. Henry of Lancaster detained in custody his cousin Edward II, who surrendered the King's Great Seal, without which it would not be possible to govern with a veneer of legality, to Isabella.

Edward II and Despenser the Younger can have been in no doubt that retribution would be swift and certain. Because the former was a crowned king as well as Isabella's lawful husband and the father of her children, great care had to be taken with how to deal with him, but this principle did not apply to the latter man. Both of them would have to be neutralised permanently. While delicacy was required in disposing of a crowned king, no such considerations were necessary when dealing with his hated favourite.

There was never any question that Despenser would suffer the same fate that he and his putative lover had meted out to Thomas, 2nd Earl of Lancaster. Brought before Isabella, he was sentenced to be executed on the 24th November. But the manner of his death was no ordinary execution. All care was taken to demonstrate to the entire country that this was one man who deserved to die in the most horrific manner possible. Condemned to depart this life as a common thief rather than the nobleman he was, and as a traitor and sodomite to boot, on the day of reckoning he was dragged from his horse in front of a vast crowd, which had gathered to witness his end. He was stripped naked, Biblical injunctions against corruption and arrogance covering his whole body, then dragged into the presence of Isabella, Mortimer and the English princes who had supported them, Henry of Lancaster included. He was then hanged, but not enough to kill him, only enough to throttle him and inflict pain. While he was wriggling on the noose, but remained conscious, his penis and testicles were cut off, in an allusion to the source of his power over the king. His body was then sliced open, his entrails removed, before he was cut down, and drawn and quartered while still alive. More than just a dire warning to others, his death eloquently demonstrated the just deserts of cruelty run riot at a time when an eye for an eye and a tooth for a tooth was the dictum of the age.

Edward II's end would turn out to be an equally eloquent indictment. Once he was captured and in his cousin Henry of Lancaster's custody, that prince removed his Great Seal – the symbol of royal power – and sent it to Isabella for her to use while ratifying royal business.

Edward II's core supporters, such as Edmund FitzAlan, Earl of Arundel and Simon of Reading, were quickly executed, after which Isabella and Mortimer demonstrated restraint against the former king's remaining followers. Many lesser nobles were pardoned for having supported Edward II, while the functionaries at the heart of government, who had been appointed by the Despensers and Stapledon, had their posts confirmed. This lessened the chaos which would otherwise have been inevitable had a whole stratum of minor officials been replaced. This also assured that the business of government would continue running smoothly, while encouraging those who would otherwise have opposed the new regime to support it.

What to do about Edward II was the main problem. He was indubitably the rightfully anointed king of England, but to permit him to keep his crown would be to invite opposition to the present regime and even encourage a counter-coup. Isabella therefore seized the Tower of London, appointed one of her supporters Mayor of London, and convened a council of nobles and churchmen to decide the king's fate. The Wallingford Council decreed that Edward should be legally deposed and detained under house arrest for the remainder of his life. In January 1327, Parliament confirmed this decision. Edward was informed that his son would succeed him if he abdicated, but if he did not, his son would be disinherited and someone else appointed in his place. Edward II tearfully agreed to abdicate and Sir William Trussell, Speaker of the House of Commons, formally renounced England's allegiance to Edward II on 21st January 1327. On 1st February, Edward III was crowned King of England; his mother was appointed his Regent until he came of age; and Trussell became the new king's Secretary. The former king was moved, from detention in Kenilworth Castle in the Midlands, to the safer and more secure location of Berkeley Castle, home of Mortimer's son-in-law Thomas, 3rd Lord Berkeley, in Gloucestershire, near the Welsh border.

It was obvious that a living ex-king was a threat to the stability and survival of the new regime. His very existence made him a rallying point for opposition. It should not, therefore, come as a surprise that he did not linger long in captivity. On the 23rd September, 1327, Isabella and Edward III received a messenger who informed them that Edward II had suffered a fatal accident. He was buried in Gloucester Cathedral and, in keeping with royal tradition, his heart removed, placed in a small casket, and taken to his widow, who would ultimately be buried with it, in keeping with royal tradition.

Also unsurprisingly, Edward II's death quickly became a source for a multitude of rumours. One compelling story centres around a well-born Genoese priest named Manuele Fieschi. A papal notary and later Bishop of Vercelli, he wrote to Edward III stating that his father had not been assassinated at Berkeley Castle. Having discovered the plot to murder him, Edward II had changed clothes with a servant, who was indeed killed. He himself killed the gatekeeper while making his escape. Having spent 18 months at Corfe Castle, he went to Ireland for nine months, before crossing the Channel into the Low Countries, through which he travelled en route to see the Pope in Avignon, ending up in Italy, where he lived for the remainder of his life as a monastic hermit near Cecima in the Diocese of Pavia. He did not try to overthrow his son, recognising that there was no support in England for his restoration.

The letter has been date tested, and is regarded as authentic. What is in doubt is whether the contents are true; whether they were merely believed to be true by Bishop Fieschi; or indeed whether the whole story was concocted by the Bishop of Maguelonne, in whose archives it is preserved to this day, to blackmail Edward III by undermining his position. The fact that Isabella chose to be buried with Edward II's heart suggests that she at least did not accept this version of events.

Less easily authenticated is the existence of a letter in Latin which Isabella and Mortimer were supposed to have sent to his gaolers stating: '*Eduardum occidere nolite timere bonum est.*' Depending on where you read the break in the sentence as occurring, it could have meant two opposing things: firstly, 'Do not be afraid to kill Edward it is good;' and secondly, 'Do not kill Edward it is good to fear.'

There is little contemporaneous evidence of Isabella and Mortimer ordering the assassination of her husband, but that in itself is hardly surprising. What would have been unexpected would have been the existence of such proof, so its absence does not add to or subtract from the likelihood of the event taking place. Isabella and Mortimer would have had to have been politically inept, which she most certainly was not, to have left behind evidence of instructions to commit regicide. Yet the fact remains, there was a body, and whether it was the servant or the master, a man was killed and buried in Gloucester Cathedral. Tellingly, after Mortimer's fall from grace in 1330, Berkeley was tried as an accessory to the murder of the deposed king. Although he was acquitted, the very fact of the trial shows that a murder did take place, and that the Crown was asserting that its victim had been the late king.

The manner of Edward II's death has gone down in history as one of the most gruesome methods of executing any human being. According to the contemporary chronicler Geoffrey le Baker, otherwise known as Walter of Swinbroke, who got his account of the king's last days from William Bisschop, a companion of the murderers, Thomas Gurney and

John Maltravers, they entered the king's quarters and while one man held him, the other pushed a red hot poker up his rectum. His screams were heard from two miles away. Death, of course, was instantaneous, but acutely painful.

Some modern historians doubt that this version can be accurate, because of the horrific nature of the despatch and the fact that the corpse would have betrayed the manner of death. This seems spurious and anachronistic, snowflake sensibilities attaching themselves to a more brutal, but also more straightforward, age than ours; as if the murderers of a homosexual king, in a day and age when homosexuality was frowned upon, when that king had brought opprobrium upon himself, his crown and his people by the scandalous way in which he had promoted his kleptocratic lovers, would have troubled themselves to conceal the method of assassination from the few people with access to the corpse's hind quarters. The fact that the king's body, while lying in state, had no visible signs of execution, would have been far more of a consideration than what lay beneath its robes. Anyone can detect the synchronicity between Despenser's death and Edward II's. Both men's sexual proclivities were pointedly highlighted in the manner of their deaths, the giver of pleasure losing his instrument, the recipient having his host organ destroyed. Both deaths were as painful as could be engineered, a figurative and literal allusion to what people regarded as being the main source of so much anguish to the nation, revisited upon them at the moment of their death so that they too shared the pain they had inflicted upon the nation through a union that had brought them riches and pleasure, but ultimately, destruction.

The month after Edward II's death, his son and heir fulfilled his promise by marrying Philippa of Hainault. Edward III was now securely upon his throne for the first time since his accession, there no longer being the prospect of his replacement with the more rightful king his father. It must be remembered, in the fourteenth century God, not Parliament, was accepted as being the fount of kingship. Until Edward II's death, Edward III's right to the throne was therefore always going to be tenuous, open to challenge from any quarter, with such support as existed for him liable to dissipate at any moment under a barrage of suspicion that God's will had been subverted by a usurper. The new king's marriage was therefore not only an attempt to draw a line under the past, with every likelihood of the arrival of new heirs to the throne, but was also paying William and Joan of Hainault back for their support in helping to fund the coup and raise the army which had resulted in Edward III's accession.

Most royal marriages at that time, and for centuries to come, followed a format. First, there was the betrothal, then the proxy ceremony before the couple had even had a chance to meet each other, at which point the marriage was deemed to have taken place. This would be followed by a celebration of the marriage once the bride had travelled from her country to the groom's. Edward and Philippa's betrothal having been agreed while they were both in Hainault before the coup, they were unusual in knowing each other before the ceremony, so when the young king sent the Bishop of Coventry to Valenciennes, the bride's birthplace and the second city of the state of Hainault, to represent him in the proxy ceremony in October 1527, Philippa at least could take her vows in the knowledge that her husband was to her taste. As subsequent events would show, she was also to his taste. Whether Philippa was objectively attractive or merely subjectively attractive to Edward III, is not known, there being no extant portraits of her. She might well have been good-looking, despite not being run-of-the-mill. There is no reason why her attributes of being dark-skinned, full-lipped, broad-nosed, and raven-haired could not have been packaged in such a way that she was her age's comparable to Sophia Loren, the movie star who in the fifties refused to alter her nose and soften her voluptuousness and in so doing was ultimately recognised as a contemporary if exceptional beauty. What is historically known is that Edward III definitely found Philippa personally attractive.

The couple's betrothal and marriage took planning, in a day and age when communications were more difficult than they now are. Further evidence of the forward planning that went into the event is the papal dispensation which they had to apply to the Pope for, prior to being married at all. This was granted the month before the proxy ceremony, Edward III and Philippa being second cousins and therefore deemed to be consanguineous, that is, too closely related for the union to take place without the Pope's consent. Only after this hurdle was cleared could the proxy ceremony proceed, following which she set out for her new country. She arrived in December, 1327, accompanied by her uncle John of Hainault, Seigneur of Beaumont and Count of Soissons. She received an enthusiastic welcome in London, before setting out for York Minster, where she and Edward III were married on 24th January 1328. He was sixteen and she about fourteen.

Although now King and Queen of England, both Edward III and Philippa were still minors. Isabella and Mortimer were the *de facto* rulers of the kingdom, and the young couple began married life at Woodstock Palace in Oxfordshire. In those days, teenagers who were married could partake of conjugal pleasures as soon as they were physically and psychologically able to do so. Whether Edward III and Philippa consummated their marriage immediately is open to speculation, but she was already six months pregnant by the time of her coronation in March 1330. This had been delayed for two years, ostensibly because Isabella was reluctant to relinquish her role as solely crowned Queen of England, but once Philippa became pregnant, the Queen Mother's sentiments became irrelevant. The mother of the future King of England had to be a crowned Queen of England herself.

In the period since Philippa's arrival in England, her mother-in-law's popularity had plummeted, while Philippa's grew accordingly. Although Isabella had proven herself to be a clever tactician in the way in which she had acquired political power for herself and Mortimer through the deposition of her husband and the accession of her son, the lovers had proceeded to repeat some of the errors which had been the downfall of Edward II, Gaveston and the two Despensers. While she made some wise decisions, such as sealing the end of the war with Scotland by agreeing to the marriage of her daughter Joan with the Scottish King David II, the lavish lifestyles and avaricious acquisition of lands at the expense of their rightful owners which had characterised the previous reign soon caused political conflict when Mortimer and Isabella began land grabs of stupendous proportions. Then Mortimer, by now created Earl of March, and Henry, now restored to the royal earldom of Lancaster, fell out. What sealed the fate of the new regime, however, was Mortimer's execution of the king's half-uncle and supporter, Edmund, Earl of Kent, in March 1330. Although Edward III was still a minor, and would remain so until his eighteenth birthday, this was deemed to be a step too far, and Lancaster now plotted with Edward III to bring Mortimer down.

Meanwhile, Philippa was earning the approbation of all who came across her. Unlike many of the foreign princesses who had married into the English Royal Family, she did not have a large retinue of foreign attendants, nor did she push her foreign connections within the land. She also possessed personal qualities that endeared her to her new subjects. The chronicler Jean Froissart claimed that she was 'The most gentle Queen, most liberal, and most courteous that ever was Queen in her days.' The writer Joshua Barnes confirmed that 'Queen Philippa was a very good and charming person who exceeded most ladies for sweetness of nature and virtuous disposition.'

Tellingly, no one thought to comment on the colour of her skin or the cast of her features, which goes to show how insignificant such details were at that time. This was not a conspiracy of silence, as we shall soon see, but silence born of absolute acceptance of the fact that the queen's brown skin, broad nose and thick lips were simply not noteworthy. What was noteworthy was her character, and that endeared her to her subjects as well as to her husband.

On the 15th June, 1330, Philippa was delivered of a baby boy who was named Edward after his father. Known contemporaneously as Edward of Woodstock because of his birthplace, he would go down in history as 'The Black Prince'.

Now that Edward III had an heir, his relationship with Mortimer degenerated rapidly. Up to this point, the king and Mortimer, who was the *de facto* ruler of England, had had a difficult relationship, with the latter pointedly disrespecting the younger in an attempt to hold sway over him. The technique of attempting to terrorise the under-aged king into submission was never a clever ploy, but it had worked for the past three years because Edward III was not in a position to openly challenge his mother's lover. As the date of his coming of age approached, however, he seems to have recognised that he had better get rid of Mortimer before Mortimer had a chance to shore up his power further. There was no telling what might happen once he came of age. Mortimer could easily do anything to hang on to power. The time to move against him was therefore while he, Edward III, was still a minor, as this produced an element of surprise which would otherwise be lacking.

The young king had already been plotting, for the previous year, to wrest power from Mortimer when the time was right, with the Pope, John XXII, and his closest friend, the twenty-nine year old William, 3rd Lord Montagu, who would subsequently be rewarded for his assistance by being made 1st Earl of Salisbury and King of Mann. Henry, Earl of Lancaster, had also been assiduous in trying to persuade his cousin to get rid of the man who had killed his brother and was abusing his power and undermining the Crown. Mortimer became aware that a plot might be afoot, and called in both Montagu and Edward III for interrogation. Although neither young man gave the game away, Mortimer was sufficiently astute to believe that his suspicions were well founded if unproven, and actually recommended to Edward that he move against Montagu on the grounds that 'It was better that they should eat the dog than that the dog should eat them.'

The dog who was up for eating, however, remained Mortimer. On the 19th October 1330, the month before Edward III turned eighteen, the plotters struck. While Isabella and Mortimer were in residence for a Parliament at Nottingham Castle in the erroneous belief that they were safe and secure – Edward III was also there – the constable of the castle guided Montagu and the small band of twenty-three plotters in through a secret, underground tunnel. These men included a grandson of Edward I, William de Bohun, (after 1337, 1st Earl of Northampton) Robert d'Ufford, (after 1337, 1st Earl of Suffolk); and John Neville, fourth son of the 1st Lord Neville de Raby. With surprise on their side, they managed to seize Mortimer after a brief scuffle. Isabella, upon being advised of what had happened, went straight to where her son and his cohorts had detained Mortimer. 'Good son,' she implored, throwing herself at his feet in an attempt to get her lover released, 'have pity on noble Mortimer.'

Edward III, however, had not only suffered sufficient personal humiliation at Mortimer's hands – Mortimer had told Montagu that his word took precedence over the king's – but had also witnessed how he had abused his powers during the nearly four years of his stewardship of the Crown. He therefore knew that the only solution to the problem was execution. Isabella herself was detained, first at Berkhamsted Castle in Hertfordshire, then under house arrest at Windsor Castle, while Mortimer was taken to the Tower of London. The charges against him included assuming royal power and other more mundane high misdemeanours such as abuse of power and treason, but no mention was made of his role as the Queen Mother's lover. Condemned by his peers in Parliament, on the 29th November 1330, exactly two weeks after Edward III achieved his majority upon turning eighteen, he was taken the 6.3 miles from the Tower of London to Tyburn, where he was hanged in ignominious fashion, as if he were a common criminal. Edward III, however, did have sufficient compassion to commute his sentence so that he was merely hanged, instead of being drawn and quartered, as traitors ordinarily were. In this, the young king seems to have considered the feelings of his mother, who was undoubtedly in love with Mortimer. Although he would not spare his life, Edward III could make his death easier, and in so doing, assuage his mother's grief. According to the Victorian historian Agnes Strickland, Isabella displayed symptoms of insanity during this period. Certainly her condition bears all the hallmarks of grief resulting in a complete nervous breakdown.

Although Isabella and Mortimer had no children together, both their bloodlines flow through the royal houses of England, Scotland, and many a European royal family. Through Mortimer's son Sir Edmund Mortimer, he is an ancestor of the last Plantagenet kings of England, Edward IV and Richard III. Through Edward IV's daughter Elizabeth of York, who married Henry VII, he is an ancestor of both King Henry VIII of England and King James V of Scotland, whose mother Margaret Tudor was Henry's sister. Through James V's daughter Mary, Queen of Scots, he is a direct ancestor of Queen Elizabeth II and all the European royals who descend from Queen Victoria or the Stuart line, meaning virtually every European royal, irrespective of the house.

Within two years of Mortimer's execution, Isabella had recovered both her health and her freedom. She was released from house arrest at Windsor, moving back to her own residence at Castle Rising in Norfolk. Thereafter, she enjoyed a life of tremendous sumptuousness and great honour. She doted on her grandchildren, especially the Black Prince, and on her late lover's descendants, including his namesake grandson, whom Edward III restored to the earldom of March in 1354. She died in 1358, covered in honours as her family's matriarch who had secured the throne of England for her descendants.

By the time of her mother-in-law's death, Philippa had been queen for nearly thirty years. In the intervening years, she had faithfully followed her husband on his travels to Scotland, France, Flanders and throughout England. She had acted as regent in 1346 and won international recognition for her compassion when, following the Siege of Calais, she pleaded with her husband to spare the life of the six burghers whose lives had been forfeit when they surrendered the city. When he did so, Philippa's reputation, already august, achieved new heights. Her last son Thomas of Woodstock, 1st Duke of Gloucester, had been born only three years before her mother-in-law's death in 1358. In the intervening decades, Philippa had produced thirteen children, including five sons who lived to adulthood and whose rivalries would form the basis for the Wars of the Roses. Her husband's claim to the throne of France would also form the basis for another war, this time The Hundred Years' War. Although some of her children were fated to fight, three of them would die of the plague during the Black Death. She herself would die aged around fifty-six of dropsy, an illness which in modern parlance has a variety of causes, such as heart failure, but manifests itself as oedema, that is, swelling of the body. Edward would outlive her by eight years, mourning the loss of a faithful companion and loving wife as well as a queen beloved of her people.

Edward the Black Prince was their most famous and popular child. Not only was he heir to his father's throne, but he was known as a great warrior. Revered contemporaneously for his prowess in battle, he would predecease not only his mother but also his father. He therefore never succeeded to the throne, but from the age of seven, Edward was marked for distinction. He became the first individual in England to be made a duke, when he was created Duke of Cornwall. The Duchy of Cornwall still flourishes to this day. Created by special Parliamentary charter to fund the lifestyle of the heir to the throne, it was endowed with the vast lands of the earldom of Cornwall, which had been given by his grandfather Edward II to his favourite, Piers Gaveston, before they were forfeited back to the Crown following his execution. Much of the Duchy lands still exist at the time of writing.

Edward III created a precedent which continues down to the present. The eldest son of each monarch of England becomes Duke of Cornwall by birth right upon his father or mother's accession, in keeping with the original charter, still in force today. Prince Charles, for instance, automatically became Duke of Cornwall when George VI died and his mother became Queen Elizabeth II. Like the Black Prince he had to be created Prince of Wales, in 1347 and 1958 respectively, but once his mother became queen, the dukedom and duchy of Cornwall became his by right. This is not a right which extends to heiresses to the throne. None of the Queens Regnant of this country has ever been a Duchess of Cornwall, because the dukedom exists by charter only for the male heir to the throne. Had George VI wanted to create his elder daughter Princess of Wales, he could have done so. He could not, however, have made her Duchess of Cornwall.

Many myths surround the Black Prince, who has historically been regarded as the most glamorous and quintessential of all the Princes of Wales to hold that title. The foremost myth surrounding the Black Prince is the reason for his moniker. Was he a Black Prince? Did it refer to his complexion or his character, or both? What did Black Prince mean? Where did it come from? There are many theories, not all of which stand up to examination. The earliest recorded use of the sobriquet originates with the antiquary John Leland, who wrote in the 1530s and 40s about Edwardi s cog: Nigri, i.e. Prince Edward cognomen: The Black, and 'the Blake Prince'. He suggested that the moniker was widely used. His sources were the 14th century *Eulogium Historiarum* and the fifteenth century chronicle of John Warkworth, and coincided with King Henry VIII's attempts to shore up his neophyte dynasty by harkening back to his Plantagenet ancestors. This was a ploy adopted by his successor and daughter, Elizabeth I. In *Toxphilius* (1545), the first English book on archery written by Roger Ascham and dedicated to Henry VIII, the author refers to 'ye noble black prince Edward beside Poeters.' Richard Grafton, who was King's Printer under Henry VIII and his son Edward

VI, states on three separate occasions in his *Chronicle at Large* (1569) that 'some writers name him the black prince', and that he was 'commonly called the black Prince.' In *Holinshed's Chronicles*, published in 1577 by Raphael Holinshed, who was a major source for William Shakespeare, the description appears several times. Shakespeare unsurprisingly used it in Richard II (1595) in Act 2, Scene 3, and again in Henry V (1599) in Act 2, Scene 4.

There is no proven source for the moniker but there are many theories surrounding its origins. Depending on who is speculating and when and where they originate, some of the theories are more far-fetched than others. Few consider the possibility that it was a simple description of the man, if only because few of the speculators nowadays have considered the possibility that a Prince of Wales might actually have been dark-skinned. In their ignorance of the fact that this might have been a possibility, even a probability, and, bizarre as it sounds, maybe even a certainty, they have plucked theories out of thin air. Rather than alight upon the obvious, they have sought out the obscure, and, in the absence of proof for their unsustainable theories, have thrown their hands up in frustration and declared that it is impossible, after this passage of time, to say with any certainty what the moniker meant, while studiously avoiding the possibility that it might have meant exactly what it said.

One theory, which really is preposterous, is that 'the Black Prince' alludes not to Edward the prince, but to his shield and/or his black armour. The only problem with this hypothesis is that no evidence exists, or has ever existed, to suggest the Edward ever had a black shield or black armour. Nor would anyone, with even the most basic knowledge of arms and armour in the fourteenth century, seriously posit the notion that an heir to a throne would wear black armour or possess a black battle shield. Armour was not made of black metal, nor was the metal dyed black. It might well have been burnished brightly, but dulled deliberately? That would have suggested a lack of chivalry, an attempt to obtain an advantage in battle through subterfuge, at a time when princes announced their positions with resplendent armour. Edward was renowned throughout Christendom for his chivalrous conduct, and codes of honour then as now prevent underhandedness, which is what black armour would have been. Plainly the proponents of this theory have never considered the implications of black armour and a black shield in terms of the values of the time, otherwise they would not suggest such a ridiculous notion.

Yes, Edward's shield for peace with the three ostrich feathers argent, which would later on transmogrify into the three ostrich feathers used by later Princes of Wales, did have a black background. His younger brother John of Gaunt had a similar shield of peace, which also had a black background but three ermine feathers. Both brothers used these shields for jousting, but as they were not black, but were strikingly white with black backgrounds, it hardly makes sense that one brother would have developed a moniker at such a stretch, while the other did not. And for a jousting shield rather than a battle shield.

A more likely source for the soubriquet Black Prince is Edward's reputation for brutality, both in battle and against his enemies. The French writer/soldier of fortune, Philippe de Mézières, who later on became Chancellor of Cyprus, described Edward as the greatest of the 'black boars' – swine whose aggressions had disrupted relations throughout Christendom. The King of France referred to 'that black name, Edward, Black Prince of Wales' in Shakespeare's Henry V, while the English cartographer and historian, John Speed, stated in 1611 that Edward was known as the Black Prince 'not of his colour, but of his dreaded acts in battell.' Thirty one years later, another English historian and churchman, Thomas Fuller, wrote that the moniker came 'from his dreaded acts and not from his complexion.'

What no one seems to have taken account of is the possibility that the description 'The Black Prince' might well have applied not only to his heart but also to the colour of his skin. John Speed and Thomas Fuller's statements can be read two ways. Their denial that Edward's complexion played any part in the award of the moniker does not necessarily mean that he did not have a dark skin. An equally valid interpretation of their statements is that he did indeed possess one, and, notwithstanding it, the description of his being a Black Prince referred not to his skin-colour, but to his black heart. This interpretation gains validity when one realises that there are claims that Edward was known as the Black Prince from early childhood. This means that the moniker was applied to him before he had ever lifted a sword or shield in battle or on the jousting field, or before he had ever begun administering his territories with the ferocity his enemies stated he employed. It suggests that he was like his mother: dark-skinned. Possibly even more dark-skinned than she was.

In a curious footnote which illustrates how small the world truly is, one of Philippa's descendants is the person from whom I bought my own castle, Castle Goring. Clement FitzRoy Somerset is descended through her third surviving son, John of Gaunt, 1st Duke of Lancaster. He and his father Fitzroy Somerset provided their DNA to substantiate identification of the corpse found in that Leicester car park as being Richard III. I suppose one way of clearing up the mystery would be to ask him to provide another sample, this time to see whether Philippa of Hainault had any Sub-Saharan African or even North African blood. That, however, is not a route down which I would consider travelling. Ultimately, it doesn't matter whether Philippa did have African ancestry, for a) according to the theory of African Adam and Eve, we all do, and b) whether she did or did not, she was indubitably dark-skinned. What does it matter where that came from? It's the possession of it that counts. That, and the fact that it was so unremarkable that few people commented upon it during her lifetime. Of course, her son's moniker, if it really was used from childhood, as some sources suggest, does draw attention to his complexion, but that does not necessarily mean that there were any racially prejudicial overtones in the description. Aside from the chroniclers who confirm that his moniker, at least in adult life, was due to his character, there is speculation that his brother John of Gaunt had reddish hair, a trait which many of his Plantagenet ancestors possessed and many of his descendants possess to this day. The moniker, in Edward III's youth, might therefore have simply been descriptive of his different colouring, in much the same way that Rufus the Red's colouring is known to us through that particular description. In those less racist days, before the prism of prejudices which ran riot throughout the world from the mid-eighteenth to the mid-twentieth centuries had distorted perceptions the way they did, there was, paradoxically, nothing racist about describing people by distinguishing features. History gives us 'The Bald', 'The Beautiful', 'The Sun King', 'The Fair', 'The Moor', and many more descriptions, all of which are simply labels of what distinguished individuals from their fellows. Such descriptions demonstrated not prejudice, but a lack of it. Hopefully one of these days, our society will progress to the stage where we can once more employ accurate descriptions without the suspicion that an accurate description of an individual is indicative of prejudice.

Chapter Four

WHEN YOU FLY into the airport of North Carolina's Charlotte, the second largest city of the south-eastern United States, you are immediately confronted by a monumental bronze statue of a woman in eighteenth century dress holding a crown aloft in her outstretched right hand, her skirts swirled by a gust of wind as if they had, anachronistically, been caught by the wind of an aeroplane. The crown she is brandishing is both her own and the symbol of the City of Charlotte, also known as the Queen's City, the most populous in the state and the 17th most densely populated in the country.

Downtown, in front of the Trade Center, there is another prepossessing bronze statue of the same woman. Again in eighteenth century costume, she stands proudly and elegantly with two dogs, one playfully jumping up towards her in confirmation of the affectionate and down-to-earth characteristics for which she was known, the other just playing nearby as it looks towards her, again conveying the benign element of her nature. Although regal, she is no beauty, and although a queen, the 'coloured' folk of that formerly segregated city have taken great pride and comfort over the centuries, from the representation of the woman after whom both Charlotte, and its county of Mecklenburgh, were named in 1763. They have always believed that Charlotte of Mecklenburg-Strelitz might well be one of them. Although they will not have known that she was verifiably the first Queen of England who had a non-European ancestress, they evidently did recognise that the features of the woman bore some resemblance to their own.

Under the 'one drop rule', the woman represented in the statue, a woman who was described by both a contemporaneous Court painter and a Court doctor as having the facial characteristics of a '*mulatto*', a woman who, in bronze, could be either white or black, or anything in between owing to the colour of the bronze and her facial features, might well have qualified as being a *'negress'*. From the days of slavery until 1971, when the federal court ruled in Swann v Charlotte-Mecklenburgh Board of Education that bussing could be used as a means of integrating the formerly legally segregated populations of black and white, those who had been excluded from integration had taken quiet, if at times cold, comfort from the fact that Queen Charlotte of the United Kingdom of Great Britain and Ireland from 1761 to 1818, as well as Electress of Hanover till 1814 and thereafter Queen of Hanover till her death, might well have been one of them. According to Melvin Luther Watts, the American politician who has been the Director of the Federal Housing Agency since being appointed by President Barack Obama in 2014 and, prior to that, the United States Representative for North Carolina's 12th Congressional District, "In private conversations, African-Americans have always acknowledged and found a sense of pride in this 'secret'." His wife Eulada concurs, stating: "I believe African-American Charlotteans have always been proud of Queen Charlotte's heritage and acknowledge it with a smile and a wink. Many of us are now enjoying a bit of 'I told you so' now that the story is out."

While there is some doubt as to whether Charlotte's non-European ancestress came from North Africa or Sub-Saharan Africa, the evidence is that she definitely came from Africa. Had European royals not intermarried to the extent that they did, there is every likelihood that the non-European strain within Charlotte's heritage would have petered out before it did. However, there are six different bloodlines traceable between her and her ancestress Margarita de Castro e Sousa, which means that the African part of the heritage inherited emanating from their mutual ancestress Madragana Bint Aloandro, was emphasised six times as strongly as it would otherwise have been. It is therefore unsurprising that Charlotte displayed characteristics which would otherwise have died out, had the gene pool not been as restricted as it was.

Duarte Nunez do Liao, the 16th Portuguese royal chronicler, states that Madragana was born around 1230 in Faro, while that province was still a part of the Muslim Kingdom of the Algarve. He states that she was a Moor. This meant that she was of African heritage. In the 16th century, Moors were taken to mean people of North African heritage. Moor was therefore something of a catch-all description, the way black has been evolving into an equally indeterminate and inclusive term which nowadays can mean wholly black, partially black, or even, in some cases, largely white with only a minute percentage of Sub-Saharan lurking several generations away in the bloodline.

To place Madragana in her proper place, many of the functionaries of the Muslim Iberian states, of which her father was one, were North African, but the description Moor could equally have applied to an African of mixed North and Sub-Saharan African descent, or indeed of exclusively Sub-Saharan African origins. There was much migration, indeed cross-pollination, during the centuries when Iberia was a Moorish state. The Berbers were the primary North African group in the Iberian caliphates, but they were not the chief peoples within the Muslim empire. These were the Arabs, who were the rulers, and who had exported their language, religion and culture throughout their empire. In the Iberian Peninsula, there were many other ethnic groups. There were the native Iberians as well as the descendants of the Vandals and the Visigoths, who had settled in both Iberia and North Africa, and a large Jewish community, which had settled during the Roman Empire, and flourished for much of the millennium they spent in these host territories.

Madragana's father, Aloandro Ben Bekr, was unmistakably Muslim, being the local Qadi, i.e. the magistrate or judge of a Sharia Court. He is sometimes referred to as having been the Governor of Faro, but this appears to be fanciful embroidery, invented centuries later when the colour question was rearing its ugly head throughout Europe as well as the Americas. Historians, acting on behalf of her eminent-ly-placed descendants, found it desirable to draw a veil over Madragana's antecedents and put as much distance as they could between her Muslim and African roots as they were able to engineer. They dexterously sought to pass her off as a Mozarab, namely an Iberian Christian living under Muslim domination, claiming that her father, her grandfather Bakr Ben Yahia, and her great-grandfather Yahia Ben Bakr were high officials, possibly descended from the Vandals or even the Jews, but definitely Christian. The only difficulty with that is that all Qadis, whether of

Faro or anywhere else, had to be Muslim. There is ample evidence to confirm that both father and daughter converted to Christianity after the Portuguese conquest of Faro, not before, but by confusing her racial and religious origins, they had whitewashed her both literally and metaphorically.

The facts are these. In 1249, Afonso III, King of Portugal (1210-1279) conquered the Kingdom of the Algarve and united the two kingdoms into one. He styled himself King of Portugal and the Algarve until he and King Alfonso X of Castile, who also claimed to be King of the Algarve, signed the Treaty of Badajoz in 1267. With that province now indisputably Portuguese, Afonso thereafter became simply the King of Portugal.

Afonso had been married since 1239 to Mathilda, Countess of Boulogne in her own right, but to date she had failed to give him children. Shortly after conquering Faro, he took Madragana as his mistress. Both Madragana and her father converted to Christianity, after which she was known as Maior Afonso and he as Aloandro Gil. It is noteworthy that Afonso obviously stood as godfather to his mistress, hence the inclusion of his name as her patronymic.

Afonso was a benevolent conqueror. In the *Cronica da Conquista do Algarve,* he is described as assuring the three major peoples of the former Moorish kingdom, namely the Muslims, Jews and Christians, that they could remain and enjoy 'the same laws in all things as they had received from their own king.' They were free to move to other Moorish lands if they wished, taking all their possessions with them, but if they chose to stay, 'all their houses, vineyards and inheritances' would be protected. Not surprisingly, many, including the former Qadi and his daughter, who was now the King's mistress, chose to stay.

Within a year, in around 1250, Madragana produced a son, Martim Afonso Chichorro. His birth possibly encouraged the monarch to divorce his barren wife, now that he had incontrovertible proof of his fertility. However, there was no question of marrying the Qadi's daughter, not when there would be no territorial or other gain to be had from such a union. Instead, in 1253, while right of possession of the Algarve was still a hotly disputed topic between him and Alfonso X of Castile, he married that king's illegitimate daughter, 11 year old Beatrice of Castile. Their first child would not be born for another six years, her birth coinciding with that of Madragana's second and final child with the king, a daughter named Urraca Afonso after his mother Queen Urraca of Castile, in 1260. This suggests that Afonso waited, as all decent men did after marrying young girls, until they were sexually mature before exercising his conjugal rights.

There is ample proof that Madragana was merely one of many mistresses. Afonso had at least six other natural offspring during the course of his relationship with her, which ended shortly after the birth of their daughter. She then married Fernao Rei, with whom she had at least one daughter named Sancha Fernandes. Rei means king in Portuguese, so historians believe that her husband was actually a member of the king's household, his name literally meaning Fernao of the King.

Martim Afonso Chichorro was acknowledged by his father and accorded all the honours and privileges that a natural son of a king of that period enjoyed. It be must be remembered that most kings had natural as well as legitimate children, all of whom were accorded the honours due to their station. Illegitimacy had not yet become the stigma it would later develop into. In 1274, when he was a young man of about 24, Martim married Ines de Sousa de Valadares. There is no doubt that this was a marriage of some significance, for she was the daughter of the Lord of Valadares and Tangil by his first wife, Maria Mendes de Sousa, herself the daughter of the eminent Count Mendo de Sousa e Sueiro Belfaguer. She and Martim, who had an established position at the Portuguese Court, during both his father and his half-brother Denis's reigns, founded what became known as the House of Sousa-Chichorro.

According to Mario de Valdes y Cocom, who describes himself as a 'historian of the African diaspora', their descendants form a black branch of the Portuguese Royal House. This is not strictly speaking accurate. Although most of the great families of Portugal have Sousa ancestry, and the Dukes of Lafoes, who are regarded as being the heads of the House of Sousa-Chichorro, are also Braganzas as a result of the marriage of Luisa Casimira de Sousa Nassau de Ligne with the Infante Miguel of Braganza, natural son of King Peter II of Portugal, the reality is, 'bastards', as they were known, were never regarded as being official members of royal families. When King Louis XIV of France legitimised his illegitimate children and included them as official members of that Royal Family, he created such offence that the ruling was reversed shortly after his death. Tolerance only went so far, and technically, the Portuguese Royal Family cannot therefore be fairly said to have a black branch.

Nevertheless, the Sousa-Chichorros were integral members of the Portuguese Court, and remained so beyond the life of the Portuguese monarchy. They were known to be connections of the royals, and, as such, possessed all the éclat with which cousins of royal houses are endowed. In 1429, when the Infanta Isabella of Portugal (1397-1471) left her native land to marry Philip the Good of Burgundy, several of them accompanied her. Two years later, Isabella de Sousa-Chichorro, daughter of Afonso Vasques de Sousa-Chichorro II, Lord of Santarem, Serva e Atei etc. etc., married one of Philip's nobles, Jean de Poitiers-Valentinois, Lord of Arcis-sur-Aube and Vadans. In 1437, another Sousa cousin of the new Duchess of Burgundy, Margarita de Castro e Sousa, niece of the newly married Lady of Arcis-sur-Aube and Vadans, married Jean II of Neufchâtel, Lord of Montagu and Fontenoy. It was this marriage which would ensure that Madragana's blood would flow throughout the entire British Royal Family, as well as many of the European royal families.

In those days, the nobility was eager to forge connections with the ruling families of their territories. Court appointments were jealously held treasures, superseded only by marital connections, although the two often went hand in hand. The advantages to be gained by a marital alliance with any connection of a ruling family were self-evident. Because ruling families usually married the legitimate progeny of other ruling families, except when legitimate heirs were sparse, or an alliance so desirable that illegitimacy could be ignored, unions between nobles and legitimate royals were ruled out. However, royal 'bastards' who had been acknowledged by the royal parent were desirable to aristocrats as marital partners owing to their semi-royal status and the wealth and prestige that went along with their background. As can be seen time and time again throughout this period of European history, neither illegitimacy nor a mixed race background trumped the obvious advantages that accrued from an alliance between a rich and well-established noble and a well-connected 'bastard', whether of colour or not, not even featuring as a part of the equation.

For this reason, the Burgundian nobles who married into the royally-connected Sousa-Chichorro family not only regarded such unions as desirable, but took pride in the royal bloodlines that would flow through the veins of their descendants. This attitude meant that generation after generation of 'bastards' made good marriages, until the once-illegitimate family was thoroughly incorporated into both the legitimate aristocracy as well as the legitimate ruling houses. For instance, Margarita de Castro e Sousa's granddaughter Antoinette de Neufchâtel married Philipp, Count of Salm. Their daughter Margarethe married Eberhard XII, Count of Erbach. Four generations later, Countess Sophie Albertine of Erbach-Erbach married Ernest Frederick I, Duke of Saxe-Hildburghausen. Their ninth child, and first surviving daughter of four, Elisabeth Albertine (1713-1761) married the Prince of Mirow, heir to the Duchy of Mecklenburg-Strelitz. She produced Princess Charlotte of Mecklenburg-Strelitz on 19th May 1744. By this time the Sousa-Chichorro line was legitimately and truly royal, on the distaff side at least, though the Braganza connection on the illegitimate side had so elevated them that they were also regarded as being one of the premier noble families of Europe.

The Infanta Isabella of Portugal, who kicked off the legitimisation of her illegitimate, mixed race, de Sousa cousins, herself had as exotic a heritage as they did. Her father, King John I of Portugal, was the natural son of King Peter I and a woman named Teresa Lourenco. He only came to the throne because the sole legitimate heir following the death of his legitimate half-brother King Ferdinand I was that king's daughter Beatrice, married to the Castilian King Juan I. The Portuguese Cortes (or Parliament), refusing to have their country's independence subsumed in the marital bed, declared the 'bastard' John king. Two years later, he married Philippa of Lancaster, daughter of John of Gaunt and therefore a granddaughter of King Edward III of England and the 'dark-skinned', broad-nosed, full-lipped former Princess Philippa of Hainault. It is through this lawful marriage that the African blood of the Portuguese royal house flows, notwithstanding the general belief that they are purely European. King John and Queen Isabella of Portugal produced two kings of Portugal, the famous Prince Henry 'the Navigator' and other sons, but only one daughter, Isabella, who would have to wait until she was 32 before being married to the twice-widowed Duke of Burgundy. It is a commentary on the desirability of the Infanta Isabella that, in a day and age when spinsterhood was a fate almost akin to death, and girls were married off in their early teens, certainly by their early twenties, she had to wait until such a relatively old age to be taken off the shelf. Nor was she rescued by a king or a prince, but a mere duke, albeit one who had the most extravagant and sophisticated Court in Europe. He was also a member of a collateral branch of the French Royal Family, but nevertheless a duke, not a king.

The Infanta Isabella's marriage would not only result in her illegitimate cousins becoming incorporated into the bloodlines of most of the legitimate royal houses of Europe, but in her own bloodline, including her African blood, flowing through the most senior royal house of Europe: the Hapsburgs. This was by way of her only child, Charles the Bold's only child Mary of Burgundy. Known as 'Mary the Rich' by virtue of being the greatest heiress of her day, she had her pick of desirable suitors, and married the Archduke Maximilian of Austria, son of the Holy Roman Emperor Frederick III and himself Emperor at the age of 20 in 1477, after his father's death.

Not only did Mary inherit her father's extensive territories in northern and eastern France, but she also produced two living children before her death in a riding accident five years after her marriage. Her son Archduke Philip of Hapsburg, known as 'Philip the Handsome', married the elder sister of King Henry VIII of England's first queen, Katherine of Aragon. Known to history as 'Joanna the Mad', she was even unluckier in her marriage than Katherine, who enjoyed nearly two decades of marital harmony before being discarded for Anne Boleyn. Queen of Castile in her own right from 1504, following the death of their mother Isabella, Joanna shared her throne and her bed with Philip and the variety of concubines he kept. She was desperately in love with him and was so tormented by his infidelities that she exhibited signs of what would today be classified as clinical depression, but was then dismissed as madness.

Philip the Handsome ruled as King of Castile *jure uxoris* as, owing to a series of deaths in Joanna's family, it looked as if the crown of Spain would be amalgamated in her person once her father King Ferdinand of Aragon died. By then Spain was on its way to becoming the world's greatest empire, and when Philip died in 1506, Joanna's father, the reigning King Ferdinand of Aragon, had his daughter declared insane, imprisoned her in Tordesillas, and had himself declared regent. There were sound political reasons for incapacitating her. Even after Ferdinand died in 1516, and while she nominally became co-monarch, Joanna's second child and eldest son, King Charles I of Spain, kept her locked up. Again, there were practical political gains from this course of action. Charles was the heir to the three greatest European dynasties of the age. In his person, Europe was united as it had never been except under the Emperor Charlemagne. He was the ruler of the Hapsburg territories of Austria, the Valois territories of Burgundy, and the Trastámara territories of Spain. Even more tellingly, he was the ruler of all Spain's overseas territories in the Indies and the Americas, the legacy of his grandparents' Ferdinand and Isabella's sponsorship of Christopher Columbus. After he became King of Spain he continued his grandparents' legacy, promoting the excursions of conquistadores such as Hernando Cortes and his second cousin Francisco Pizarro, who colonised much of the North and Central American continent as well as the South American as far as Peru. Four years after succeeding to the throne of Spain, Emperor Charles V was himself elected Holy Roman Emperor in succession to his grandfather Emperor Maximilian I.

While Joanna's son Charles became Europe's most powerful monarch, she languished in captivity, as powerless to influence her own fate as she was to influence the fate of her subjects. She would remain a prisoner until her death in 1555, by which time her sister Katherine of Aragon was dead, her grandson Philip of Spain nominal King of England through marriage with her great-niece Queen Mary I, 'Bloody Mary', and her son the Emperor Charles V had started to turn over some of his tremendous responsibilities to his son and heir, King Philip II of Spain, by abdicating.

If Joanna La Loco's fate was unfortunate, her descendants would do far better. Each and every Spanish king and queen regnant who sits, or has ever sat, on the throne of Spain is descended from her. Through Philippa of Burgundy and Philippa of Hainault, they also have dark-skinned ancestors. The result is that this bloodline devolves upon the crowned heads of Europe several times over, through many different bloodlines.

While Mario de Valdes y Cocom is technically wrong when he asserts that there is a black illegitimate branch of the Portuguese Royal Family, if Philippa of Hainault was mixed race, all the legitimate descendants of Philippa of Lancaster would also, of necessity, be. Under the 'one drop rule', both the Portuguese and Spanish Royal Families would therefore not only have mixed race ancestry, but would qualify for categorisation by racists as black.

While there may be some doubt as to whether Philippa of Hainault had African ancestors, there is none where Margarita de Castro e Sousa is concerned. This means that virtually all the members of the royal houses of Europe have African ancestors. Through her, there is practically no member of a European royal family connected to or descended from Queen Charlotte and her granddaughter Queen Victoria, who does not have Sousa's African blood flowing through his or her veins.

It has to be said, Queen Charlotte was an outstandingly successful and popular queen at a time when she could have been anything but. Both the American War of Independence and the French Revolution took place while she was queen. Nor was her popularity limited to her subjects. Personally, she was held in high regard, even by people she never met but with whom she nevertheless had letter-writing relationships. She and Marie Antoinette, for instance, had a warm friendship despite never having met. At a time when travel was more onerous than it now is, people often had close relationships which were forged and maintained by way of letter. They were regular correspondents, who shared similar tastes in music, decoration and family life, and, when the French queen was executed in 1793, Charlotte was distressed, not only by the method of her end, but also by the loss of a friend for whom she felt genuine affection.

By this time, Charlotte was well-established on the British throne. She had endeared herself to her husband and her people alike by keeping well away from politics and by being the archetypal good wife and mother. Domesticity was the byword for the private life of the king and the queen. Indeed, George III had chosen her partly because she was from an obscure, albeit royal, background, and would therefore have neither knowledge of nor interest in political intrigues and party politics.

Mecklenburg-Strelitz was a minor duchy in the north-east of Germany near the Polish border, abutting Swedish Pomerania in the north and Brandenburg in the south. Charlotte's father had never even been the reigning duke. He was the second son of a second marriage, so, when his father died, his elder half-brother acceded to the ducal throne while he lived the life of a nobleman on his estate in the Castle of Mirow; hence his title, Prince of Mirow. He died when Charlotte was eight. Six months later his half-brother died and Charlotte's brother Adolphus Frederick succeeded as Duke of Mecklenburg-Strelitz. The family moved from Mirow to Strelitz, which gave them only the merest of glimpses of Court life, for Mecklenburg-Strelitz was one of the poorest states in Germany.

At the time of Charlotte's betrothal to King George III, the diplomatic reports state that she had been given a very mediocre education. According to Percy Hetherington Fitzgerald in the nineteenth century, her upbringing was similar to that of the daughter of an English country gentleman. This meant that she did not benefit from either a royal or an aristocratic upbringing. She lacked the style, polish and exposure which girls of superior rank would ordinarily have had inculcated into them. But she did benefit from the quietude of a simple country existence, being brought up as a good *hausfrau* whose education focussed on household management and religion, with her tutors imparting only the most rudimentary lessons in such subjects as languages, botany (which would become a lifelong interest for her, leading to the creation of Kew Gardens), and natural history. She was also notoriously plain, but this did not matter to George III. Two years before, he had fallen in love with Lady Sarah Lennox, daughter of the 2nd Duke of Richmond. He had wished to marry her. The problem was, her grandfather the 1st Duke of Richmond had been the illegitimate son of King Charles II, the penultimate king of the Stuart dynasty which the Hanoverians had replaced at the invitation of Parliament. It would hardly have done for the Prince of Wales, as George still was while his grandfather reigned as King George II, to marry a mere aristocrat, and one, moreover, whose title had the dual disadvantage of the taint of illegitimacy and a link to the exiled Stuart dynasty. How could an illegitimate great-granddaughter of King Charles II end up being a Queen of England while the legitimate grandson of the last Stuart king was in exile abroad? Only fourteen years before there had been the Jacobite Rebellion which had sought to replace King George II with the 'Old Pretender', still regarded by Legitimists as the rightful King James III of England. So when George's mother, the Dowager Princess of Wales, and George's mentor, tutor, and chief political advisor, the 3rd Earl of Bute, advised against the marriage, the dutiful heir to the throne abandoned his dreams, writing, 'I am born for the happiness or misery of a great nation and consequently must often act contrary to my passions.'

Being of a dutiful as well as scholastic disposition, once he had made the decision to marry for reasons of state rather than passion, the character of his bride, rather than her appearance, became George's overriding consideration. He seems to have genuinely not minded that Charlotte was plain, or, as some people said, ugly. Certainly, when he was informed by his scouts that she was anything but a beauty, he did not allow her appearance to deflect him from choosing her on the basis that she would be a good, dutiful wife. Portraits show that Charlotte was decidedly no oil painting. The Johann Georg Ziesenis picture of 1761 captures a sumptuously dressed young woman whose most markedly attractive feature is her clothing. The Johann Zoffany portrait of 1765, with her two eldest sons, does the same, while the Francis Cotes pastel of 1767 depicts a staggeringly unattractive woman with heavy features. Lady Mary Coke, the authoress of a journal whose observations bring Court life in that period alive, observed that the sketch was 'so like [the Queen] that it could not be mistaken for any other person.' The famous Scottish painter Allan Ramsay depicted Charlotte many times. He did the state portraits of her and George III in their coronation robes shortly after her marriage. So successful were these that 150 orders of the pair as well as 26 of the king on his own and 9 of the queen, flooded in from other sovereigns, heads of state, royals, ambassadors, governors of colonies, corporations, institutions and courtiers. The Ramsay depictions of George III and Queen Charlotte, which ended up all over the world, became amongst the most familiar images of the day. In all his renderings of her, her dignity, kindness, benevolence and plainness are obvious, but what is even more marked is what Baron Stockmar called her '*mulatto face*'.

Of all the people who have described her, the most trustworthy is this most eminent of courtiers. Christian Friedrich von Stockmar was a physician and statesman who had been born in Coburg. He came to England with Prince Leopold of Saxe-Coburg-Saalfeld at the time of that prince's marriage to Princess Charlotte of Wales, only child of the Prince Regent, George III's eldest son, who would subsequently reign as King George IV. She died in childbirth on 6th November 1817, a year before her namesake grandmother, leaving the nation bereft. Not only had she been a popular heiress to the throne, but with her gone there was no legitimate heir to the throne in her generation. All her first cousins were illegitimate. The vacancy caused her uncles to scramble to find wives with whom they could produce legitimate children. It was as a result of her death that Queen Victoria was born.

Baron Stockmar was Comptroller of the Household and Private Secretary to the widowed prince, Leopold, who remained in England after his wife's death. He lived in some style at Claremont House, having been raised to the dignity of Royal Highness by her father the year after her death. Stockmar's stock, always high, rose higher and higher as he graduated to become Leopold's principal advisor. Four British Prime Ministers, Lords John Russell, Melbourne and Aberdeen, as well as the Duke of Wellington, had the utmost respect for his integrity and intellect. In 1830 Leopold was offered the crown of Greece, which, after careful consideration, he turned down, only to be offered that of Belgium shortly afterwards. This he accepted, moving to Brussels as the first King of the Belgians in July 1831.

Although Stockmar remained central to Leopold, he wisely did not accompany him to Brussels, preferring to advise from a discreet distance away in their native Coburg. This was wise, for it prevented the Belgians from becoming suspicious of their nominated king's foreign coterie, thereby making the process of settling into Belgium smoother. Nevertheless, Stockmar remained Leopold's most trusted advisor, even after his marriage the following year to Princess Marie-Louise of Orleans, the daughter of another nominated king, Louis-Philippe of the French, who would prove to be the thorn in his son-in-law's side as France jealously sought to take over the newly independent and neutral kingdom, while Belgium's other neighbour, Holland, had similar ambitions. As Leopold's reign went from success to success amidst the difficulties caused by French and Dutch acquisitiveness, Stockmar remained in the background, all the while invaluable to his master.

Meanwhile, Leopold's family continued to flourish through a series of dynastic marriages. One sister married the heir in line to the Russian throne, Grand Duke Constantine Pavlovich, while Victoria, the widow of Charles, Prince of Leiningen, married Prince Edward, Duke of Kent, brother of Leopold's father-in-law the Prince Regent, in the hope of producing an heir to the British throne to replace Leopold's late wife. In this Victoria, Duchess of Kent, was resoundingly successful.

When Leopold's niece Princess Victoria of Kent acceded to the British throne in 1837, he immediately ordered Baron Stockmar to return to England as her confidential advisor. Stockmar not only helped the eighteen year old queen navigate the treacherous shoals of British party politics embodied by Lord Melbourne, Sir Robert Peel and the Duke of Wellington, but he also helped to edge the young queen into the arms of Leopold's nephew and her first cousin, Prince Albert of Saxe-Coburg-Gotha. In his memoirs, Stockmar explains how Victoria hoped to keep Albert dangling for three or four years before she made up her mind whether she would marry him, and how he gradually made her realise that she would have to make a decision sooner. In the process, Stockmar gained the trust of the young couple, and became their most influential advisor. He remained one of their closest and most trusted advisors until Albert's death. It is therefore inconceivable that he would have described Victoria's grandmother Queen Charlotte as possessing a real '*mulatto face*' if she had not had one.

There is a fanciful theory, first propounded by Mario de Valdes y Cocom in a 1996 episode of the PBS TV series *Frontline*, that Allan

Ramsay emphasised Charlotte's *mulatto* appearance in the portraits he did of her as a way of supporting the anti-slave trade movement. This is propounded on the slenderest of grounds. Ramsay's wife Margaret Lindsay was the eldest sister of Sir John Lindsay, whose daughter Dido Elizabeth Belle features so prominently in the early chapters of this book. It might be remembered that Dido and her cousin, Lady Elizabeth Murray, were the subjects of a famous portrait, once thought to be by Zoffany, which used to hang at Lord Chief Justice Mansfield's Kenwood House residence until that family sold the property at the beginning of the last century. Undoubtedly, Lord Mansfield made two judgements which helped with the abolition of the slave trade. Equally certainly, he embraced his illegitimate and legitimate wards, but what Valdes seems not to have taken into account is that, despite the long and happy marriage of Allan and Margaret Ramsay, producing two daughters and a son, her father Sir Alexander Lindsay of Evelick never forgave her for marrying a mere artist. Eminent though he was, Ramsay was a member of the artisan class. He was not, according to the stratifications of the age, a gentleman. This rendered him unsuitable for matrimony with a lady. While Dido Elizabeth Belle was accepted within the family circle despite her mother's antecedents and because of her father's, Ramsay, who was of another class entirely, was not. This demonstrates more plainly than any other example how class was a far more important consideration than colour, even in the latter part of the eighteenth century, by which time prejudice against the '*Negro*' race had begun to tear through Europe and the Americas. There is, moreover, no evidence to support Valdes's contention that Ramsay exaggerated the '*negroid*' features of Queen Charlotte. While it is likely that Ramsay did possess sympathy for the abolitionist cause, everything concrete indicates that he did not exaggerate the African cast of Queen Charlotte's features any more than Francis Cotes did. Indeed, anyone who has trained as an artist can immediately see the synchronicity between both artists' work. This leads to the unmistakeable conclusion that both men captured good likenesses of their subject.

Allan Ramsay was one of the most eminent portraitists of his time. Thomas Gainsborough was another. While Gainsborough's 1781 portrait of Queen Charlotte can be accused of being flattering (the subject bears only the slightest of resemblances to Ramsay's), it seems incredible that an artist of Ramsay's stature would have been exaggerating the '*negroid*' features of England's queen at a time when colour prejudice against the black race was beginning to build to a crescendo. It seems even more unlikely that the highly-educated and cultivated king would then have promulgated this caricatured version of his beloved wife throughout his empire, for he is the individual who gave permission for the Ramsay versions of the portraits of himself and Charlotte to be distributed worldwide, becoming, in the process, the most famous images of their day. What seems more likely is that Ramsay was simply rendering an accurate and less flattering portrait than his competitor Gainsborough, and that it is the latter, rather than the former, who was playing with reality.

Ramsay also seems to have been expert in painting black subjects. He is believed to have painted the famous 'Portrait of an African' which hangs in Exeter Museum and probably represents Ignatius Sancho, the erudite, socially acceptable freedman who was bequeathed a small fortune and an annuity by the Duchess of Montagu in 1751. This would have been a commission in much the same way that his many commissions arose, prior to 1767, when his appointment as painter to the king resulted in his thereafter working more or less exclusively for George III. It also confirms that even at this stage of the century, 'people of colour' were still acceptable in Society as long as they had the qualifications that all others needed to possess, namely education, civility, money and position.

Ramsay's appointment as painter to the king also suggests that Ramsay did not exaggerate Charlotte's facial characteristics in any way whatsoever. It is hardly likely that the king would have appreciated having his wife's visage distorted, especially when they were both artistic and so happily married that he is the one king of England who is accepted by all reputable historians as never having had a mistress. He and Charlotte had fifteen children together, of whom all but two survived into adulthood. Moreover, both he and she were not only artistic but also cultured and erudite. Although Charlotte had not had a good education, she was an intelligent as well as a sensible woman who grew into the role of queen, while he was the best educated monarch Britain has ever had. He was also possibly the most erudite and intelligent. The hypothesis, therefore, that Ramsay might have distorted Charlotte's image to further the abolitionist movement, and that neither the king nor the queen would have noticed the disfigurement while allowing the distortion to be disseminated worldwide, seems far-fetched to say the least. Charlotte was well known to lack vanity, while George III was so down-to-earth that he was known as 'Farmer George'. Far more likely is that Ramsay's representations of the queen were accurate and that neither king nor queen minded. Indeed, they were so pleased with the images Ramsay created that they appointed him to copy them repeatedly, which he did for the remainder of his career. At the time of his retirement, he had fifty outstanding commissions for portraits of the king and queen which had to be completed by his studio.

Hindsight is a wonderful thing, especially when one is looking back onto the past from a platform with a racial message. The evidence suggests, however, that no one in Court or Establishment circles, looking at Queen Charlotte, ever made the link between her facial features and the fact that she might have had black blood. It seems very unlikely that Baron Stockmar, Allan Ramsay, or the many other people who observed that Queen Charlotte looked like a '*mulatto*', which at the time had a very specific meaning, namely half white and half black, would have commented upon the resemblance, had it occurred to them that she might actually have been what was then called '*coloured*'. It is inconceivable that any white person anywhere in the British Isles or British Empire could have imagined such an eventuality as a possibility. It is for that reason that they were so free in noting the cast of her features, little realising that they might well have hit upon ancestors they could never have suspected existed. After all, white royalty in the eighteenth century, especially in its second half, when colour prejudice was on the increase, was unthinkingly accepted as possessing 100% Caucasian heritage. It would never have occurred to anyone that a queen of England might actually have African blood, nor that that African blood might actually be visible owing to the repeated intermarriages that had taken place in royal families over the centuries, with the result that one African ancestor popped up on several branches of the family tree, thereby making her presence felt in a way that would have been wholly unthinkable had she remained perched on only one branch.

Chapter Five

IN THE EIGHTEENTH CENTURY, the further east you went into the heartlands of Europe, the higher up you went in social circles, the more desirable black people became. They were treasured as employees, especially in Russia, and would remain so until the downfall of the Romanoff dynasty in 1917.

In Western Europe, while King George III was losing the American colonies and colour prejudice began to take root against the '*Negro*', black staff were still viewed as being more exotic and desirable than white. This had been true for at least a century and a half, if not longer. For instance, Louis XIV of France's queen, Maria Theresa of Spain, had a black dwarf in her retinue, and was so fond of him that, when her second child died six weeks after birth in 1664, there was a rumour that the baby had been born black and was killed to cover up that fact. So widely did the story spread that her sister-in-law, Liselotte of the Palatinate, wife of the king's younger brother the Duke of Orleans, alluded to it in her memoirs before making a categoric denial.

Ladies and gentlemen of distinction not only had superb jewels, magnificent clothing, and housing and modes of transport which announced their rank to the world, but also black attendants who were the jewels in their households' crowns. Yes, these blacks were servants, but at a time when the upper classes did not work and industrialisation had not yet come into being to provide alternative forms of employment, household service was one of the few respectable and desirable modes of employment for people without means. Now that we live in a world where service is regarded as undesirable, we might be tempted to frown upon those who, in an earlier age, were happy to be employed as servants, but history is the story of the past *as it was,* not the past as we would like it to have been, and certainly not something to be seen through the distorting lens of present-day values. It is therefore necessary to remember that what we might be tempted to frown upon today, might actually have been something that was desirable yesterday.

A case in point is how desirable black household staff had become by the eighteenth century. While they would ordinarily have worn the uniforms or livery of their household - as would all the other members of staff, irrespective of '*colour*' but determined by function within the household (a butler wearing a different uniform from a footman, for instance) - for special occasions black staff were sometimes bedecked in '*Blackamoor*' costumes. These were today's equivalent of a movie star like Scarlett Johansson wearing a ball gown and jewels from Harry Winston on the red carpet: ludicrous if worn at home for no reason, but appropriate when worn to the Oscars. Nowadays, however, by neglecting the context, there is the growing belief that '*Blackamoor*' costumes were racist. Yet at the time they would have heralded glamour and distinction, and been extremely expensive to boot, and it is very doubtful that anyone who wore one would have felt that they were being denigrated. Is Scarlett Johansson a candidate for sympathy because she is bedecked in a garment worth hundreds of thousands and jewels worth millions?

In much the same way that the wife of a cheapskate, dressed in cheaper clothes than her husband could afford, would have been jealous of the silks and satins of the wives of more generous men, so too would the white household staff have felt outshone by their more sumptuously-at-tired black colleagues. It must be remembered that cloth was extremely costly in the eighteenth century. Even queens such as Marie Antoinette and Charlotte darned their clothing, needlework and embroidery being activities that all ladies did. Dressing up a servant in extravagantly expensive brocades was therefore no insult, either to the wearer or the viewer. Nor was the costume of the '*Blackamoor*' a racist putdown of the antecedents of the Sub-Saharan Africans who wore them. Firstly, the costume itself was not Sub-Saharan African, but a rendering of the extravagant costume privileged Moors wore. Exotica was a mark of distinction, whether in the form of clothing, or in decoration such as the Rococo, or in plants, such as the pineapple, which was so valuable that the middle classes actually used to rent that fruit for special occasions and offer it to their guests, the protocol being that you always declined, as it would have to be returned intact or paid for, and pineapples were ruinously expensive.

The mundane had not yet achieved the status of desirability that it would in the twentieth and twenty first centuries. Clothing remained a means of declaring your position in life, and the sumptuously dressed employee of a grandee was not announcing his inferiority, but the superiority of his own and his master's station. The purpose of the message was to elevate. Far from being creatures of revilement or mockery, '*Blackamoors*' were the exotic representations of a contemporary as well as an ancient culture which both valued the sumptuous. '*Blackamoor*' costumes did not represent the clothing worn by Moorish slaves, but by rich Moors. They were therefore never intended to represent the costumes of slaves. This was at a time when ladies and gentlemen were dressed to the nines, when certain costumes and fabrics were reserved for the exclusive use of the nobility, when their staffs were bedecked in magnificent livery. Dressing up their most desirable employees in ancient costumes representing a former elite was not only a way of making a statement about the household's position in society, it was also a way of 'aristocratising' members of their staff, while also maintaining the distinction between employer and employee. It must be remembered that only superior ranks in society were allowed to dress sumptuously. The middle classes dressed plainly, in sombre colours and dark fabrics, their staff equally plainly attired. While the poor wore rags, even the working class, when in service to households of rank, were more richly dressed than the middle classes. Indeed, it is fair to say that servants attired in '*Blackamoor*' costumes would have been like today's movie stars, bedecked in borrowed couture garments and borrowed jewels on the red carpet. It would hardly be credible to say that an actress who has on a dress worth $250,000 and jewels worth ten times that is being taken advantage of, or that her costume represents a putdown, yet the corollary has been gaining traction as regards '*Blackamoor*' costumes.

Black staff were extremely desirable, and it is this desirability that accounts for one of the most extraordinary trajectories in history. Uniquely, a black slave ended up as a Russian nobleman, a revered general, the great-grandfather of Russia's greatest poet, with his descendants heading up branches of the British royal family and two of Britain's greatest ducal houses, amongst other eminent descendants.

The man in question was definitely what was once called a '*Negro*'. There can be none of the fudging that has surrounded Madragana, if only because there is a famous bust of him in Petrovskoe which shows an unmistakably Sub-Saharan African, and there are portraits of him showing an obviously black man of Sub-Saharan cast. There is also a portrait of his son Ivan by the School of Dmitri Levitzky, which is of a bi-racial man of obvious Caucasian and Sub-Saharan African parentage. But most important of all, his line is so eminent that there has been considerable research into its origins.

Despite this, the man's son-in-law attempted a fudge, writing a biography claiming that he was from Ethiopia rather than Sub-Saharan Africa. This was to give him Hamitic rather than Negroid antecedents, for, while the family enjoyed the status of aristocrats, as the century wore on, the prejudice against Sub-Saharan Africans was beginning to be felt even in far-off Russia. The veil of Ham, however, would be torn asunder as the family achieved ever-greater heights and researchers discovered that it was indeed descended from Sub-Saharan Africans.

The man in question has gone down in history as Abram Petrovich Hannibal. The most reliable source of information about his past is his great-grandson Alexander Pushkin's unfinished biography, *The Negro of Peter the Great*, published after that author's death in 1837.

No one knows exactly when he was born, or where, for Abram Hannibal was kidnapped as a child and taken as a slave to Constantinople. Even he did not know his birth date, or where his place of birth was. He celebrated his birthday on the day of his Christening, though he did write and tell the Empress Elizabeth Petrovna that he was from a town called Logon or Logone. The only problem with that is, there are several Logons and Logones in Africa. The Russian anthropologist Dmitri Anuchin speculated that he could have been from Logo-chewa in Eritrea, while the noted author Vladimir Nabokov came to the conclusion in 1962, while doing research on his origins, that Hannibal was referring to the Logona region of Equatorial Africa, south of Lake Chad. This dovetails with the extensive research undertaken by the Beninean historian and Russian expert Dieudonne Gnammankou, who surmised in 1995 that Hannibal was born about 1698 in or around Logone-Birni, by Lake Chad in the central African republic of present day Cameroon. It is also possible that he was the son of a minor chief, who had several wives and 19 children, and died in battle defending his land from the invading Ottoman Turks. What is certain is that the boy was captured and taken to the Ottoman capital, where he was bought by the Sultan and pressed into the service of Mustafa's younger brother Ahmed, who had been condemned to live his whole life in a gilded cage to prevent him from being a threat to his brother's throne.

After about a year serving in this profoundly depressing environment, Hannibal, who would later on, once he had become a successful soldier, endow himself with that surname in honour of the great Carthaginian Hannibal, was bought by the Russian Ambassador. Count Sava Lukich Vladislavich-Raguzinsky's brief from Peter the Great had been to acquire a 'few clever little African slaves' for the Russian Court, in keeping with the craze for black attendants. As soon as the Count owned Hannibal, he sent him to Moscow, where the boy, by now about six or seven, maybe even eight, was presented to the Tsar. Peter was drawn to his intelligence and not only agreed to stand as his Godfather when Hannibal was baptised the following year, but ensured that he had a superb education as a member of the royal household. A quick learner, the boy displayed an early aptitude for mathematics and geometry, and was soon fluent in several languages. There seems to have been genuine affection between Peter, his daughter Elizabeth, and Hannibal. Whenever the Tsar travelled, the youngster accompanied him as his valet, which was a position of considerable honour. As he grew up, he continued to be nurtured by both Peter and Elizabeth, who treated him more as a ward than a slave or servant. As a teenager, he slept in the Tsar's bedroom (an honour reserved for the most trusted attendants), while acting as his secretary and studying science and mathematics. He was also a natural linguist, and accompanied Peter on his trip through the Netherlands and France in 1717, when Hannibal was about 19. Peter decided to leave him in France, sending him to Metz to be taught the arts, sciences and warfare at the most progressive institutes of the day.

It was obvious that Peter was training him up for a brilliant future. Hannibal understood that the way to flourish was to please his godfather, so the following year he joined the French Army to learn more about military engineering. This did indeed please Peter, so two years later he enrolled in the Royal Artillery Academy at La Fère. War broke out between France and Spain, so Hannibal, who began using that name around this time, fought for France, rising to the rank of Captain. There is no question that the young man was treated as a privileged visitor. Class once more trumped race, and he was embraced by such Enlightenment figures as the philosopher Baron de Montesquieu, Diderot, and the young Voltaire, who is alleged to have quipped that Hannibal was 'the dark star of the Enlightenment'.

After five years in France, Hannibal returned to Russia. Unfortunately, Peter died in 1725, and while his widow sat on the throne as Empress Catherine I, Prince Menshikov, who became the *de facto* ruler of Russia for the next couple of years, disliked the young man. He therefore exiled him to Siberia, and though Hannibal was freed after three years, he was compelled to remain there for another three, building a fortress and overseeing other construction projects. Nevertheless, his accomplishments were considerable. He wrote a textbook on Geometry and Fortification that was six inches thick, became the Russian Army's chief engineer, worked on a secret howitzer that was a precursor of the first rockets, and even assisted in designing the system of canals which would be built two centuries later by Josef Stalin.

Only when Peter the Great's daughter Elizabeth became Empress in 1741 did Hannibal return to favour. She ennobled him the following year, and gave him the 6,000 acre Mikhailovskoye Estate in Pskov Oblast, on the border of Estonia in the west, along with hundreds of serfs. He was appointed the Superintendant of Reval (modern-day Tallinn in Estonia) for the next ten years, before he finally became a Major-General of the Army in charge of the construction of sea forts and canals in Russia. How this former slave assumed mastery over thousands of other souls says much about him as an individual, as well about contemporaneous attitudes to slavery. There was no question of freeing the serfs. Had he done so he would have ruined the estate financially. Serfs were property just like slaves, and if they did not exist, who else would do the work they did? Freeing them, moreover, would have been a revolutionary action which would have criticised the status quo at a time when slavery was the norm internationally, and serfdom but a less extreme form of enforced servitude. No one would have employed his freed serfs, who would have been viewed as threats. He would also have ruined his prospects with the Tsarina, who would have rightly regarded his action as overt criticism when gratitude would have been a more appropriate response. So he did what millions of masters have done over the centuries. He became as good a master as he could be. When he rented out the estate to a German aristocrat, he stipulated that the 'present contract is...void if... the peasants....are mistreated in any way.' After two of the peasants complained, he successfully sued the tenant, thereby enshrining peasants' rights in Russian common law.

Plainly, Hannibal's race was no preventative to success. Although he complained that on occasion he suffered 'insults and offences', and although these sometimes had racist overtones, the fact is that all successful people are subject to revilement and jealousy from their less successful peers. If they are tall, their height is alighted upon as a weapon with which to beat them. If they are short, the same rule applies. If they are fat, they are called tubs of lard, and if they are thin, match sticks. When they are pale, their pallor is commented upon, and when dark, that becomes the brickbat. Although Hannibal's race might therefore have been used to insult him from time to time, the argument that he was somehow the victim of racial prejudice does not stand up to in depth examination. Indeed, the 19th century military expert General Christoph von Manstein (1711-1757) believed that Hannibal's race and foreign origins could have helped him to become the success he did, because 'soldiers repose more confidence in strangers than in officers of their own nation.' Therefore his very visible difference, allied to his high intelligence and obvious ability, meant that he enjoyed the confidence of his men and the Tsar and Tsarina in a way that he would not otherwise have done had he been just another Russian.

The acid test of racial prejudice lies in the marriage bed. No one who is prejudiced would consider marrying someone of another race.

Co-mingling lives and blood is one thing, if it is done in the shadows. Marriage, especially in those days, involved more than pleasure or desire. It was as much a worldly contract as a religious sacrament. It involved overt declarations that included such important considerations as status and, through the progeny, the future bloodline of one's descendants. History is full of examples of couples being forced to marry for worldly gain against their better instincts. This is what happened with Hannibal's first marriage. Although there has never been any evidence to suggest that his first wife Evdokia Dioper, who was Greek, was racially prejudiced, there is much which confirms that she had taken against him and did not wish to marry him. At the time, however, girls were made to marry whomever their families had chosen for them. The Dopiers regarded Hannibal, by then in his early thirties and relatively prosperous with the cachet of having been Peter the Great's godson, a good match, and when Evdokia baulked, they forced her to marry him. From the outset, the marriage was not a success. Hannibal began to suspect that she was being unfaithful, a fact which was confirmed when she gave birth to a white daughter. Incensed, he had her arrested and thrown into prison for eleven years.

His second marriage was a greater success. He began living with a noblewoman of Scandinavian and German origin named Christina Regina Sioberg, shortly after Evdokia had been thrown into prison. In 1735, she gave birth to their first child, and the following year, he married her bigamously. It would be another seventeen years before his first marriage was legally dissolved. After paying a fine, his second marriage was deemed to be legal and his first wife was banished to a convent for the remainder of her life.

Abram and Christina Hannibal had ten children together and appear to have had a long and successful union. Their eldest son Ivan helped to found the city of Kherson while another son, Osip, produced the daughter, Nadezhda Osipovna Hannibalova, who gave birth to Russia's greatest poet, Alexander Sergeyevich Pushkin.

The mere fact that the Pushkins were a noble family who traced their ancestry back to the twelfth century eloquently proclaims that the African heritage of the Hannibal family was no preventative to a good match.

As Peter the Great put it, Abram Hannibal's gifts disproved 'that odious prejudice which assigns to the *Negro* race a reputation of intellectual and moral inferiority.' Nevertheless, his son-in-law Rothkirch was taking no chances, and managed to lighten the matter literally as well as metaphorically when he declared in his biography of Hannibal that his father-in-law had been an Ethiopian prince. The Ethiopians, despite being relatively dark skinned, were not regarded as being '*Negro*', and of course, princes were regarded as superior beings. The historian Dieudonne Gnammankou has rather pointedly noted that the Russians thought that 'Ethiopians are practically white', so in one dextrous move Rothkirch had managed to neutralise any potential future prejudice against his own, as well as his in-laws', progeny, by whitewashing him.

Quite how useful Rothkirch's fig-leaf was in covering what he obviously saw as a sore point is open to question. Alexander Pushkin, his niece's son, was avowedly mixed-race. This did not prevent him from enjoying the most glorious career as a writer, or from being venerated as Russia's finest poet, both during his lifetime and thereafter, up to the present day. Nor did it exclude him from enjoying an acknowledged social position of eminence as an aristocrat, sometimes enjoying the favour of the Tsar. Even at the height of the Soviet Terror, in 1937, Pushkin's reputation was such that Josef Stalin allowed the former Tsars' enclave of summer palaces outside St. Petersburg, Tsarskoye Selo, to be renamed Pushkin.

When he was not being exiled for revolutionary ideas, the poet was also a favourite writer of Nicholas I, and married to one of the great beauties of the Russian Empire: Natalia Goncharova. To Russians, Pushkin is a great Russian writer, pure and simple. He is the author of some of Russia's greatest literary works: *Eugene Onegin, Boris Godunov, Ruslan and Ludmilla*, and *The Queen of Spades* being but a few. His works have been set to music by some of Russia's greatest composers, including Tchaikovsky, Mussorgsky, Glinka and Rachmaninoff. No one before him had ever used the Russian language the way he did, and it is possible no one after him ever will. His exotic ancestry might have had more significance had he not been so great, had he needed some jazzing up, but because his works have been such gifts to the Russian people, his literary accomplishments render everything else utterly insignificant. To

Russians, Pushkin is truly Russian, even as they acknowledge the fact that he was mixed-race, proving that race and nationality are not necessarily one and the same, and that civilised societies celebrate the accomplishments of their nationals irrespective of any racial mixtures that exist.

Pushkin had four children with Natalia. She then compromised his honour by embarking upon an inappropriate relationship with a French émigré named Baron Georges-Charles d'Anthès, her sister Catherine's husband. This resulted in Pushkin challenging his brother-in-law to a duel. On 2th January 1837, d'Anthès shot Pushkin in the stomach, fatally wounding him. He took two days to die, during which time he sent a message to his brother-in-law absolving him of any wrongdoing. Duelling, however, was illegal in Russia, so d'Anthès was arrested, imprisoned in the Saints Peter and Paul Fortress, before being called to Court by the Tsar. Pardoned for the duel, he was nevertheless cashiered out of the Army, escorted to the frontier, and expelled from Russia.

Pushkin's death unleashed national mourning. Despite this, rumours soon circulated that the Tsar was having an affair with Natalia. True or false, she remarried with his blessing seven years later, producing three more children with her second husband.

Her two sons with Pushkin would not make waves, but her two daughters did. The elder, Maria, is regarded as having been the prototype for Tolstoy's heroine Anna Karenina, while the younger, Natalia Alexandrovna Pushkina (1836-1913) was a ravishing beauty like her mother. Unlike her mother, however, she possessed the spicy exoticism of her father's heritage to distinguish her from the competition. Her first husband was the Russian General Mikhail Leontievich von Dubelt, with whom she had a daughter, then in London on the 1st July, 1868, the 32 year-old divorcee married Prince Nikolaus Wilhelm of Nassau (1832-1905).

Natalia had well and truly struck gold. Nikolaus was the only son of the tremendously rich, truly regal Wilhelm, Duke of Nassau (1792-1839) by his second wife, Princess Pauline of Württemberg (1810-1856). It is no understatement to say that Natalia had married into a family that had links to the most important thrones in Europe. What Wilhelm's side of the family didn't provide, his two wives' did. There were his cousins the

King of the Netherlands and Prince Adolphe, who was the heir to the Grand Duchy of Luxembourg. His first wife had been Princess Louise of Saxe-Hildburghausen (1794-1825), his second, the namesake daughter of her younger sister, Charlotte. Both had been named in honour of another eminent relation, only recently deceased, the late Queen Charlotte of the United Kingdom of Great Britain and Ireland.

This, of course, made them mixed race as well, but this fact had been buried by the sands of time. Nevertheless, through a series of intermarriages within the royal houses of Saxe-Hildburghausen and Mecklenburg-Strelitz, Madragana's descendants had become Queen Louise of Prussia, wife of King Frederick William III (ancestors of the modern Kaisers of Germany), Queen Therese of Bavaria (whose descendants became Grand Duchess of Hesse and the Rhine, Duchess of Modena, King of Greece, and married into the Spanish and Austrian royal families) and Queen Frederica of Hanover, consort of King Ernst August of Hanover.

This Queen of Hanover demonstrates how bad behaviour rather than colour or class could render someone unacceptable, even when their antecedents were impeccable. Her husband was George III's fifth son. Known as the Duke of Cumberland until he acceded to the Hanoverian throne when his first cousin Victoria ascended the British and he the Hanoverian, Salic law preventing a female from becoming ruler of Hanover, his mother, Queen Charlotte, refused to receive his wife, who was also her niece, the daughter of her brother the Grand Duke of Mecklenburg-Strelitz. Frederica had jilted Charlotte's other son, the Duke of Cambridge, something Queen Charlotte never forgave, so she refused to acknowledge the existence of her niece as her daughter-in-law. Frederica and Ernst August's son would become the last King of Hanover, the blind George V, and their descendants flourish to this day. They include King Constantine of the Hellenes, Queen Sophie of Spain, and the present Prince of Hanover, who married Princess Caroline of Monaco.

The splendidly royal Nikolaus of Nassau was one of twelve children, all of whom made splendid matches. There were eight progeny from his father's first marriage, and four from his second. Natalia's eldest surviving half sister-in-law was married to one of the Tsar's cousins, the immensely rich Duke of Oldenburg, son of Tsar Alexander I of Russia's favourite sister Grand Duchess Catherine Pavlovna, and grandfather of the famous Grand Duke Nicholas Nickolaievich who was the Commander in Chief of the Russian Imperial Army until the closing days of the Romanoff dynasty. Another half sister-in-law was married to the Prince of Wied, whose daughter Elisabeth would become the first Queen of Romania, while her full sister-in-law Helena married the Prince of Waldeck and Pyrmont. Their daughter Helena would become the Duchess of Albany when she married Queen Victoria's haemophilic son Leopold, and their granddaughter Princess Alice would marry Queen Mary's brother Prince Alexander of Teck, later Earl of Athlone. Last but not least, Nikolaus's youngest sister Sophia became Queen of Sweden until her death in 1913, and Queen of Norway until her husband King Oscar II lost that throne in 1905. The union of the King and Queen of Sweden and Norway had been a love match, as was Wilhelm of Nassau's and Natalia Puskhina, and though the king kept mistresses she wielded considerable influence over her husband, whose political views were significantly less liberal than hers. Historians credit her with helping to popularise her husband during his reign, and their reigning descendants include King Carl XVI Gustaf of Sweden, King Harald V of Norway, Queen Margarethe II of Denmark, King Philippe of the Belgians, and the Grand Duke of Luxembourg; all of whom are therefore cousins of Natalia's descendants.

It is unlikely that Nikolaus and Natalia would have been aware that both of them descended from Africans, though there is no doubt that they would have known about Hannibal. Thanks to Pushkin's celebrity, there was no question of ignoring him. The poet's visage was famous through Europe, his mixed-race heritage to the eye. It is speculation whether that would have become a source of objection to the marriage of his daughter and her royal prince, but in the event, the main bone of contention was not racial, but the class difference. Although an aristocrat, Natalia was not royal. The German royal families had strict House Rules, forbidding unequal marriages, i.e. marriages between royals and non-royals. In Europe the mechanism of the morganatic union had been created to accommodate such pairings. The royal would retain his royal rank, style and title, while his wife and any children of the marriage, though legitimate, would have non-royal names, styles and titles - if the morganatic wife managed to acquire a title in her own right from a sympathetic relation.

Frowned upon by many of the European monarchs, morganatic marriages had nevertheless recently begun the transition from unacceptable to tolerable.

There were ample precedents for such unions, all somehow connected to Nikolaus. Prince Alexander of Hesse, the brother of Tsar Alexander II of Russia's Empress Marie Alexandrovna, in 1851 had married Countess Julie von Hauke, a ward of the previous Tsar and lady-in-waiting to his sister. She had been created firstly Countess, then latterly Princess, of Battenberg by her brother-in-law the Grand Duke of Hesse. At the time of Nikolaus and Natalia's marriage, there were five Battenberg children, all received at the major courts of Europe. Two of the sons would marry into the British Royal Family, the eldest brother Louis marrying Queen Victoria's granddaughter Princess Victoria of Hesse, while a younger son, Prince Henry, would marry her youngest daughter, Princess Beatrice. Their daughter would become Queen Victoria Eugenia of Spain, consort to King Juan Carlos's grandfather, King Alfonso XIII. Another granddaughter, Princess Alice of Battenberg, would marry Prince Andrew of Greece and produce Queen Elizabeth II's consort, Prince Philip.

On the Württemberg side of Nikolaus's family, there was the rackety Prince Francis of Teck, recently elevated from Count of Hohenstein and married off, two years previously, to Queen Victoria's grotesquely fat first cousin, Princess Mary Adelaide of Cambridge. His parents were Duke Alexander of Württemberg, nephew of King Frederick I of Württemberg and Empress Marie Feodorovna of Russia, Consort of Tsar Paul I, and the Hungarian Countess Claudine Rhédey von Kis-Rhéde. She had died tragically when her son was only four, trampled to death by a cavalry charge during a military review. At the time of the Nassau-Puskhina marriage, her Teck granddaughter, who would one day become the world's most splendid queen consort as Queen Mary, was one year old.

The Battenberg and Teck marriages had helped to take some of the stigma out of morganatic unions, if only because the two greatest empires on earth, the Russian and the British, accepted them with a previously unknown alacrity. Queen Victoria and Empress Marie Alexandrovna had put the happiness of their respective cousin and brother first, and, as with so much in life, once the precedent had been set by the powerful the less splendid followed in their wake, even if, on occasion, they did so reluctantly.

It would have been embarrassing for both Nikolaus and Natalia if she had not been given her own title. Just such a humiliation would happen, later on, when Tsar Nicholas II's younger brother Grand Duke Michael Alexandrovich married the twice-divorced commoner Natalia Sergeyevna Wulfert. While still married to her second husband, she had given birth to Michael's son George. To prevent the child being legally Vladimir Vladimirovich Wulfert's under the laws of presumption of legitimacy, Michael had the Wulfert divorce backdated so that he could acknowledge the child as his own. Although his brother Nicholas strongly disapproved of Natalia, he nevertheless created the boy Count Brasov, after Michael's estate of Brasovo. The young count was given the surname Romanovsky-Brasov in acknowledgement of his status as a non-royal member of the Romanoff family, but, even after Michael married Natalia, the Tsar refused to give her a title. Taking matters into his own hands, when Michael went into exile with her, he referred to her as Countess Brasova. It would only be in 1928, eleven years after the abolition of the Russian monarchy, by which time Michael had been declared legally dead for four years, that the Tsar in Pretence, Grand Duke Kirill, elevated Natalia, creating her Princess Brasova and making George Prince instead of Count. Gilding the lily, in 1935 he created her Her Serene Highness Princess Romanovskaya-Brasova, but by then such honours were pointless, as she was so poverty-stricken that she was barely able to survive.

To ensure that his sister-in-law would not suffer as ignominious a fate as awaited Grand Duke Michael Alexandrovich of Russia's wife, Prince Nikolaus of Nassau's brother-in-law, George Victor, Prince of Waldeck and Pyrmont, created Natalia Alexandrovna Pushkina Countess of Merenberg in her own right. This act alone demonstrates how much more relevant class was than any element of a mixed-race heritage. While Grand Duke Michael Alexandrovich's non-aristocratic but wholly Caucasian Natalia was deemed unsuitable to be created a Countess in her own right, Prince Nikolaus's aristocratic but mixed-race Natalia was.

Eleven months after the newly minted Countess of Merenberg's marriage, she gave birth in Geneva to a daughter who was known as Countess Sophie von Merenberg. This suggests that the couple had still not decided where to live. It was bad enough to marry morganatically and live discreetly in another state while nevertheless visiting family, but quite another to flaunt one's union by taking up residence in one's native land. Discretion was the order of the day in a world where marriage had both a dynastic and a procreational aspect, morganatic marriages therefore failing on two fronts. Prince Nikolaus and Natalia displayed commendable tact in keeping away from the duchy of Nassau until the dust settled. However, they had one thing militating in their favour when they decided, the year later, to live in Wiesbaden, the capital of the duchy of Nassau and therefore the heartland of Nikolaus's family. Three years before, in 1866, the kingdom of Prussia had annexed the duchy as punishment for supporting the losing side in the Austro-Prussian War. It had been incorporated into the state of Prussia and amalgamated with the state of Hesse-Cassel, thereafter to be known as the Province of Hesse-Nassau. So when Nikolaus and Natalia moved to Wiesbaden and she was delivered of another daughter, Alexandrine, in 1869, followed fifteen months later by a son, George, the family had lost its territorial rights though not its wealth. With the creation of the German Empire following the Franco-Prussian War in 1871, there was even less hope of the deposed Duke of Nassau being restored to his throne. This had the unexpected effect of being advantageous for Nikolaus and Natalia, as it meant that their unequal status had, in a way, extended to the other members of the family. Being dethroned but royal, the ducal Nassaus (as opposed to those who were the Kings of Holland) now occupied the anomalous positions of being both equal to all other royals but no longer equal to those with thrones. This took some of the sting out of Nikolaus and Natalia's marriage, and theirs would prove to be a long and happy one, lived in style and comfort, as they travelled between their many royal and aristocratic relations, bringing up their three children, all of whom were accepted in family circles despite their morganatic status. The African heritage of the Merenberg children was not an issue, at least not so that it caused problems, and when their Uncle Adolphe regained a throne, this time becoming the Grand Duke of Luxembourg, in 1890, they were so fully incorporated into the family circle of the Nassau Royal House that their morganatic status was of scant consequence, except to diehard reactionaries.

Admittedly, some of those reactionaries still occupied thrones, Kaiser Wilhelm II and Tsar Nicholas II being the prime examples. Despite this, two of Nikolaus and Natalia's children would grow up to marry members of the Russian Imperial Family. To give an idea of the significance of these unions, at the time they took place the Romanoffs were the grandest and richest royal family on earth, regarded by many as the world's foremost ruling family. At twenty four, George von Merenberg married, in Nice, Tsar Alexander II's morganatic daughter, Princess Olga Alexandrova Yurievskaya. They had two sons and a daughter, who in turn produced a wealth of aristocratic descendants, all of whom lived in Germany or Switzerland, but, because they chose to live on the Continent as throne after throne was lost, their branch of the family plateaued.

But this is to anticipate the future. At the time of their marriage, Princess Olga Yurievskaya had some of the cachet that attached to all the Romanoffs. It was well known that Olga would have ended up a fully-fledged member of the Imperial Family had her father not died prematurely. Tsar Alexander III had been arranging to make an Empress of her mother, the former Princess Catherine Mikhailova Dolgoroukova, whom he had married morganatically and had created Princess Yurievskaya in her own right following the death of his first wife, Marie.

In the web of connections which were characteristic of European royals, Marie's brother Alexander was the morganatic husband of the Princess of Battenberg whose marriage had done so much to make morganatic marriages more acceptable. However, in Russia at least, Tsar Alexander II managed to dissipate all those advances when he began a torrid and flagrant affair with the teenaged Catherine. The letters he wrote to her convey the full extent of the passion between them. He wrote longingly about how erotic he found her vaginal juices as they flowed over his penis.

While his son and heir, Alexander III, might have understood his father's lust for Catherine once he had read the letters, what he could never forgive was the way the relationship had tormented his mother.

She and the Liberator Tsar had once had a great passion as well. He had married her despite the rumour that she and three of her siblings, including Prince Alexander of Hesse, were the natural children of the Grand Duchess Wilhelmine of Hesse and Baron August von Senarclens de Grancey, Grand Master of the Horse of Grand Duke Ludwig II. When told of Marie's questionable paternity, he had said, 'Is she listed in the *Almanach de Gotha* as the Grand Duke's daughter?' Assured that she was, he said, 'Then we marry.' However, eight children and incipient tuberculosis ruined her health, and with it, her desirability. When her youngest child was six years old, the Liberator met the nineteen year old Catherine. It is arguable that any young girl, well- bred or not, would have been able to withstand the ministrations of a Tsar, and certainly not a vigorous, sexually impassioned 48 year old one like Alexander II.

He soon moved Catherine into a suite of rooms above Marie's in the Winter Palace. In time, she produced four children. Marie could hear the patter of their feet above her rooms as her life gradually seeped away downstairs and the husband who had once loved her focussed on his new family.

Five weeks after the empress's death in 1880, the Liberator Tsar married his young mistress, legitimising their children and creating an international scandal in the process. The 'unseemly' haste with which he 'regularised' his domestic relations astonished and offended in equal measure, but his writings show that he felt that time was not on his side. There had been several assassination attempts made against his life, and he was worried that he might be killed before he had time to marry Catherine. Within a year he would be blown apart by a bomb, ruining his plans to give Russia a constitution and his morganatic family Imperial status.

As a result of his mother's sufferings, Tsar Alexander III had a pronounced antipathy to morganatic unions as well as to infidelity. Upon his father's death, he cancelled all plans to elevate his half-siblings, expelled them and their mother from the palace, and ensured that his step-mother took up exile on the French Riviera. Although she was cushioned by the 3.4 million roubles with which her late husband had endowed her, she was such a scandalous figure, as a result in large measure of her husband's haste in marrying her, that her existence put back the acceptance of morganatic unions by years. This would have an adverse impact upon the status of both the Merenberg children who married into the Russian Imperial Family, for Alexander III's horror of morganatic marriages was shared by his wife. Both Sasha and Minnie, as the Imperial couple was known within the family, passed on this distaste to their son Nicholas II, and he in turn found it impossible to accept Sophie von Merenberg being married to his cousin Grand Duke Michael Mikhailovich of Russia, a grandson of Tsar Nicholas I.

Sophie and Michael's love story might easily have been written by her grandfather Alexander Pushkin, so full of passion, improbability, tragedy and good fortune was it. They met in Nice when he rescued her from a bolting horse. It was love at first sight. She was a statuesque, good looking young woman, not a ravishing beauty like her mother but very attractive nevertheless, while he was a typical Romanoff grand duke: extremely tall, handsome, well-built and physically fit owing to the military training which was obligatory for all the men of the dynasty.

Each of the grand dukes was provided with an annual allowance, laid down by law, which ran into several million US dollars in today's money, as his brother Sandro would later reveal in his memoirs. While the Nassau royal family was also rich, the difference was nevertheless stupendous. The Romanoffs were known to be the richest ruling family on earth, far richer than any other, including the British, who were hamstrung with constitutional restrictions which meant that they were custodians of their apparent wealth rather than the owners of it. No such restrictions applied to the Russian Imperial House.

By all accounts, Michael Mikhailovich, known as Miche-Miche in the family, was as amiable and sociable as he was handsome and rich. He was a popular member of St Petersburg society and something of a romantic. Nowadays, he would be regarded as having been damaged by his childhood. For the first twenty-one years of his life, he had been raised in Tiflis, Georgia, where his father was Viceroy of the Caucasus. His childhood was, in some ways, freer than it would have been in St. Petersburg; Georgia was exotic, wild even, the Viceregal Court a splendid and less rigid version of the capital's or Moscow's. His father was a busy and distant military man, kindly and unimaginative, but his mother, the former Princess Cecilie of Baden, was a cold, well-educated, highly intelligent, waspish-tongued and unmaternal disciplinarian who lived for gossip. Miche-Miche's brother Sandro described her in his memoirs as showing her children no affection but making endless demands upon them.

To ensure that they would not be spoilt and that they would grow up to reflect well upon her and be worthy of their exalted positions, all the Mikhailovichi children were deliberately deprived of creature comforts in their personal quarters. While being surrounded by unbelievable luxury in the public rooms of their palaces, in their nurseries and bedrooms everything was Spartan. They were made to sleep on hard bunk beds in plain rooms decorated no more lavishly than cells, and had cold baths even in winter. Taught by private tutors, their days were mapped out with all the rigidity of Cecilie's Germanic heritage. Harsh as this regimen was for all the children, Olga Feodorovna, as Princess Cecilie became upon marriage, made it clear that her second son was her least favoured child. He was less intelligent and gentler than his six siblings, and she dismissed him as stupid. So too did his first cousin, Tsar Alexander III, calling him a fool.

Like many an emotionally deprived child, Miche-Miche grew into a romantic who wanted to marry young and create the loving family he had never had. He had also been witness to the joys a long and happy marriage can bring, for, ironically, his parents were a devoted couple, polar opposites wrapped up in each other to the exclusion of everyone else. After the Mikhailovichi moved back to St. Petersburg when he was twenty one, he set about building himself a magnificent Neo-Renaissance palace with an entrance on the splendidly situated Admiralty Embankment, in preparation for the marriage he intended to make. Its design showed that Miche-Miche had taste and was innovative. It was kitted out with such new-fangled inventions as gas, electricity and telephone lines, and within a year of construction beginning he was in England, looking for a wife. His first choice was Princess May of Teck, the morganatic cousin of Queen Victoria who would ultimately become Queen of England. Fortunately for them both, she turned him down, her

Carl Linnaeus (1707-1778) was one of the greatest scientists who ever lived and the first person to classify plants, animals and minerals in Systema Naturae. His opus magnum was later twisted by racists into something he had never intended.

The childless William Murray was the poor fourth son of a Jacobite nobleman who ended up being the 1st Earl of Mansfield, the Lord Chief Justice, and the judge whose rulings in the famous Somersett and Zong cases led to the abolition of the slave trade. His two wards, whom he raised as his own daughters, were his great-nieces, the white Lady Elizabeth Murray and the mixed race Dido Elizabeth Belle.

I

Ignatius Sancho was born on a slave ship in the Middle Passage before coming to England, where his intelligence was spotted by the 2nd Duke of Montagu, who encouraged his education. Known as 'the extraordinary Negro', he was painted by such artists as Gainsborough and became a symbol to the Abolitionists of how opportunity and education could change a former slave's destiny.

The famous double portrait of Lady Elizabeth Murray and her first cousin Dido Elizabeth Belle, once thought to be by Johann Zoffany but now accepted as being by David Martin. Hung at Kenwood House, the London residence, of the Earls of Mansfield, till it was taken over by Grand Duke Michael of Russia, the Tsar's cousin who was in exile in England because of his morganatic marriage with a woman of colour.

II

King George III's consort was born Princess Charlotte of Mecklenburg-Strelitz. Allan Ramsay painted the most famous portrait of her. Her resemblance to a 'mulatto' was much commented upon by her contemporaries, including Baron Stockmar, one of the most eminent courtiers of the nineteenth century. She was indeed descended from a woman of colour, Madragana of Faro, who cropped up on some six branches of her family tree, compounding the genetic heritage as a result of the royal practice of intermarriage.

Abram Petrovich Hannibal was a Sub-Saharan African captured as a child in a slave raid in Cameroon. Taken to Istanbul, he was sold to the Sultan before being bought on behalf of the Russian Tsar Peter the Great, who became his godfather and patron. Rising to the greatest heights under Peter's daughter Empress Elizabeth, his descendants have married into a host of European imperial, royal and aristocratic families.

III

Natalia Pushkina was a ravishing beauty whose escapades triggered the death in a duel of Russia's greatest poet, her celebrated husband Alexander Pushkin. A great-grandson of Hannibal, his daughter with Natalia would end up marrying into one of Europe's leading royal families.

Grand Duke Michael Mikhailovich was the handsome younger son of the Tsar's first cousin. His elopement with Pushkin's granddaughter caused the death of his mother and resulted in his perpetual banishment: a punishment that would save his life when the Russian Revolution claimed the lives of many of his Romanoff relations.

IV

Countess Sophie Merenberg was the daughter of Prince Nicholas of Nassau and Natalia Pushkina, who was created Countess Merenberg in her own right so that her children would be spared the ignominy of being untitled. History repeated itself when Sophie married Grand Duke Michael and her uncle created her Countess Torby in her own right, so that her progeny would have aristocratic status. Interestingly, the great objection to Sophie wasn't her Sub-Saharan ancestry, but the fact that she was a mere aristocrat, and therefore deemed unsuitable for marriage into the Russian Imperial House.

The father of modern Russian literature, Alexander Pushkin was famously and obviously a man of colour, which has never made a scrap of difference to Russians, who have embraced him since his youth as being the greatest writer of all time in the Russian language, and, as such, the archetypal Russian man of letters.

V

Sacha (Duchess of) Abercorn, with (left to right) her husband James and cousin Prince Philip, was the proud descendant of Pushkin, Hannibal, Russian Emperors as well as sister of the Duchess of Westminster and mother of the next Duke of Abercorn. She more than anyone else is responsible for the extensive recognition her Sub-Saharan ancestors have received.

One of the greatest royal dynasties of all time was the Habsburg dynasty, which ruled over Spain, Austria, the Holy Roman Empire and the North, Central and South American colonies for centuries. Although dethroned, they retain immense prestige. The Archduke Geza's son Franz Ferdinand von Habsburg was one of the first European royals to marry, with the blessings of his family, a Sub-Saharan African. Known as Dr Frank von Habsburg, he is photographed with his second wife, Lei Greenspan, an African-American from South Carolina.

Count Ferdinand von Habsburg is Archduke Geza's second son. Like his brother, he has made his life in Africa. Married, with the approval of the Head of the House of Habsburg, to Mary Nyanut Ring Machar, a Dinka from South Sudan, he is the father of four children.

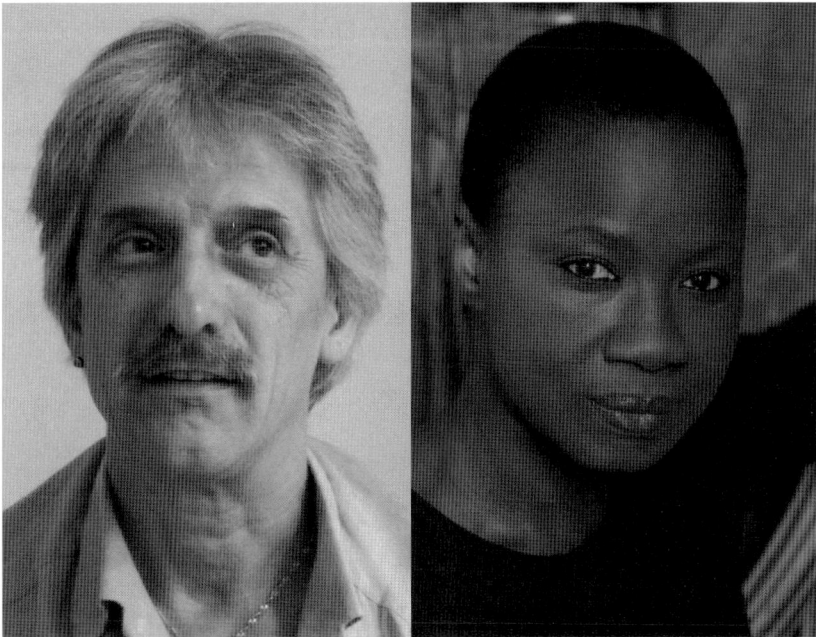

The Hon James Lascelles on the left is the second son of The Queen's first cousin George, Earl of Harewood, whose grandfather was King George V and mother was the late Princess Royal. He was the first member of the extended British Royal Family to marry, with the Sovereign's approval, an African. On the right is his wife Joy Elias-Rilwan, herself a scion of an aristocratic family.

Prince Maximilian of Lichtenstein is the second son of the ruling Prince of Lichtenstein Hans-Adam II, the richest monarch thanks to the family-owned LGT Group, which is the largest private banking and asset management group in the world. He has been happily married to the Panamanian-born, American dress designer Angela Gisela Brown since 2000, and is the father of 28 year old Prince Alfons.

Christian, Baron de Massy's mother was Prince Rainier of Monaco's troublesome sister Antoinette, who tried to supplant her brother and place her son on his throne. Married four times, his last wife Cecile Gelabale was born in Guadeloupe and gave birth to their son Antoine in 1997. She founded the prestigious charity Ladies Lunch Monte-Carlo and enjoys a good profile in the principality.

The marriage of the Marquis of Bath's heir Viscount Weymouth to Emma McQuiston, the half-sister of his half-uncle by marriage, inadvertently established a whole new code of acceptability which helped pave Prince Harry's way when he met the American actress Meghan Markle. The beautiful, glamorous and capable Viscountess Weymouth has gone from strength to strength and enjoys well-earned success within both aristocratic and national circles.

uncle the Duke of Cambridge and her father, by now elevated to Duke of Teck, being against the union on the grounds that the Romanoffs made bad husbands. It is arguable, taking into account Tsar Alexander III's objection to the products of morganatic unions, whether he would have agreed to a match involving his first cousin and this morganatic princess, and helps to explain why that Emperor thought him a fool.

Miche-Miche, however, did not allow himself to be deflected from his chosen path. Within months, he had proposed to Queen Victoria's granddaughter, Princess Irene of Hesse, whose elder sister Elizabeth, known as the most beautiful princess in Europe, had married his first cousin, Grand Duke Serge Alexandrovich of Russia. Though not nearly as good looking as her elder or younger sister Alix, who would ultimately marry his cousin Tsar Nicholas II and die as the Tsarina Alexandra, Irene was nevertheless attractive. However, she was in love with her first cousin, Kaiser Wilhelm II's younger brother Prince Henry of Prussia, and when she in turn turned him down, he proposed marriage to her first cousin Princess Louise of Wales, eldest daughter of the Prince of Wales and the former Princess Alexandra of Denmark, whose sister Dagmar was Empress Marie Feodorovna, married to his first cousin Tsar Alexander III. She too turned him down.

Returning to Russia, where the Imperial marriage pool was shallow, Miche-Miche plunged into the cold waters of the aristocracy, falling in love with Countess Catherine Nikolaievna Ignatieva. Her father had been a Minister of the Interior, but was a mere aristocrat. Miche-Miche nevertheless proposed marriage and took his father along in the hope of convincing the Tsar to give his permission. However, Alexander III remained implacably opposed to morganatic unions, as did his wife and Miche-Miche's mother, who condemned her son for 'openly provoking her' and showing her a 'lack of respect, affection and attention'. With permission refused, the grand duke was packed off to the South of France to lick his wounds and get over his latest ill-fated attempt at marriage.

His wounds were healed the instant he saved Sophie von Merenberg from being trampled to death. Their romance took off with the immediacy *coups de foudre* usually do. Within weeks, on the 26th February 1891, they married in San Remo. That town had become, along with Cannes and Nice, one of the fashionable Riviera resorts, where royalty and the nobility gravitated when ill, or just to have fun. Because Miche-Miche knew that neither his parents nor the Tsar would give permission for him to marry morganatically, he did not even bother to ask for permission. This meant that his marriage was unequal as well as technically illegal in Russia, being in defiance of the Pauline Rules of the House of Romanoff.

Although Prince Nikolaus of Nassau had not objected to the marriage, the Tsar was apoplectic when he discovered what Miche-Miche had done. He stripped him of his military rank (a disgrace for any army officer), dismissed him from his post as one of his adjutants (a position of high honour unsustainable without an army rank), suspended his grand ducal income, and banished him from Russia for life. Miche-Miche would have been penniless had he not had private investments: in particular, a plant that bottled water near Borjomi in Georgia, which would keep him afloat financially until the Revolution sank that source of income as well.

Worse was to follow. When Miche-Miche's mother found out what he had done, she collapsed with a heart attack. Sent to recover in the Crimea, the Imperial Family's favourite vacation spot in the empire, she had another heart attack on the train and died at Kharkov en route. Miche-Miche was blamed for her death and, when he asked for permission to return to Russia for her funeral, the Tsar refused it.

Despite the tragic start to the marriage, the couple was happy. Sophie's uncle, the Grand Duke of Luxembourg, did for her what her Uncle George of Waldeck and Pyrmont had done for her mother. Adolphe created Sophie Countess Torby in her own right, thereby enabling her and any future children to enjoy aristocratic rank. This was necessary because the customs of the day decreed that a woman lost the rank of her birth and adopted that of her husband upon marriage. With morganatic marriages, however, this meant that women had no rank at all unless they were given titles of their own, for morganatic unions specifically excluded the female partner from assuming her husband's rank. Moreover, the children of morganatic unions took the rank, style and titles of their mothers, which meant that they would have no rank, style or title if she had none, unless, of course, they received titles specific to them alone. It was to avoid this ignominious state of nothingness that sympathetic relations would come to the rescue and endow a morganatic wife with a rank of her own.

There is no doubt that had the Merenberg and Torby children not possessed the aristocratic dignities which they did, they would not have flourished to the extent that they did. They would have been unassigned embarrassments in a world where everyone else had the dignities they lacked. As it was, they not only assimilated completely into the aristocratic tribe with their Merenberg and Torby titles, but, in the case of the Torbys, achieved heights that were truly dazzling.

Grand Duke Michael and Countess Torby, as Sophie was thereafter known, started out their married life in Wiesbaden, where her parents also had a home. Their elder daughter, Anastasia (1892-1977) and youngest child and only son, Michael (1898-1955) were born there. Their middle daughter Nadejhda (1896-1963), was born in Cannes, where they had a villa called Kazbek in honour of a mountain in Georgia which held fond memories from his childhood and became their main home towards the end of the century. There they lived in some style with several gardeners, a chauffeur, five footmen, a butler, a valet, a lady's maid, a governess, a nursery maid, six chefs, housemaids and laundresses. Miche-Miche acutely felt the loss of his marginalisation by the Tsar, but any hope he had of lessening the ostracism when his younger cousin Nicky acceded to the throne in 1896 was short lived. The *froideur* continued even though Nicky's elder sister Xenia was married to his younger brother Sandro (Grand Duke Alexander Mikhailovich). Nicky, as the Tsar was known in the family, refused to withdraw Miche-Miche's banishment. He shared his parents' antipathy towards morganatic marriages. In this, he was backed up by his wife Alix, despite the fact that her eldest sister Victoria was herself married to a morganatic son, Prince Louis of Battenberg, and their great-aunt Empress Marie Alexandrovna of Russia had condoned her brother Alexander's morganatic marriage which had resulted in the self-same Battenbergs.

Can any of this have been racist? Hannibal's son-in-law might have put about the red herring that he had been an Ethiopian prince, but the Imperial Family knew only too well that he had been Sub-Saharan African. I gather from friends of mine who are members of the Imperial

Family that their grandparents waited with bated breath each time Sophie was pregnant, wondering, 'Will the baby be *black?*' Like many people who had no working knowledge of intermarriage the way Jamaicans do, they believed the fallacy that someone with '*negro*' blood, though looking white, could produce a black baby. What they did not realise was that '*throwbacks*' are never black. They might be darker-skinned than the rest of their family, or they might simply look '*negroid*', to use the vernacular popular at the time. Queen Charlotte had been a '*throwback*', her African heritage evident from the cast of her features. But she had hardly been black. Had the Romanoffs known this simple fact, they would have been spared the anxiety which went along with ignorant speculation.

Despite each baby's arrival being greeted with bated breath, this did not impact upon the friendship of the Tsar's sister and her husband with his brother and sister-in-law. Miche-Miche and Sophie spent what would now be called 'quality time' together in the South of France with Alexander Mikhailovich and Xenia who stayed, sometimes for extended periods, especially after Sandro and Xenia's relationship with the Tsar and Tsarina became strained over Alix's reliance on Rasputin.

Also there for six months every year, from November to May, were the brothers' sole sister Anastasia and her husband, Grand Duke Frederick Francis III of Mecklenburg-Schwerin. They had built one of the most palatial villas in the South of France, Villa Wenden, on the side of the mountain overlooking the Bay of Cannes. He suffered from a variety of chronic ailments, including asthma and eczema, and she had not wanted to marry him. Forced to, they ended up having a happy marriage, and she mourned 'the loss of my best friend' when he committed suicide by hurling himself off the 25 foot high retaining wall of their villa in 1897.

The Romanoff double grand duchess was a true character: warm, funny, intelligent, eccentric, regal, down-to-earth, generous and kind. She did much to incorporate Sophie into the imperial fold, paving the way so that she and Grand Duke Michael Mikhailovich were socially acceptable. She was as sociable an animal as her brother Miche-Miche, who was by then known as 'The Uncrowned King of Cannes'. Against all the odds, Anastasia's private life had been as successful as her public one. She and her husband had had three children: a daughter, Alexandrine, who became

Queen of Denmark, another daughter, Cecilie, who became Crown Princess of Germany, and Frederick Francis IV, the last Grand Duke of Mecklenburg-Schwerin. Widowed at only 36, she began an affair with her personal secretary, Vladimir Alexandrovich Paltov. After developing a swelling that she initially passed off as a tumour, she withdrew from public view with a purported case of chicken pox, and gave birth in Nice to an illegitimate son on 23rd December 1902. Thanks to her daughter Alexandrine's father-in-law, King Christian IX of Denmark, the baby was granted the aristocratic style of Alexis Louis de Wenden, and though not publicly acknowledged as her son was nevertheless brought up by her. To what extent the priggish Kaiser Wilhelm II, whose son and heir had married her daughter, knew of her 'private arrangements', is uncertain, but she was allowed to attend the Berlin Court only twice: for the marriage of her daughter, and when the Crown Prince and Crown Princess's first son was born.

If the Kaiser disapproved of the irregular living arrangements of the Mikhailovichi grand duke and grand duchess, the siblings' father, Grand Duke Michael Nicolaievich, was much more tolerant once he became a widower. Having been disabled as a result of a stroke, he moved from Russia to live near his rackety children in the South of France, lingering on until 1909. He left his vast fortune to his only daughter, and in so doing preserved at least that portion of the Romanoff hegemony which would otherwise have been subsumed by the Bolsheviks at the time of the Revolution.

From Miche-Miche and Sophie's point of view, it was one thing to be received by their close relations within the Imperial Family in an outpost like Cannes, but quite another to be marooned permanently in a republican environment. To him especially, there was Court life, which was where life was at, and there was everything else, which was a pale facsimile. Seeing his father, sister, cousin and brother when they were all together in the South of France was a pale substitute for benefitting from a Courtly existence, so he set about laying down roots of a sort in England when it became apparent that his banishment would not be lifted by the Tsar. Little did any of them realise that this enforced exile would result in his descendants achieving heights unimaginable at the time.

In Britain, royal customs had been keeping pace with the changes in society in a way they no longer did in Russia. Queen Victoria's youngest daughter was married to the morganatic Prince Henry of Battenberg. The heir-in-line to the throne, Georgie, Duke of York, was married to the morganatic May of Teck who had turned down Miche-Miche's proposal of marriage. The bugbear of unequal status would hereafter not rear its ugly head and bother them, any more than her African ancestry would. He and Sophie proceeded to maintain their imperial stature in England without the loss of dignity that was evident in Germany under the snobbish Kaiser and his prickly, status-obsessed cabal of imperialists; was impossible in Russia owing to his banishment; and was equally impossible in republican France, where Court life had been rendered obsolete with the deposition of Emperor Napoleon III.

At the turn of the century, Miche-Miche took a ten year lease on Keele Hall in Staffordshire which would prove decisive in establishing his immediate family's fortunes in the country that was about to become the world's premier monarchy. He entered into local life with such enthusiasm that he was made Lord High Steward of Newcastle-up-on-Lyme. As would later on happen with the Duke of Windsor, he so acutely felt the loss of opportunities to play the part in national life that his royal upbringing had prepared him for since birth, that he seized upon any opportunity to partake in public life, enjoying each crumb as if it were a whole meal in itself. This was equally true of his time in Cannes, where he laid many a cornerstone and cut many a ribbon ceremonially, the uncrowned king of the town now that the country had no crowned heads to fulfil such ceremonial roles. To him, any recognition seemed to be better than none, but the best came from those of his kinsmen who were reigning monarchs. He was therefore touchingly gratified when King Edward VII invested him with the Honorary Knight Grand Cross of the Royal Victorian Order, the House Order of the British Royal Family. Even though he could not return to Russia, he was still a Grand Duke of Russia, and it mattered greatly to him that he was accorded the recognition due to his rank.

By 1908 it had become apparent to him that his hopes of Cousin Nicky lifting his banishment were misplaced, especially as how his cousin

Grand Duke Paul Alexandrovich had also married morganatically and other grand dukes were involved with unequal paramours. Nicky felt he had to 'hold the line', otherwise he would lose all control over his family and the Romanoff dynasty would become top heavy with non-royal or -imperial spouses. So Miche-Miche did something people nowadays can identify with, but which at the time was truly exceptional. He went public with his bitterness, publicly expressing his sentiments about the way he, and other Grand Dukes who had made morganatic marriages such as his cousin Paul Alexandrovich, were still being treated. He wrote a novel, *Never Say Die*, about a morganatic marriage, bemoaning in the preface: 'Belonging, as I do, to the Imperial Blood, and being a member of one of the reigning houses, I should like to prove to the world how wrong it is in thinking – as the majority of mankind is apt to do – that we are the happiest beings on this earth. There is no doubt that we are well situated, but is wealth the only happiness in the world?' He had lobbed a grenade into the glass house, but it still did him no good. While he bemoaned his fate contemporaneously, he did not realise that his continuing banishment would be instrumental in the future success of his descendants.

Meanwhile, as the heyday of the Edwardian Age continued to unfold with an elegance and a security that were providing onlookers with a deceptive impression of what the future held for the world, in England, at least, Miche-Miche and Sophie maintained a degree of imperial dignity. They were regularly received by King Edward VII and Queen Alexandra, the disparity in their rank being glossed over as much as possible, while their acceptance at Court signalled to the wider world that they remained *persona grata* in England. Every year, they stayed as houseguests at Windsor Castle and Sandringham, and attended luncheons, dinners and balls at Buckingham Palace. This went some way not only towards palliating the indignity of his banishment, but also affirmed his position and that of his wife and children as members of the extended royal world.

When Miche-Miche's father Grand Duke Michael died in 1909, Tsar Nicholas II relented enough to allow him back to Russia for the funeral. Sophie, however, was not permitted to enter the empire. This confirmed their worst fears. They would never be allowed to return to the fold. As soon as Miche-Miche returned to England, they therefore decided to sink down even deeper roots. They gave up their lease on their house in the country and moved nearer to London, taking a lease on Kenwood House overlooking Hampstead Heath. This was still owned by the Earls of Mansfield, whose ancestor had housed his wards Lady Elizabeth Murray and Dido Elizabeth Belle there. They continued to be received everywhere, the glamour of the Romanoffs encasing them in an aura of desirability that made them one of the most appealing couples and fixtures on the Edwardian social circuit.

Meanwhile, the Tsar was fighting a losing battle to prevent the other Grand Dukes involved with non-royal women from marrying unequally. His uncle Paul Alexandrovich had seven years before married a divorcee commoner with four children from her first husband and three from the grand duke, while his youngest brother Grand Duke Michael Alexandrovich had married a double-divorcee commoner who had given birth to their illegitimate son just weeks before their uncle's death.

The relationship between the two morganatically married Grand Dukes Michael demonstrated, in a surprisingly clear way, how much more important class was than colour, even in Edwardian England. The Tsar's younger brother Grand Duke Michael Alexandrovich and his by-then wife Natalia Brasova, had taken a lease for £3,000 per annum in 1913 on Knebworth House in Hertfordshire, hoping that they would be able to settle in England and live the respectable, respected life of acceptance that the other Grand Duke Michael and Sophie Torby did. However, the older grand duke and his wife refused to receive the younger grand ducal couple. This was a snub of the highest order. In royal circles, where precedence reigns supreme and even today juniors defer to seniors by curtseying or bowing, it was unheard of for a more junior member of a reigning family to refuse to receive a family member who ranked above him. Yet that is precisely what Grand Duke Michael Mikhailovich, the mere grandson of an Emperor, did to the son, grandson and brother of Emperors and heir-in-line to the Imperial throne.

One did not have to look far for the motive. Miche-Miche and Sophie were protecting not only their own positions in Society, but also their children's. By the time the other Michael and his wife came on the scene, their two daughters, Anastasia (Zia) and Nadejhda (Nada) were 'out'. They had made their debuts at Court and were actively hunting for husbands the way all well-bred girls did at a time when marriage was the only route to a truly satisfying and satisfactory way of life. The Great War derailed everyone's life, but this did not stop both daughters from marrying brilliantly, nor could they have foreseen, when they were isolating Michael and Natasha, that the war which would end the Russian Empire and the monarchic way of life that had prevailed for over a thousand years, would begin in a matter of months. So Miche-Miche and Sophie excluded Michael and Natasha, while their two daughters began the process that would ensure that their descendants achieved the greatest heights.

First up the aisle was Nada. In November 1916, before her father lost all his money during the October Revolution of 1917, she married Prince George of Battenberg, eldest son of Queen Victoria's grand-daughter Princess Victoria of Hesse and Prince Louis of Battenberg. This was a superb match. Nada became a Princess as well as a Serene Highness. Though morganatic, the Battenbergs were now so well-established that they were grander than many fully-fledged royals. Victoria's younger sisters were, in chronological order, Elizabeth Feodorovna, Grand Duchess Serge of Russia, Irene, Princess Henry of Prussia, and Alix, Empress of All the Russias. Her brother was the reigning Grand Duke of Hesse. Prince Louis of Battenberg's niece Ena was Queen Victoria Eugenie of Spain, his daughter was Princess Andrew of Greece, his brother Franz Josef's wife Ana was the daughter of the King of Montenegro and sister of Queen Elena of Italy as well as the notorious Grand Duchesses Militza and Anastasia, the 'Black Witches' who had married two brothers, Grand Dukes Peter and Nicholas Nikolaievich, and introduced Rasputin to Empress Alexandra. Nada had pulled off a neat hat-trick, being accepted as royal while also managing to leave the question of 'throwbacks' behind, for, while the Romanoffs were concerned each time her mother had produced a child, the question did not even arise with the Battenbergs, who either did not know or then were so unaware of the possibility that the thought never occurred to them.

Irony of ironies, when Nada became Princess George of Battenberg she also became niece by marriage to the Empress Alexandra and Tsar

Nicholas II. This was despite the fact that the Tsar had refused to allow her father to return to Russia and serve his country in any capacity, military or otherwise, at the outbreak of the war in 1914. Yet he had allowed his brother Michael and uncle Paul to return with their morganatic wives and children, restoring their military ranks and even, in 1915, upgrading Paul's wife from the Bavarian title, Countess of Hohenfelsen, with which the Prince Regent had ennobled her, to Her Serene Highness Princess Paley. Only Grand Duke Michael Mikhailovich had been prevented from returning. No one knows the actual reason why. There has been speculation that Nicholas II might have disapproved of having someone with African blood in his family, but it is equally likely that it was easier to take a firm stand against a man to whom he was not close, who was merely a cousin, than it was to exclude a beloved brother and uncle. Other grand dukes, such as Andrei Vladimirovich, who was living with the Tsar's former mistress the great ballerina Mathilde Kschessinskaya, would have broken ranks at the slightest sign of weakness and married morganatically, so continuing to exclude Miche-Miche might have been a warning to them. Whatever the reason, Nicholas II's refusal to reverse Miche-Miche's banishment saved his life and assured his progeny of British lives.

Meanwhile, Nicholas II's forgiveness of his brother and his uncle cost them their lives, and the life of Paul's morganatic son, Prince Vladimir Pavlovich (Volodia) Paley, during the Russian Revolution. At 3am on the morning of morning of 28th January, 1919, Miche-Miche's two brothers Nicholas and George were taken along with their cousin Grand Duke Dmitri Konstantinovich and Paul, stripped to the waist despite the temperature being -20 C, and shot at the Saints Peter and Paul Fortress in St. Petersburg. Paul was too weak to stand, so he was strapped to a stretcher.

At least their deaths were quick. Six months before, on the night of 18th July 1918 – the day after the execution of the Tsar, Tsarina and their five children, as well as their various attendants – Miche-Miche's brother Serge had been taken along with his secretary, Feodor Remez , Paul's morganatic son Volodia (Prince Vladimir Paley), the Tsarina's sister Ella (Elizabeth, Grand Duchess Serge Alexandrovich) who by then was a nun, Varvara Yakovleva, another nun from Ella's Moscow convent, and the three sons of Grand Duke Constantine Konstantinovich, to a disused iron mine. After beating them up, the Bolshevik secret police, the Cheka, threw them down a disused mine shaft 66 feet deep. With perverse inversion of courtesy, Ella was hurled down first, to be followed by the others. According to Vasily Ryabov, who was one of the executioners, when it became apparent that they had survived the fall, he hurled a grenade into the shaft hoping to finish them off. Only Feodor Remez, however, died immediately. This became apparent when the others started singing an Orthodox hymn. To silence them, Ryabov lobbed another grenade in, but even that failed to still the voices of the injured Imperial Family and their attendants, whose devotional singing disturbed their executioners. So they gathered up brushwood, stuffed it down the mine shaft, set it on fire, and waited for the prisoners to suffocate or burn to death.

The Russian Revolution had far-reaching effects, not only for the Imperial Family and people of Russia, but for all the other participants in the Great War. One unexpected effect was to strengthen Britain's enemies. For that, and other equally valid political reasons, King George V changed the name of his dynasty from Saxe, Coburg und Gotha to Windsor. At the same time, he ordered all the junior members of the British Royal Family to cease using their German titles. The Battenbergs lost their princely rank. If Georgie and Nada were not particularly upset, his younger brother Dickie, now Lord Louis Mountbatten instead of Prince Louis of Battenberg, was furious. For the rest of his life, he bemoaned the loss. His father, the elder Prince Louis, became the 1st Marquis of Milford Haven. Nada's husband George became Earl of Medina until his father's death in 1921, at which time they became the 2nd Marquis and Marchioness of Milford Haven. In Germany, however, they remained princes and princesses of Battenberg, though by then being known as collateral members of the British Royal Family meant more than being even fully-paid up members of the former German reigning houses, all of whom had been stripped of their constitutional rights and privileges when Germany became a republic in 1918.

As for Nada's African heritage, while known within royal circles, it was unknown to the general public in Britain, and would remain so until her great-niece Sacha, Duchess of Abercorn began actively broadcasting this while promoting Russia's heritage and Pushkin's work. Public ignorance at the time was most likely just as well, for while the upper classes were adept at 'rising above' inconvenient facts until they withered on the vine and ceased to be a factor in day-to-day living, the general public was far less able to rise above their expectations, and far less tolerant of any deviation from the norm. As 'anti-black' prejudice was at its height a hundred years ago, the last thing collateral royals needed was to be stigmatised racially. Especially when, like Nada, they were already breaking a host of other taboos.

Although Georgie Milford Haven was basically a conventional man with a pleasantly individualistic streak, Nada deviated from the norm more starkly. Both of them were classically aristocratic in demeanour and presentation, with the exquisite manners of the truly well bred, but they nevertheless were a bohemian, sociable, progressive couple whose way of life was unconventional while paying lip service to convention. Nada developed into a well-known lesbian, and the only thing that seems to have saved her from becoming a perpetual figure of scandal was that her sister-in-law Edwina, Lady Louis Mountbatten, was even more notorious for her rampant sex life with a host of lovers, some of whom were black. Edwina was also of Jewish origin, her maternal grandfather being the august German-Jewish financier Sir Ernest Cassel. Edwina and her sister Mary Cunningham-Reid, later Lady Delamere, were the only children of Sir Ernest's only child, so both young women were among the greatest heiresses of their age. They needed every penny they had, for while royalty and the aristocracy accepted intermarriages as long as there was sufficient money involved, the same was not true of people lower down the social order. Moreover, between the wars, anti-Semitism was at its height, and would result in the Holocaust during the Second World War.

While Nada and her sister-in-law cut a swathe through fashionable society with their sexual antics, all remained well as long as the public knew nothing. This was the period before newspaper intrusiveness ensured that the private lives of the privileged were violated. What happened in drawing rooms and historic houses stayed in them. As long as one 'didn't frighten the horses,' as Mrs Patrick Campbell put it, one could pretty much do as one pleased. And people did. Without any adverse consequences.

Both Mountbatten brothers and their wives were close to the younger generation of the senior members of the British Royal Family, despite their rackety private lives, or maybe because of them. Indeed, their closest friend David, the Prince of Wales, had an equally complex private life. But the pool of choice amongst royals for both friends and matrimonial partners had shrunk because of the war, with the result that the British royals had an incentive to, on the one hand, become less picky about their fellow royals and, on the other, to look outside the royal circle for companionship.

The end of the war in 1918 had brought peace, but it had not brought forgiveness. Many of the British royals simply refused to have anything to do with those of their relations who had been avid supporters of the German cause. Even when they would privately forgive, they could not publicly associate with the former enemy, for in the aftermath of the war, with Bolshevism and then Nazism on the rise, the established social order itself seemed to be under threat. In Britain, a new sense of insecurity had entered the picture. It was not limited to any one particular segment of society either. Even the royal world, so cohesive before the war, had splintered into two camps. Those who had been on the British side, irrespective of petty drawbacks like '*black blood*' or morganatic status, were now deemed to be desirable, while those who had been on the German, and now deposed side, were not. This burnished the status of families like Nada's in a wholly unexpected way. It also provided opportunities for advancement that might not have hitherto existed. Dickie Mountbatten became such a close friend to their cousin the Prince of Wales, that he accompanied him on the royal tour of India and Japan in 1921. They remained the closest of friends until the Abdication. There are countless pictures of the Mountbattens at Fort Belvedere in the years before David became King Edward VIII, and the Duke of Windsor never forgave Dickie Mountbatten for jumping ship and trying to cosy up to George

VI and Queen Elizabeth once he ceased to be king.

Georgie and Nada were also friendly with their royal cousins, but less so than Dickie and Edwina with David. The brothers came from a naval background and both were officers in the Royal Navy. Their father had been First Sea Lord at the start of the war, but had been hounded out of office owing to anti-German prejudice. Although Dickie was determined to vindicate his father by filling the same role, and would ultimately do so, Georgie was less driven. He remained a median-ranking naval officer until 1932, when he retired from active service holding the rank of Commander.

According to his niece by marriage, Queen Elizabeth II, Georgie 'was one of the most intelligent and brilliant of people.' A mathematician by inclination, he used to work out complicated gunnery problems in his head and read calculus for pleasure. Nada was less accomplished, but she too was a popular member of the wider British Royal Family. This was quite an accomplishment for someone of her background, but in those less intrusive days people could go about their business without being subjected to prejudice disguising itself as the right to know.

Home for the Milford Havens was Lynden Manor, a thirteenth century house in Bray, Berkshire, near Windsor Castle. Prior to moving there, while Georgie was serving in the Navy, they lived in Edinburgh, where their two children were born: Tatiana, who was disabled, in 1917, and David on 12th May 1919. Their son would become 'the brother I never had' to his first cousin, Prince Philip of Greece, who spent the years between the ages of ten and seventeen living with Uncle Georgie and Aunt Nada while his mother was locked up in mental institutions, his father residing in the South of France or in Greece with a mistress, and his four much older sisters married to German princes.

The Russian Revolution and the downfall of so many of the European dynasties at the end of the Great War had affected all royals deeply. Georgie's father was as badly affected as Nada's. All Lord Milford Haven's Russian investments and properties, residues of his father and his aunt Empress Marie of Russia, had been seized by the Bolsheviks. The former Prince Louis had to sell Kent House in England and Heiligenberg Castle near Darmstadt, the beautiful schloss which had been the meeting place for many a visit between the Hesse and Russian royal families up to 1914. The collapse of the mark made the castle valueless and he no longer had the money to keep it up, and regrettable though it was to let it go, he felt he had no choice.

Nada's father had also lost all his money and was being kept afloat by his other son-in-law, but at least Georgie's mother, being a granddaughter of Queen Victoria, would always have a roof over her head. Lady Milford Haven was entitled to an apartment in Kensington Palace, not that it was one of the grand ones. But it was a convenient and desirable address in Central London, and, being a palace, it had a cachet beyond what money could buy.

In 1921, shortly after returning from Jerusalem, where Victoria's murdered sister Ella's body had been taken for burial in the Church of Mary Magdalene at Gethsemane after the White Army discovered it when they recaptured that part of Russia, the 1st Lord Milford Haven's heart gave out in the annexe of the Naval and Military Club. Within weeks, yet more tragedy hit the family when his son-in-law Prince Andrew of Greece was condemned to death by a military junta in Athens. It was only a combination of Princess Andrew's courage, and the pressure she and her brothers put on their cousin, King George V, who was guilt-ridden for having refused to provide a refuge for the Tsar, Tsarina and their family, resulting in their murders, that mobilised that Sovereign into action. He sent an emissary and a battleship to negotiate for his cousin's release, and, when it was successfully achieved, Prince and Princess Andrew, their daughters and infant son Philip (together with Nanny Roose), sailed out of Greece on the British cruiser *HMS Calypso*, en route to Brindisi and exile. This was the first of the many steps which would lead to Prince Philip ending up living with his Uncle Georgie and Aunt Nada between the ages of ten and seventeen.

People who knew Georgie and Nada Milford Haven said that they had a good marriage. Although different in many ways, they had a bond of genuine affection between them. Theirs was an affectionate, relaxed, indeed Bohemian household, where intellectual discussion, thoughtfulness and fun ranked before such worldly considerations as rank or advantage. Nada's sister Zia was particularly scathing about her sister's lifestyle, strongly disapproving of its informality and unconventionalism, but the Milford Havens seem to have had a genuinely happy family life.

Theirs was not your typical marriage. Georgie seems to have been rather lowly-sexed, as indeed was his brother Dickie, but Nada's Sapphic friendships were well known in social circles. Then, in 1934, she was named as the lesbian lover of Gloria Morgan Vanderbilt by her maid, Marie Caillot, in a New York court during the most sensational custody trial of its day. This was the battle between Gertrude Vanderbilt Whitney and Gloria Morgan Vanderbilt for custody of Gloria's daughter, known as 'Little Gloria'. It was front page news every day, full of the most sensational allegations of misconduct, glamour, and privilege. The roster of names was strictly A List. These included Gloria's identical sister Thelma, Viscountess Furness, who was the acknowledged lover of the Prince of Wales. When Caillot described the Marchioness of Milford Haven, cousin of the King of England, kissing Mrs Vanderbilt, the explosion was heard throughout the world. Prince Philip's sister, Princess Margarita of Greece and her husband, Prince Gottfried zu Hohenlohe-Langenburg, who had once been engaged to Gloria Vanderbilt, travelled to New York to testify in her favour, while Nada, after publicly announcing that the maid's claims were 'lies', stated that she was sticking by her friend to the end.

In civilised circles, scandal may be undesirable, but it passes, like any other stink. After Gloria Vanderbilt Senior lost custody of Junior, Georgie and Nada picked up the pieces and continued to parent both their children and Philip of Greece, while enjoying their lives. Four years later, however, tragedy struck. Georgie slipped and broke his leg. When it failed to heal, they discovered that he had terminal bone cancer. He died at the relatively young age of 45, leaving a devastated widow, a grief-stricken nephew (Prince Philip has said that his Uncle Georgie's death was one of the great sadnesses of his life) and his eighteen year old son, who became the third Marquis.

David, now 3rd Marquis of Milford Haven, became the head of the Mountbatten family before he had even achieved his majority. His first great love, Robin Dalton, is a chum of mine, so I know that he was a delightful man, albeit not driven like his uncle Dickie or his cousin Philip.

He would ultimately marry another old chum and neighbour of mine, the former Janet Bryce, a great beauty. In the incestuous world of the upper classes, where everyone is somehow connected to everyone else, she was a first cousin of his first cousins, George, Gina and Myra Wernher. David and Janet had two sons, George, the present Marquis and therefore now the head of the Mountbatten family, and Ivar. Last year Ivar had the distinction of being the first member of the extended Royal Family to enter into a same sex marriage. His ex-wife Penny attended as well as their children. George's first wife, Sarah, is not only the mother of his heir but also the daughter of the multimillionaire businessman George Walker, who started out life as a Billingsgate porter. I used to see her sometimes when she came to visit her mother-in-law when we lived in the same complex of flats. She was a charming, attractive, down-to-earth girl, with excellent manners and the dignity befitting the mother of the future head of the Mountbatten Dynasty.

If Zia disapproved of her sister Nada's private life, it was not on social grounds. Nor was it jealousy. She too achieved a splendid match during the Great War when, on 20th July 1917, she wed Harold Augustus Wernher, second son of Sir Julius Wernher, 1st Baronet. Sir Julius was a financial genius. So rich was he that even the Romanoffs were impressed. Together with Cecil Rhodes, Jules Porges, and Alfred Beit, he had cornered the South African diamond market, enabling Wernher, Beit & Co to acquire a controlling interest in De Beers Consolidated Mines. He was a Protestant, born in Darmstadt, Hesse, but his wife, Alice Sedgwick Mankiewicz had her own ancestry, attracting prejudice in certain quarters, her father being a Jewish merchant from Danzig who married an Englishwoman, Ada Susan Pigott, of Colchester.

If Nada's marriage could be fairly said to have catapulted the Torby family into the extended British Royal Family, Zia's ratified those connections to that royal family in a wholly unexpected way. Once Prince Philip married the present Queen, the Wernhers became amongst their very closest personal friends. Every year, they celebrated their wedding anniversary at the Wernhers' magnificent stately home, Luton Hoo.

Two things above all trump prejudice when grand families are considering marriage. The first is status (there being no higher stature than being royal or imperial), and the second is money. The more there is of the latter, the greater the tolerance of family trees with twisted branches. So it proved with the immensely rich Harold Wernher and Countess Zia Torby. Sir Julius had died in 1912, leaving Luton Hoo to Harold. Notwithstanding that the Romanoffs had a(n often unjustified) reputation for anti-Semitism, there was no question of Harold's Jewish blood preventing such a welcome marriage. Zia would be chatelaine of Luton Hoo, one of the greatest stately homes in the United Kingdom, housing one of the world's great art collections.

Grade I listed, Luton Hoo had once been a neoclassical house in Bedfordshire which had been remodelled by Robert Adam for the 3rd Earl of Bute, King George III's mentor and first Prime Minister, who features earlier in this book. In the next century, it was remodelled further by the fashionable architect Sir Robert Smirke, who kept the south façade but altered the rest. Capability Brown designed the grounds, enlarging the park from 300 acres to 1,200. He also dammed the River Lea to form two lakes, one of which is 60 acres, with formal gardens added later. The house and contents were destroyed by fire in 1843, but it was purchased by a property speculator and Mayor of Liverpool, who rebuilt it before selling it on to the Gerard Leigh family. They rented it to Sir Julius in 1899, and he bought it four years later. He turned loose on Luton Hoo the Ritz Hotel's architects, Charles Mewes and Arthur Davis. They added the Mansard roof, which had the dual effect of giving the house more staff quarters while also evoking the style of the Second Empire despite retaining the Neo-Classical facade. They also redesigned the interior in the Belle Époque style, providing the perfect showcase for the world-renowned Wernher Collection.

The year after Zia's marriage, King George V stepped into the fray the way the Prince of Waldeck and Pyrmont and the Grand Duke of Luxembourg had done for her mother and grandmother. Upon marriage, Zia had ceased to be a Countess of the House of Torby and had become plain Mrs Harold Wernher. Because Harold Wernher was the second son of a mere baronet, he had no courtesy title beyond Mister. His brother Derrick had succeeded their father as the second baronet and, though unmarried, was expected to be at some time in the future. He ultimately would, but only had a daughter, with the result that when he died in 1948, Harold unexpectedly succeeded to the title. Nevertheless, in 1918 it seemed unlikely that Harold would ever be anything but a Mister, so, to spare Zia the ignominy of living her whole life as a rich but untitled woman, King George V issued a warrant granting her the style and precedence of an earl's daughter. Thereafter, Mrs Harold Wernher was known as Lady Zia Wernher, even when he became Sir Harold Wernher, Bt.

Harold and Zia had three children. Their son George Michael Alexander was born in 1918 and would die in a tragic, almost silly, accident in Egypt in 1942, when he was crushed by a slipping vehicle while serving in the Army. He had been like a brother to Prince Philip, who wrote a touching letter of condolence to Zia, and is on record as saying that his cousin's death was another of the great losses of his life. The loss to his parents can only be imagined.

There were also two daughters. The elder, Georgina (always known in the family as Gina), was born in Edinburgh in 1919 and the younger, Myra, in 1925. At one point, Gina was mooted as a prospective bride for Prince Philip, but she discounted the idea as ridiculous. They were more like brother and sister, and she also declared that she had no intention of marrying anyone with a title, for she did not plan on spending her whole life cutting ribbons and attending fetes. In 1944 she married Lieutenant Colonel Harold 'Bunny' Phillips of the Coldstream Guards, the '6'5" former lover of Edwina Mountbatten. According to Edwina's daughter, Lady Pamela Hicks, Bunny was 'thrillingly handsome' and more or less moved into the family home, Broadlands in Hampshire, for the duration of the relationship. It devastated Edwina when he left her and married Gina Wernher, but they were happy together, producing five children, two of whom would become duchesses, and in so doing, take Hannibal's bloodline into two of the most important families in the land.

Their eldest daughter Alexandra Anastasia (1946-2018) married the present Duke of Abercorn. Her son will be the next duke. It is largely due to Sacha Abercorn that the Sub-Saharan ancestry of her ancestor Alexander Pushkin is now so openly acknowledged. But for her pride in that part of her heritage, and her dedication to the Pushkin Trust, which promotes creative writing in schools, it is likely that only people connected to the Romanoff family would have known. She was a delightful woman, a committed Jungian with a highly developed sense of social responsibility who believed in using her privileged position to make the world a better place for the less fortunate.

Bunny and Gina Phillips' youngest daughter made an even more spectacular marriage. Thirteen years younger than her eldest sister, Natalia Ayesha (known as Tally) married the handsome Gerald, Earl Grosvenor on the 7th October 1978. Within months, her father-in-law, the 5th Duke of Westminster, died, making Gerald and Tally Grosvenor the 6th Duke and Duchess. For years Gerald Westminster had the distinction of being regarded as the richest man in England. The Grosvenor Estate owned much of Mayfair and Belgravia, the two smartest areas in London, with vast property holdings throughout the world as well. The Westminsters were much richer than the Royal Family and close to all the royals. Indeed, Queen Victoria had elevated the 3rd Marquis of Westminster to a dukedom, stating that someone of his wealth deserved the rank. She became godmother to his first son, Victor. The family also married into the extended Royal Family, the 1st Duke's daughter, Lady Margaret Grosvenor, marrying Queen Mary's nephew Prince Adolphus of Teck, later 2nd Duke of Teck, and after 1917, 1st Marquis of Cambridge.

The Westminsters were often to be found entertaining, or being entertained by, the Royal Family, whether in this or any other generation from Queen Victoria's to today's. Gerald and Tally and their siblings either were close personal friends of the Queen, her sister, and her children, or had Court appointments. For instance, Gerald's sister Leonora was one of Princess Margaret's ladies-in-waiting. She was also married to the 5th Earl of Lichfield, son of Princess Anne of Denmark, niece of Queen Elizabeth the Queen Mother. Indeed, so grand were the Westminsters that it would have been infra dig for them to have been awarded the highest Court appointment a woman can have: Mistress of the Robes. They had such great social responsibilities, being a Duchess of Westminster akin to being a full-time, working royal, that they were never considered for the honour in the knowledge that it would be a burden they would not be able to fulfil.

In the early days of the marriage of the present Prince of Wales and the late Princess, Gerald and Tally were amongst their closest friends. According to Diana, this was because they were the right age, right background, and two of the few couples she and Charles found jointly acceptable. The Westminsters were also members of the inner personal circle of the Queen and Prince Philip. The age difference was of no account. Philip was like a brother to Tally's mother Gina, and the extraordinary privilege of being so rich meant that there were attendant responsibilities to which only people like the Queen and Prince Philip, burdened with similar responsibilities, could relate without such unworthy sentiments as competitiveness, envy, and the awkward awareness of one's substantially lesser endowments.

There were dynastic elements to the marriage, but also a human side. Gerald Westminster was not only stunningly handsome, especially as a young man, but also decent, and I have never heard anyone utter a word against Tally. Nevertheless, both of them were acutely aware of the necessity to produce male heirs, for primogeniture requires a son to succeed, and there was a dearth of male heirs in the family. Gerald was an only son and his father one of only two sons, both of whom became duke. The 3rd duke had never married and the 2nd, Bendor, had an only son who died aged four following an appendectomy. The 1st duke had had seven sons, but the sole male heir from all of them was Gerald. Tally had to get cracking.

Fourteen months after marrying Gerald, the twenty year old duchess produced a daughter. Lady Tamara would go on to marry Edward van Cutsem, whose parents were great friends of the Prince of Wales and neighbours of mine. Two years later, Tally produced another daughter, Edwina, who was Diana, Princess of Wales's goddaughter. She would marry the historian and tele-journalist Dan Snow. There was a ten year gap between Edwina and the much needed heir, Hugh, the present Duke of Westminster. He is one of Prince George's godfathers and the youngest and richest duke in the country. Clearly hoping for a second son, Tally and Gerald had a fourth child a year later. Another daughter, Lady Viola Georgina Grosvenor, was born. She was named after her paternal great-grandmother Viola, 5th Duchess of Westminster, and her maternal grandmother Gina Wernher, who remarried that same year and thereafter was known as Lady Kennard.

In case anyone doubts the degree of pride the family has in its Sub-Saharan ancestry, when Tamara and Edward van Cutsem had their first child, they named him Jake Louis Hannibal van Cutsem. If '*a touch of the tar brush*' had once been cause for concealment, it was most certainly not any longer. Indeed, it was a mark of honour and a symbol of pride.

Chapter Six

IF THE DESCENDANTS OF Hannibal grew prouder of their mixed-race heritage as the last decade of the second millennium approached, those of Eliza Kewark, who included Diana, Princess of Wales, were not even aware that they too had the distinction of possessing an ancestor of colour. They would only discover that they were partly Anglo-Indian when this author's 1992 biography of the Princess, which had begun as an authorised work before she turned elsewhere and I proceeded to write what I had discovered, was published.

Amongst the many unexpected things I happened upon while researching the book was that Diana's very grand and hyper-correct, blue-eyed, blonde-haired, fair-skinned grandmother, Ruth, Lady Fermoy, a Woman of the Bedchamber to Queen Elizabeth the Queen Mother, and as Anglo-Saxon a grandee as it was possible to be, was a descendant of a dark-skinned Indian girl named Eliza Kewark. Ironically, *Diana in Private: The Princess Nobody Knows* was so full of other revelations that it would take another two decades before the *Telegraph* and *Times of India* picked up on this revelation. When it was finally confirmed through Mitochondrial DNA (mtDNA) testing, Diana's maternal aunt, the Hon. Mary Gunningham, said, in keeping with the inclusiveness that now characterises current values, 'I always assumed I was part-Armenian so I am delighted that I also have an Indian background.'

Attitudes had changed a lot between when Diana got married in 1981 and 2013, when the mtDNA results were published. Even between the publication of *Diana in Private* in 1992 and *The Real Diana* in 1998, attitudes had shifted sufficiently for this author to write, 'Eliza Kewark was a dark-skinned native…who had lived, without benefit of matrimony, with her great-great-grandfather Theodore Forbes while he worked for the East India Company. Unsavoury as the taint of illegitimacy was at that distance of time, it was nothing compared with the stigma of what was then known as '*coloured blood*'. Had it been generally known that Ruth and her children were part-Indian, they might never have made good marriages. Eliza's true race was therefore expunged from the family tree and she re-emerged as an Armenian. This fiction was maintained even when Diana married the Prince of Wales.'

What made confirmation of this fact especially exciting for the *Telegraph* and *Times of India*, in 2013, was that Diana's Indian ancestry, revealed in 1992 and 1998 but not verified scientifically, was beyond dispute after Prince William took a mtDNA test. Dr Jim Wilson, the genetics expert at the University of Edinburgh who carried out the research, confirmed that Diana's matrilineal ancestry through Eliza Kewark could only have been Indian. It was most decidedly not Armenian. Regrettably, William and Harry will not be able to pass on the proof of this strain, which is carried through the female bloodline alone.

The result of the test showed that William is one of only 14 other people, out of 65,000 tested, who belong to the extremely rare haplogroup, R30b. Of the remainder, 13 were from India and 1 from Nepal, which borders India and has always had cross-migration, thereby proving that only people of Indian ancestry can belong to that haplogroup.

One needs to cut through a lot of cant when establishing the antecedents of royals and aristocrats. Puffing up certain aspects of their ancestry, while down-playing or even eradicating others, is par for the course. The family had been fed the line that Eliza Kewark was the Armenian wife of their ancestor, Theodore Forbes (1788-1820). He was the third son of a landowner from Forgue, Aberdeenshire, Scotland. There was therefore never any question but that he would have to seek his fortune elsewhere, in keeping with the age-old custom of the first son inheriting the land, the second and third sons going into the church or army or, being Scots, business. The Scots had been building up formidable connections in India once Henry Dundas, later 1ˢᵗ Viscount Melville, took charge of the East India Company. The Foreign Secretary, George Canning, observed that Melville had a system of 'pillage and patronage'. He had no interest in colonising India, merely in commercial exploitation and monopoly. The Rev. Sydney Smith hit the nail on the head when he stated: 'As long as he is in office, the Scotch may beget younger sons with the most perfect impunity. He sends them by loads to the East Indies.' Lord Minto, Governor-General of India between 1807 and 1813 and a fellow Scot, maintained that there was scarcely a family in Scotland without an obligation to him. Theodore Forbes was one of the many young Scotsmen who sailed out to India, joining the East India Company as an officer. That in reality meant that he was a median level merchant. He was first posted to Surat, a southern port in Gujarat, the westernmost state in India abutting the Arabian Sea.

Before leaving Britain for India, in 1808 Forbes had fathered an illegitimate son, Frederick, with a local Aberdeenshire girl named Ann MacDonnell. Both are mentioned in his will, with Frederick being bequeathed the sum of 20,000 rupees. The boy would be absorbed into the family of his uncle Alexander, and subsequently became a surgeon, which, while a worthy profession, was not then as prestigious as it would become as the nineteenth century progressed. The Forbes family, though perfectly respectable, was neither grand nor aristocratic.

Soon after arriving in India, Forbes met Eliza Kewark through her brother-in-law Arrathoon Baldassarian, who was his agent. He quickly formed a relationship with her. In his will, he described her as his 'housekeeper'. It is possible that he thought it more decorous to give some official standing to the woman to whom he left the small annuity of 100 rupees a month, rather than describing her more truthfully as his concubine. However, it is also possible that his description accurately reflected the original status of the relationship, for Eliza wrote to Charles Forbes in 1834 complaining that the annuity left by her 'beloved master' had been halved. Whatever her status at the beginning of the relationship, relations between the nineteen year old Eliza and the twenty three year old Forbes soon turned sexual. Certainly, she became pregnant quickly, giving birth to their daughter Katherine Scott Forbes (1812-1893) within a year of his arrival. By this time, Forbes had been posted to Mocha in Yemen, where Kitty was born. In a sign that Eliza would have recognised as hopeful, the baby was named after his mother. Two years later, she was delivered of a boy, Alexander. They returned to Surat the following year, and two years later she gave birth to another boy, Fraser, who died aged six months.

Shortly after the birth of this third child, Forbes left the East India Company to take up a partnership in Bombay in Forbes & Co., a trading company whose senior partner was his distant cousin, Sir Charles Forbes. This was a step up in the world, but it came at a cost. Eliza was not welcome in the more sophisticated environment of Bombay, where inter-racial unions were starting to be frowned upon. As India became more important to Britain, there began the first of the many waves of British girls who were sent out to the Sub-Continent to bag husbands. Necessity no longer needed to be the mother of invention or anything else, so Forbes left Eliza and their two surviving children in Surat. There are letters she wrote, begging him to come and see her and, more especially, the children. 'Our beloved Kitty and Alexander thank God they are in good health and often hope to see their beloved father,' was but one of the many heart-rending letters she sent.

According to the historian Mohan Meghani, Forbes sent another Scotsman who was a close friend, Thomas Fraser, to visit Eliza. It was Fraser who recommended that he send Kitty back home to Scotland. The little girl was fair-skinned and could pass for white. In Scotland her prospects for a good life were infinitely superior to those in India, where she would be known as a mixed-race child at a time when prejudice was starting to bite. So Kitty was sent to Scotland, aged 6, to live with her paternal relations and await the arrival of her father, who was due to leave India a year later. Alexander, however, was ordered to remain in India, which suggests that he was darker-skinned and therefore less likely to fit into Scottish life as easily.

Forbes set sail for Scotland on the *Blenden Hall* in 1820. En route, he fell ill, and made a will. It was in this instrument that he described Eliza as his 'housekeeper'. He halved her allowance, leaving her just 100 rupees a month, while leaving 50,000 to his 'reputed natural daughter by Eliza Kewark' and 20,000 rupees to his 'reputed natural son Alexander'. Since he plainly stated that Eliza was the mother of his natural children, one is left with the impression that his description of her was, more likely than not, truthful.

Until my researches uncovered the fact that Eliza was at least half Indian, she had been passed off as Armenian by her Scottish descendants. So successful were they in suppressing the facts that Diana's aunt Mary stated: 'My mother appeared to have no knowledge of this, so perhaps it was hidden.' The Armenians, of course, are Caucasian, while the Indians are Mongoloid. In his excellent and readable tale of intermarriage in the early days of the East India Company, before India became a British colony in 1857, William Dalrymple, himself a descendant of an Anglo-Indian union, describes how many a Briton lived with or married Indian girls. Class was often the deciding factor. British men would marry grand Indians but keep more humble ones as their mistresses. Usually, they acknowledged paternity. Failing to do so was a sign of an accidental pregnancy between a low-born woman and a higher-born man, but even when there was a disparity in class it was unusual for a man not to acknowledge his children.

It was while the economic power of the West Indies waned and India became more important, indeed crucial, to Britain's economy, that the vicious prejudice used to keep the Indians down came to be viewed as a necessary tool of subjugation. It was then that 'going native' became frowned upon. Forbes and Eliza's relationship was on the cusp of this change in attitude. Prior to that, mixed unions had been neither remarkable nor unacceptable. It was basically economics, pure and simple, that decreed that racism should replace tolerance.

Nevertheless, by the time Forbes arrived in India, there was an element of the 'shadow' family that one also saw in the West Indies and the Southern States of the Americas. There remained a sharp difference between a wife and a concubine. Eliza Kewark was, off any reasonable examination of the facts, the latter. Her father was Habok Kevork and might, or might not, have been of Armenian extraction, but what is certain is that her mother was not Armenian. This much the mtDNA results confirm.

Surat had a small Armenian population at the time of Eliza's birth. There is speculation that Kevork could have been short for Kevorkian, which is an Armenian name. Kevork or Kewark could equally have been a Muslim name, the Q sound being classically Arabic. Transcribed as

Qwakh instead of the more anglicised Kewark, the name itself gives away its possible origins.

Quite why Eliza's father's name would have been shortened from Kevorkian to Kevork has never been satisfactorily explained. The Armenians took pride in their culture, clinging to their habits, alphabet and names. As far as we know, no other Armenian of that time and place lost the classical *ian* so typical of Armenian names, so if Kevork did, it was either because he was not Armenian, or he was partly Armenian and partly Indian, and by shortening his name he was acknowledging both his cultures.

Historians such as Mohan Meghani speculate that inter-racial relations between Europeans and Indians were more likely if the girl was Muslim as opposed to Hindu. With their rigid caste classifications, and the absolute disgrace of co-habiting outside of their own caste, Hindu unions of this kind were unheard of. Even if Habok Kevork had been patrilineally Armenian, it is likely that he too was mixed race, hence the shortening of the name. The Armenians had been in Surat for five hundred years, and while they had retained something of their language and culture, theirs was a sufficiently small settlement for inter-marriage, or at least inter-breeding, to have been likely.

There is also speculation amongst the optimists, who would like Diana's ancestors to have been Armenian, and white, rather than Indian, that a man named Gevorg, who died in 1811 and whose tomb, now in the City Museum cellar, was once in the Surat's Armenian cemetery, is the same person as Hakob Kevork. Their speculations extend further, to try to turn three different names into a version of one. However, there is no proof that Kewark, Kevork and Gevorg, whom they would like to believe was one person, was actually one individual as opposed to three different people, as the difference in the names suggests. They even hypothesise that Mrs Elizabeth Farbessian, a woman with an Armenian name who lived in the Armenian community, was Eliza Kewark. They extend their hopes on the grounds that Farbessian might have been an Armenianised version of the name Forbes, which Eliza assumed once Theodore Forbes had deserted her.

This is all fanciful speculation. What is known to be factual is that Eliza never used the name Forbes. She always signed herself as Kewark, not Kevork, and definitely not Farbessian, and in so doing suggests that she was Forbes's concubine and not his wife. Had she been Mrs. Forbes, she would have used that surname, and used it proudly too, for, whether Armenian or Indian, it was prestigious to be the wife of a Scotsman, while *infra dig* to be a concubine. One appreciates the motivation of those who seek to glamorise Eliza, to elevate her from concubine to respectable wife, to convert her from mostly Indian to mostly if not entirely Armenian, using the slenderest of possibilities to advance their case. Armenians too have been an oppressed people. Who are we to condemn them if they wish to have as one of their own this ancestress of the future King of the United Kingdom? Claims, however, do not amount to substantiation, at least not if one is seeking historical fact.

Yet what happened to the Armenian community in Surat in the first two decades of the nineteenth century is a fascinating feature that is now lost in the sands of time. But something happened in the space of two decades to annihilate them. According to the Armenian historian Mesrovb Jacob Seth, 'The decline and dispersion of the Armenians at Surat must have been very rapid.' During the last two decades of the 18th century, 'there were 33 Armenian merchants besides many others in the humbler walks of life.' At a time when most families were large, this must have been well over two hundred people, if not more. Yet by 1820 there were only seven 'souls' remaining, including Mrs Elizabeth Farbessian, 'the only well-to-do amongst them.' No one knows what happened, but as she qualified as well-to-do and Eliza's allowance had been cut to fifty rupees a month, it seems even less likely that they were one and the same person. Nor does anyone know what became of Eliza, who is not buried locally, and whose death is not recorded accessibly.

What is known as historical fact, however, is that her daughter Kitty flourished in Scotland. She married James Crombie, whose family manufactured the coats of the same name. This confirms the family's status as solidly mercantile, but by then, Scottish merchants were becoming an elite of their own. Although neither the Forbes nor the Crombie family flew high like the other Scottish mercantile families such as the Jardines, who would be responsible for Hong Kong becoming a British colony, and in the process became mercantile princes whose wealth rivalled Croesus as well as being elevated to aristocratic status, they were nevertheless what was then categorised as 'gentlemen and ladies'. Mr. and Mrs. James Crombie had eight children, including Jane, who married David Littlejohn, another gentleman of no illustrious background or position, but solid nevertheless. Their daughter Ruth married Colonel William Smith Gill, who was both an army officer and prosperous. Her namesake daughter Ruth Sylvia Gill was decidedly a lady, but an untitled one. Musically gifted, she studied piano under the great Alfred Cortot at the Paris Conservatoire of Music, where she met the older, richer and much grander Edmund Burke Roche, 4th Lord Fermoy. He and his brother had been heirs to a great American fortune on their mother's side, and while the Fermoys were of middling rank in aristocratic terms, they nevertheless became close friends of King George V and Queen Mary's dull but worthy second son, Bertie, and his resolutely old-fashioned but extremely bright and ambitious wife, Elizabeth.

By this time, Ruth Fermoy had changed from being a freewheeling pianist of obvious artistic temperament into the paradigm of the impeccable and predictably non-threatening lady of breeding. Although she remained bright, charming and humorous, she developed a patina of rectitude which both royal couples found appealing. The Fermoys' special status as personal friends of the monarch, his consort, his second son and daughter-in-law, was confirmed when they were granted a lease for Park House on the Sandringham Estate. To show how close the families became, on the 19th January 1936, only hours before George V's death, Queen Mary tried to cheer up her dying husband with the news that 'dear Ruth Fermoy' had been safely delivered of a daughter, Frances, at nearby Park House.

Disappointingly, this was their second daughter, but three years later the treasured heir, Edmund James Burke Roche, was born. Their family complete, Lord and Lady Fermoy settled down to the sedate and ultra-respectable life of personal friends of the monarch and his consort. The Second World War only partially disrupted the even tenor of this life, with Edmund joining the Royal Air Force until 1943, when the local

Member of Parliament died on active service and he replaced him until Parliament was dissolved at the end of the war in 1945.

Thereafter, until his death in 1955, Edmund lived the life of a rich, retired gentleman, while the much younger Ruth found an outlet for her musical talents. She founded the King's Lynn Musical Festival in 1951, which remains, one of the leading musical festivals in the country. She persuaded Queen Elizabeth the Queen Mother to become its royal patron, and also roped in her extensive circle of friends to support it. These included every top musician of the time, from Benjamin Britten and Peter Piers to Richard Adeney, the leading flautist of his day. No one without world-class talent would have been taught by Alfred Cortot, and while Ruth did not have a musical career, she remained a top-flight pianist. Occasionally, she performed in public, for instance under the baton of the Austrian conductor Josef Krips at the Royal Albert Hall in 1950, or under Sir George Barbirolli with the Halle Orchestra at King's Lynn in 1966.

Widowhood presented a wholly unexpected opportunity for Ruth when Queen Elizabeth the Queen Mother, who liked her ladies-in-waiting to be widows like herself, invited her to become an Extra Woman of the Bedchamber in 1956. This worked out so well that four years later the appointment was made permanent, lasting for the remaining thirty-three years of Ruth's life. It would prove particularly useful for the advancement of her family, especially when her granddaughter Lady Sarah Spencer caught the Prince of Wales's eye. Regrettably, Sarah mucked up her chances of walking up the aisle to him by talking to the press, but this did not prevent the youngest granddaughter from ultimately succeeding where her eldest sister had failed.

By then, Ruth had embedded herself so firmly in the royal constellation that another of her granddaughters, Lady Jane Spencer, had married in 1978, the Sandringham Land Agent Major Sir William Fellowes' son Robert. He was then Assistant Private Secretary to the Queen, and would work his way up to becoming Private Secretary by the time his sister-in-law Diana was Princess of Wales.

This presented the family with a dilemma when the Wales marriage broke down. To whom should they be loyal? Diana or the Prince? Ruth and Robert both took the view that they should put their principles before personalities and elected to distance themselves from Diana, who had undertaken a vendetta not only to glorify herself at the expense of her husband but, if possible, to eliminate him from the line of succession and replace him with her son. By the time Ruth died in 1993 she was no longer speaking to her illustrious granddaughter, and by the time Diana herself died four years later, neither was her brother-in-law on cordial terms with her. But that is another story.

Both Ruth and her younger daughter Frances were chic, stylish, good-looking women. They were tall, willowy, slim, blue-eyed, fair-skinned blondes. Looking at them, you would never have guessed that they had anything but European ancestors. Because their '*touch of the tar brush*' was unknown, possibly to them and definitely to others, they did not have to contend with silly speculation about *throwbacks* the way the morganatic Romanoffs had to.

When she was 18, on 1st June 1954, Frances made an even better marriage than her mother had done. The Queen, Prince Philip, the Queen Mother and Princess Margaret attended the ceremony at Westminster Abbey as well as the reception at St James's Palace along with *tout-Londres*. While Lord Fermoy was rich and titled, he had nevertheless been an Irish peer and half American. The 30 year old Johnnie (Viscount) Althorp (1924-1992), however, was heir to one of England's great titles as well as the magnificent treasure-trove, Althorp House, with its spectacular paintings by artists such as Reynolds, Gainsborough, Kneller, Van Dyck and Rubens; fabulous furniture; tapestries; a 600 acre deer park and 13,000 acre estate, only 75 miles northwest of London in Northamptonshire. His father was the 7th Earl Spencer, head of the Spencer family whose junior branch was the Spencer-Churchill Dukes of Marlborough. Johnnie was tall, strapping, charming but, according to his father, who despised him, none too bright. Nevertheless, he was regarded as a great catch. As a former equerry to King George VI (1950-52) and Queen Elizabeth II (1952-54), he had even more impeccable Court credentials than the Fermoys. His mother Cynthia had been a Lady (as opposed to a Woman) of the Bedchamber to Queen Elizabeth the Queen Mother since 1937, a position she would retain till her death in 1972. She was a daughter of the Duke of Abercorn and also a great-granddaughter of the 5th Duke of Richmond and Gordon. As a result, she was descended from King Charles II, albeit on the wrong side of the blanket. This also made her a descendant of Philippa of Hainault, though she was not a descendant of Madragana, her royal blood preceding the advent of Queen Charlotte.

Johnnie and Frances had five children: three daughters, of whom Diana was the youngest, a son who predeceased Diana's arrival, and Charles, who was their youngest child and the Queen's godson. By the time of his birth, the marriage was rocky. Ruth had turned over Park House to her son-in-law and daughter. Until Johnnie became Earl Spencer in 1975, this was the family's main home. To put it mildly, the 7th and 8th earls drank entirely different brands of tea. In one respect, however, they were similar. Both men beat their wives. While Cynthia bore Jack's abuse valiantly, Frances took steps to bring Johnnie's to an end. The route she chose, however, proved to be disastrous for her and her two youngest children. Upper class gossip claims that she had an affair with Sir James Goldsmith, but whether this is so or not, she certainly had one with Peter Shand Kydd, a scion of the well-established firm Shand Kydd Wallpapers, dating back to 1891. They met at a dinner party in 1966, following which the Althorps and the Shand Kydds became a foursome, even sharing a skiing holiday together. Peter and Janet Shand Kydd were actually happily married, but Frances's passionate nature – something which her daughter Diana inherited – allied to her unhappy marriage, proved so seductive that Peter began an affair with her. This was the catalyst Frances needed, and, after a particularly ugly quarrel at a party, shortly after the two eldest girls, Sarah and Jane, were sent to boarding school at West Heath in September 1967, Frances decided that she had had enough. She walked out, moving into a flat in Cadogan Place in London's Chelsea near Sloane Square, where her two youngest children joined her along with a housemaid, Violet Collinson, who acted as cook and would remain with her for the remainder of her working life. Frances enrolled Diana in a nearby day school and Charles in kindergarten, and continued to pursue her relationship with Peter Shand Kydd. He, however, seemed reluctant to leave Janet, with whom he had hitherto been happy, and who would later say, 'I still find it hard to believe' that the marriage had come to an end.

Frances's big mistake was to return with Diana and Charles to Park House to celebrate Christmas *en famille* with Johnnie and the two older girls. When the time came to return to London, Johnnie refused to allow her to take Diana and Charles back with her. He hoped that by digging in his heels Frances would be encouraged to return to him. She, however, had decided that she wanted a divorce whether Peter Shand Kydd left Janet and married her or remained with his wife. She initiated a suit for custody and divorce, citing cruelty.

To Frances's lifelong horror, her mother decided to testify against her. This was as clear a demonstration of snobbishness beating family loyalty as could be imagined. Ruth was intent on keeping her family within the royal circle. Queen Elizabeth the Queen Mother disapproved of divorce. Also, the Shand Kydds were 'in trade' while the Spencers moved in Court circles. Ruth was determined that her grandchildren would remain part of that treasured fold. If her daughter was unworldly enough to want to run off with a 'wall paper merchant', she had no compunction about cutting her loose. However, she intended to preserve the position of her son-in-law and grandchildren. So she protected the wife-beater by testifying against Frances at the trial – something her daughter never forgave.

Yet the evidence confirms that Ruth made the right judgement call in terms of keeping them in the magic circle, for, rather than being cut loose the way they might have been had Johnnie not won custody of them, all three daughters ended up with some sort of royal connection. This they might well have not had the opportunity for had Ruth not behaved 'treacherously' (in the eyes of her daughter), or 'sensibly' (in her own eyes and those of the courtiers and royals who were her *raison d'être)*.

Ruth's choices would have had little or no effect outside her family circle, had she not helped to traumatise her daughter on the one hand while promoting her granddaughters on the other. By Diana's own account, every time Frances had to hand back her children to Johnnie, the caterwauling would be so distressing that it caused lifelong distress for them. This undoubtedly damaged Diana psychologically. There is much evidence to suggest that she suffered from borderline personality disorder.

By her own admission, as her marriage broke down and she sought her freedom, she so feared history repeating itself that she took steps, many completely unnecessary and unreasonable, to protect herself against the Royal Family in case her husband should want to take her children away from her. This was despite every effort being made by Charles and the Royal Family to assure her that no such thing would happen.

Diana's fears did untold damage to her own position, the position of her husband, and the health of her children. Although she loved her sons, she used them as weapons against her husband, even going so far as to wage a press campaign to convince the public that Prince Charles was a bad father. In the notorious Martin Bashir BBC TV interview in 1995, she even went to the lengths of suggesting that he was not fit for the crown. This attempt to manoeuvre him out of the line of succession was so outrageous that it triggered the Queen's demand that her warring daughter-in-law and son divorce. This act of treachery, so reminiscent of Ruth's equally cold-blooded calculation to sacrifice her daughter in the interests of maintaining the family's Court links, caused Establishment doors to slam in Diana's face. She became marginalised, and until she died was fighting a rearguard struggle to regain acceptance within her peer group.

This was not obvious to the general public, who still believed that because she remained Princess of Wales she enjoyed the prestige she had once possessed. But she did not. Her friends were no longer well-connected Establishment figures. They were people on the periphery of 'Café Society' or so unsophisticated that they actually thought that Café Society was real Society. This, ironically, only added to Diana's public appeal, for now the press had an endless stream of stories with which to titillate their readers. But no well-established British or European man would touch her with a barge pole. Her lovers were all from outside the sort of circles she and her sisters had been brought up to associate with. The recently-married, England rugby captain Will Carling was a case in point, as indeed was Dodi Fayed. As her distant cousin Lady Caroline Waterhouse, mother of David with whom she used to play two-hand Bridge in Lennox Gardens, observed: 'Diana is an embarrassment.'

With hindsight, however, it is possible to see that Diana made a valuable contribution to race relations and to the lessening of class prejudice even as her pariah status was forcing her to seek new friends and lovers from less established worlds. It is arguable whether the middle class girls who Prince Edward and her two sons married would have gained the acceptance they did had Diana not blazed the trail she did. Mavericks often suffer opprobrium, while those who come after them benefit from the breaches in the walls of prejudice that they have created. She was the first British princess to have an acknowledged affair with a Pakistani, as well as the first to openly cavort half-naked on yachts in the Mediterranean with a Muslim lover. This was pretty shocking stuff at the time, but it also helped to loosen up attitudes, with the public believing: If Diana, Princess of Wales can do it, it must be okay for me as well.

It is tempting to think that one of the elements that gave her the licence to pursue inter-racial relationships was her own mixed-race heritage. Before this was made public, she never had a non-European boyfriend. Afterwards was another story altogether. Inadvertently or otherwise, she cast off the old limitations of her perceived European origins and became a real game-changer.

Chapter Seven

WHEN THE AFFAIR OF Diana, Princess of Wales and the Pakistani-born heart surgeon Hasnat Khan first hit the news in the summer of 1995, it could not have come at a better time for two other royals: Prince Joachim of Denmark, second son of Queen Margarethe II (1940 -) and Franz Ferdinand of Hapsburg-Lorraine, eldest son of Archduke Geza of Austria.

The Danish Royal Family is close to the British. Queen Margarethe is a good friend as well as cousin of the Queen and Prince Philip, who are all descended from two brothers, King Frederick VIII of Denmark and King George I of the Hellenes, and their sister, Britain's Queen Alexandra. Technically, Prince Philip was also a Danish prince until he renounced his Greek and Danish titles to become British in 1947. Because of this closeness, what happens in one family inevitably has a knock-on effect in the other.

Like Queen Elizabeth II, the chain-smoking Margarethe had made a love match in 1967, when she married the former French diplomat known as Count Henri de Laborde de Monpezat. Therefore, when her son Joachim informed her that he had met a mixed-race girl named Alexandra Manley in Hong Kong towards the end of 1994 and wanted to marry her, the queen gave her blessing.

It is doubtful that Margarethe would have realised that she too had mixed race ancestry. At the time, few of the descendants of Philippa of Hainault and Madragana of Faro realised just how colourful their backgrounds were.

Alexandra was part Chinese and part European. Her father, Richard Nigel Manley, had been born in Shanghai in 1924 to a British father and Chinese mother. Her mother, Christa Maria Nowotny, was Austrian and

Czech. When China became Communist in 1949, the only people on the mainland who were free were residents of Hong Kong. The Manley family lived there, Richard working as an insurance executive and Christa managing a communications company. Because Czechoslovakia had also become Communist after the war, the Manleys had the additional bond of Communist regimes having taken over both their countries. They were prosperous without being rich: solidly bourgeois. After spending her school years in Hong Kong, Alexandra was sent to the Vienna University of Economics and Business, before finishing off her studies in Japan and England. She was thoroughly international, something most royals, but few other people, are. Upon returning to Hong Kong, she got a job at GT Management (Asia) Ltd. By the time she met Joachim, she was the deputy chief executive of Sales and Marketing. He was in Hong Kong working for the Danish shipping company, Maersk.

Theirs was a whirlwind romance. Within months of meeting, Joachim took Alexandra, who was five years his senior, on holiday to the Philippines, where, whipping out a diamond and ruby engagement ring while on bended knee, he proposed.

Six months later, the couple was married by Queen Margarethe's Chaplain-in-Ordinary in the chapel of Frederiksborg Castle, with their reception being held at Fredensborg Castle on the eastern shore of Lake Esrum. The bride wore her wedding present from her mother-in-law, the stunning Mecklenburg-Schwerin tiara which Queen Alexandrine had brought into the family, along with the Romanoff wealth inherited through her mother who features earlier in this book in the section dealing with Grand Duke Michael Mikhailovich and Countess Torby.

From the outset, Prince Joachim and Princess Alexandra, as she was now styled, were welcomed by one and all, from the highest to the lowest, as a desirable couple. The fact that she was a quarter-Chinese was unmistakable, but regarded as exotic. There has never been the degree of prejudice against the Chinese and Japanese that there has been against darker-skinned non-Europeans.

I met them in St. Moritz a few years after their marriage. While he is a nice looking man but nowhere near as attractive as his elder brother the Crown Prince Frederik, she was, and remains, a very good-looking woman. Soignée too, in the way that so many sophisticated international women are.

What eased the new Princess Alexandra's path to acceptability was a combination of good looks, good style, good behaviour, and a willingness to fit in. She endeared herself to the Danish people by immediately setting about learning their language, stating: 'It would have been terrible to have to stand up and speak English at an engagement, or thank someone for something. It would have been utterly wrong. This is my home, so there is no other option.' She threw herself into philanthropic work, supporting such charities as the Danish Society for the Blind, the Children's Red Cross, and UNICEF, serving as its Ambassador when she visited places such as Thailand on behalf of HIV/AIDS patients. It also helped that she always looked glamorous, had a kind word for everyone, and was thoughtful and sympathetic without trying to grab the limelight. She gave birth to two sons, Prince Nikolai William Alexander Frederik on 28th August 1999 (now a top model in Europe), and Prince Felix Henrik Valdemar Christian on 22nd July 2002.

By 2004, however, rumours were circulating that the marriage was over. These would prove to be true. On 16th September, their separation and intention to divorce were announced. It was the first divorce in the Danish Royal Family since 1846, but their British cousins had trodden a well-worn path by this time, and in so doing, had made divorce acceptable. Rather than the end of their marriage seeming like a disaster, it was accepted as just another manifestation of modernity.

Alexandra had made it clear from the beginning of her marriage that her adoption of Danish nationality was permanent. Her two children were the heirs-in-line to the throne, the Crown Prince having married only earlier that year and therefore still childless. As a mark of Alexandra's popularity, the Folketing (the Danish Parliament) chose to put her on the Civil List for life, voting her an annual allowance of 2.1m kroner (about $330,000). It was announced that she would remain Her Royal Highness Princess Alexandra of Denmark until her divorce, at which time she would become Her Highness Princess Alexandra of Denmark.

Ten years later, Alexandra began a relationship with another younger man. Martin Jorgensen was fourteen years her junior. A photographer whose father Jacob is well known in their native country as the owner of the JJ film production company, he married Alexandra in 2007. In so doing, she lost the rank of princess, becoming Countess of Frederiksborg in her own right. She also went into business, sitting on the board of Ferring Pharmaceuticals. By 2015, however, that marriage was also over. Nevertheless she remained a popular if semi-detached member of the Danish Royal Family, going about her life and her duties with a discretion that Diana, Princess of Wales and Sarah, Duchess of York could have emulated.

She also achieved a dignified *modus vivendi* with her former husband which meant that, after he remarried in 2008, and had another son and a daughter, the families could mingle without the anomalies that seemed to bedevil the divorced British royals, whether with too much or too little integration.

Of course, having to live in the public eye has its difficulties, but so too does being royal and living outside of the public eye. The exiled royals, especially, have the problem of being neither truly ordinary nor truly extraordinary any longer. Caught between the devil and the deep blue sea, many of them have opted for an approximate form of royal life, while others have chosen to embrace ordinariness. This has not always been as easy as it might appear. The exiled European Royal Houses all have house laws, many of which have constitutional force to this day (e.g. the German families), while others have clung onto defunct values, making life hell for those who wished to live relatively normal lives without turning their backs on their heritage. Marriage has been the most contentious issue. Unbelievable as it is, there have been families that have refused to change their house rules to permit unequal unions. This has caused real problems at times. For instance, the late Fürst (Ruling Prince) of Leiningen disinherited his eldest son, Prince (Prinz) Karl Emich, because he had married Gabriele Renate Thyssen (no relation to the steel family of the same name). At stake was a fortune of tens if not hundreds of millions, so Karl Emich sued in the German courts for his right as eldest son to be recognised. The court, however ruled that his father was well within his rights, for the house laws of the former royal states have constitutional force even today, and the German nation cannot alter them, though the head of the relevant family can. So the Fürst disinherited Karl Emich, who remains a mere Prinz as opposed to a Fürst, and substituted him with his younger brother Andreas, who became Fürst when he died in 1991. Along with the title and leadership of the family go all the constitutional rights still enjoyed under German republican law by the former ruling houses, including the right to dictate to his family members who they can and cannot marry, as well as absolute command over the vast Leiningen fortune.

Another family which was obsessed with equal marriages was the Habsburgs. Once rulers of most of Europe and the Americas, after the last Emperor, Karl I, was deposed in 1919, the family was banished from Austria. The head of the family, Archduke Otto, former Crown Prince of Austria, Hungary, Bohemia and Croatia etc. etc., was a stickler for equal marriages. That is, until his son and heir, Karl of Habsburg-Lorraine, wanted to marry the stupendously rich Francesca (Chessie) Thyssen, daughter of Baron Heini Thyssen-Bornemisza and Fiona Campbell-Walter. Although I have only met Chessie briefly on a few occasions, we have friends in common. She also has a house in Jamaica and actually knows the place better than I do, notwithstanding it being where I was born. I can attest to the fact from personal knowledge that she is the antithesis of class or colour prejudice. I also knew and liked Fiona's parents, Rear Admiral Keith McNeil Campbell-Walter, who adopted the Campbell in honour of his wife, the former Frances Henriette Campbell, daughter of Sir Edward Campbell, 1st Baronet. I was also friendly with Fiona's brother Geoffrey, who worked with the Simpson's group of companies in public relations and could not have been more charming. The family claimed to be related to the Dukes of Argyll, and were so proud of their link that Fiona named her son Lorne, the subsidiary title of the dukedom. But the duke of the day, my poisonous brother-in-law Ian, asserted that they were no more related than a bar of soap is to a toothbrush. Since he treasured putdowns and had scant regard for the truth, it is difficult to assess the merit of his observation, but the fact remains, it illustrates a point. Although a perfectly acceptable family, the Campbell-Walters did not possess parity with a Scottish duke, much less a royal or an imperial family.

Nor did the Thyssens. Heini Thyssen, however, was one of the richest men in the world. Heir to the vast steel and armaments empire of Thyssen Krupp, which armed Germany in both world wars as well as providing armaments and materials to literally half the world, his father had been Mr. Heinrich Thyssen until he married Margit, the daughter of the monarch's chamberlain in Hungary. Baron Gábor Bornemisza de Kászon et Impérfalva had no sons, and his immensely rich son-in-law no title, so the baron adopted his son-in-law. This made his daughter her husband's sister by law, but legalised incest was of no account, and in 1907 they applied to the Emperor Franz Josef for permission to extend baronial status to Heinrich and his male-line descendants. This was granted, but being a Hungarian baron was not on a par with even a comital or ducal title, much less a princely, regal or imperial one. The lure of the Thyssen fortune, however, had such an equalising effect upon Archduke Otto that he managed to surmount a lifetime of opposition to unequal marriages within the Habsburg family, and, balancing Chessie's money with his son's heritage, consented to the union by decreeing it equal.

Sadly for Archduke Otto's cousin, Archduke Geza of Austria (1940-), no such equalising factor could be found when he married Monika Decker (1939-) in 1965. Their marriage was deemed to be morganatic. Notwithstanding Geza's impressive career as an art and Fabergé expert who was Chairman of Christie's Switzerland before becoming chairman of Habsburg Fine Art International Auctioneers, as well as the author of books and the curator of several exhibitions featuring Fabergé and other Russian *objets de vertu*, and notwithstanding Geza and Monika being one of international society's most glittering couples, she remained Countess Monika von Habsburg. To drive home the morganatic status of the marriage, their three children, Franz Ferdinand (1967-), Ferdinand Leopold Joseph (1969-), and Maximilian Philip (1974-), were also Counts, not Archdukes, though many people all over the world regarded them all as archducal and referred to them accordingly, ignoring Archduke Otto's ruling in much the same way that half of French and American society ignored George VI's ruling rendering Wallis Windsor a mere Grace as opposed to an HRH.

It is difficult to know whether the morganatic status of Geza's family, allied with their artistic tendencies and the generally more modern tenor of their lives, contributed to a commendable degree of broadmindedness, or whether their attendance at Ampleforth Abbey and College, the noted Roman Catholic boarding school near York in England, in conjunction with their family's highly developed social conscience, encouraged them to break new ground, but the fact is, two of Geza and Monika's three sons ended up marrying black girls. And one did so twice.

Their eldest son, Franz Ferdinand, was the first European royal to marry a fully-fledged, Sub-Saharan African when he wed the Mozambiquean Theresa Joao Manuel Carlos (1973-) on the 12th January 1995. A graduate of the London School of Economics, he is known professionally as Franz von Habsburg. He moved to Tete, Mozambique, where he was the CEO of ProIntel Africa, an accounting firm. Ten months after the wedding, the latest of the Habsburg's countesses gave birth to a daughter, Anna Monika, named after both her great-grandmother Anna Monika, Archduchess Joseph Francis of Austria, a daughter of the last king of Saxony, Frederick Augustus III, and her grandmother, Countess Monika von Habsburg. A son, Count Philipp Paolo von Habsburg-Lothringen, followed two years later, in Harare, Zimbabwe. The family then moved back to Tete, Mozambique, where they were joined in 1999 by Franz's mother. She had been living in Scotland after her divorce from the archduke, but, upon being assured by her enthusiastic son that there was scope for new adventures if she wanted them, she opened up a B&B called Villa Habsburg in a manor house on the banks of the Zambesi River. She has been a devoted grandmother to her Mozambiquean grandchildren.

Because my children mix in the same social circles, I know Anna Monika von Habsburg somewhat. She is a charming, pretty, delightful young woman. Without being pretentious, she is regal, and without being inelegant, she is down-to-earth. She is a fully acknowledged member of the young elite that exists in London and stays in one another's castles and stately homes. These youngsters go about their lives with a grace and dignity that the flashier, more public 'rich kids' would be well advised to adopt. She will be a desirable daughter-in-law for anyone of distinction and sensibility, including any reigning sovereign, and is more desirable, because of her looks, demeanour and character, than many a blue-eyed, blonde brat of equally regal ancestry.

Regrettably, Anna Monika's parents' marriage was dissolved after fifteen years. Three years later, on 18th May 2013, in Cape Town, South Africa, Franz married another lady of colour, this time an Afro-American from Columbia, South Carolina. LeOntra (Lei) Breeden Greenspan was a lawyer who had attended George Washington University and had been called to the Bar in New York in 2007. She grew up in her southern hometown before moving north to the traditionally black neighbourhood of Bedford-Stuyvesant in Brooklyn, New York City, where the family ultimately settled. When asked by the *New York Times* about the attitude of the Habsburg dynasty to his marriage, Franz said, 'The family modernised its rules to survive [following Karl's marriage to Chessie]. For the modern Habsburgs, the importance of who your wife is, is more about whom you have fallen in love with than how they fit into the aristocratic family.' Fit in both his wives and children nevertheless did. The couple still lives in South Africa, where their daughter, Countess Sofia Gabriela Louise von Habsburg, was born in October 2014.

Anyone who has lived amongst people of colour knows that the average black person is generally much warmer and more immediate than his or her white peers. Whether this is what accounts for the oft-used adage, 'Once you try *black*, you never look back,' or whether the appeal lies elsewhere, is open to question. But Archduke Geza's second son, Count Ferdinand Leopold Joseph von Habsburg-Lothringen (1969-), followed the trail blazed by his brother and also fell in love with, and married, a lady of colour in Nairobi, Kenya, in August 1999. Mary Nyat Ring Machar was a Dinka from South Sudan. Ferdinand had been posted there in his capacity as a consultant with the United Nations Development Program following studies at Fordham University in New York, the University of Bradford and the University of Durham, whence he received a PhD in Social Sciences. Dr. von Habsburg, as he is known professionally, has worked for some years as a consultant with UNICEF (United Nations International Children's Emergency Fund). Based in Juba, South Sedan, and Nairobi, where his children were born, he and his countess have produced four children: Countess Luisa Aluel von Habsburg (2000-),

Count Laszlo Rum von Habsburg (2002-), Countess Gisela Aluk von Habsburg (2004-), and Count Matyas Malith von Habsburg (2009-). Count and Countess Ferdinand von Habsburg lead an African life, committed to improving their world. Worthy they are; spurned they have never been. They are as accepted in the society as any other members of any other royal family. What is edifying is how enlightened the upper reaches of society can be. They think nothing of accepting inter-racial unions, but will draw the line at bad behaviour, irrespective of whether it emanates from a prince, a priest, or a pig of the human kind.

It would be a mistake to think that the Habsburgs have been side-lined in royal circles just because they have lost their thrones. Franz and Ferdinand's cousin, Archduke Lorenz of Austria-Este is also Prince Lorenz of Belgium. He married the present King Philippe of the Belgians' sister Astrid on the 22nd September 1984. All of their children are not only princes and princesses of Belgium but also archdukes and archduchesses of Austria-Este. This branch of the Habsburgs descends from Lorenz's father Robert, the second son of the last Emperor and Empress of Austria, and therefore the younger brother of Archduke Otto the Equaliser. The d'Estes were one of the great Renaissance dynasties of Europe. One of Leonardo da Vinci's most famous paintings is of Beatrice d'Este, wife of Ludovico 'The Moor' Sforza, Duke of Milan. The d'Estes became Dukes of Modena and provided consorts for a plethora of monarchs, including King James II of England and VII or Scotland. They were known to be one of the richest families in Europe. They were also intermarried with the Habsburgs, and were Archdukes of Austria-Este, Royal Princes of Hungary and Bohemia etc. etc. When they were ousted from their duchy during the Second Italian War of Independence in 1859, prior to the unification of Italy under King Vittorio Emanuele II in 1861, the last reigning Duke of Modena, Francis V, retired to Austria, taking up residence in Vienna at the Palais Modena. He died in 1875, bequeathing his immense fortune to Emperor Franz Josef's nephew, Archduke Franz Ferdinand, in an act of secundogeniture, on the condition that he assumed the style of Archduke of Austria-Este. Little did the duke or his beneficiary realise that fourteen years later Franz Ferdinand would become heir to the Austrian throne following his first cousin Crown Prince Rudolf's suicide at Mayerling. Or that he would marry morganatically, so his children would not be able to become Archdukes and Archduchesses of Austria-Este, though there is every possibility that he might have changed the house rules had he lived to succeed to the throne.

Be that as it may, the Austria-Este branch of the family has flourished in a way that few other parts of the Habsburg dynasty have. Reflected glory is not only a fact of life, but a very useful one, and, between the Austria-Estes having been absorbed into the reigning House of Belgium, and the head of the Habsburg dynasty marrying into the Thyssen family, all the Habsburgs have benefitted from those boosts to their status, while the marriages of Franz and Ferdinand have catapulted them into the vanguard of a new royal way of being.

Another, even richer, family which has also spearheaded bi-racialism, is the ruling House of Liechtenstein. The head of state, Prince Hans-Adam II, is the richest monarch in Europe. Liechtenstein is a tiny country (160 square kilometres), the fourth smallest in Europe after the Vatican City (0.44 sq.k.), Monaco (1.95 sq.k), and San Marino (61 sq.k.). It is bordered by Switzerland on its west and south and Austria on its east and north, meaning that it has no natural wealth beyond snow-capped mountains. Its population is less than 40,000. At the end of the Second World War the country was so broke that the Ruling Family kept on selling treasures to keep itself, and the state, afloat. As late as 1967 it sold Leonardo's Ginevra de'Benci to the National Gallery of Art in the USA for the then record-price of $5m (about $39m in today's prices). Now, Liechtenstein is one of the banking centres of the world. LGT Bank, which has a 46% share of the entire market, is owned and operated by the Princely Family. It has benevolent tax and inheritance laws, all of which came about because necessity proved to be the mother of invention. Because the country is so small and mountainous, with no natural resources of any consequence, and, with nothing to sell and no assets to strip save those acquired by the Ruling Family, in desperation the Prince and the Government created an asset out of thin air by lowering taxes, welcoming foreign depositors to its banks, with no questions being asked and con-fidentiality assured. In the process, Liechtenstein turned itself, in three decades, into one of the richest countries per capita in the world, while its Ruling Family became one of the richest in the world and its Ruling Prince the richest monarch in Europe.

Technically, the Liechtenstein Ruling Family is not royal. That is a status which it shares with that other financially canny Ruling Family, the Grimaldis of Monaco. Because they are neither Imperial, Royal, Grand Ducal, Ducal, nor simple Highnesses, all of which denote royalty, but are merely Serene Highnesses, which usually implies aristocracy or par-royal (morganatic) status, they have always had more freedom to choose their husbands and wives than their royal peers. Nowadays, when royalty is thin on the ground and even royals are permitted the latitude that only Ruling Families enjoyed previously, these distinctions are no longer significant. But they do still exist. And they mean that the Ruling Families, being used to greater freedom, have continued to exercise it, even as they have seamlessly joined the Band of Royals to which they still technically do not belong, but which everyone, from the general public to royalty itself, regards them as being an intrinsic part of.

The first Prince of Liechtenstein who exercised his right to buck tradition maritally was Franz I (1853-1938). A younger son, he was not expected to accede to the throne. His elder brother Johann II was the sixth child but first son of Aloys II and his wife Countess Franziska Kinsky, whose father Count Franz Kinsky was the younger brother of Ferdinand, Prince Kinsky. Both men were the sons of yet another Liechtenstein princess, and Ferdinand's son Karl would have thrown caution to the wind and married Sir Winston Churchill's mother Jennie Jerome, Lady Randolph Churchill, had she not refused to divorce her dying husband. The Kinskys, though one of Austria's great noble families, were definitely not royal or imperial. Princess Aloys, as she remained until her husband acceded to the throne of Liechtenstein, had to deliver another four daughters before she finally managed to produce a second son, at which point her child-bearing came to an end. Johann II succeeded to the throne shortly after his eighteenth birthday. He would go on to enjoy the distinction of being the longest reigning monarch in Europe without a regent, reigning for 70 years and 91 days, and while Louis XIV's reign would be longer by 1 year and 356 days, for nearly two decades his mother was Regent, with Cardinal Mazarin the actual ruler of France. Johann II would distinguish himself even further by earning the moniker, 'Johann the Good'. He died, childless and unmarried, aged 88, leaving his younger brother by 13 years his heir.

Prince Franz I of Liechtenstein was not the first monarch in Europe to marry someone who had been born Jewish, but he was publicly perceived in this way. Elisabeth (Elsa) von Guttman (1875-1947) was the daughter of Sir Wilhelm Isak von Gutmann, a Jewish businessman from Moravia whose trading and mining company, Gebrüder Gutmann, was a market leader. Austria under Franz Josef was not anti-Semitic. Indeed, the Emperor had a policy of encouraging Jewish immigration. Successful Jews were rewarded as readily as their Christian equivalents, so there was nothing exceptional when the Emperor knighted both Wilhelm Gutmann and his brother, endowing them with the Order of the Iron Crown and the hereditary knighthoods that went along with it. For a while, Isak was even President of the Vienna Israelite Community. This did not stop him condoning the conversion of his daughter to Catholicism preceding her marriage to the Christian Hungarian, Baron Geza Eros von Bethenfalva.

Widowed nine years later, the Baroness met Prince Franz of Liechtenstein at a relief benefit for soldiers at the start of the First World War. They quickly became a couple, but Prince Johann II did not approve of the match, so they could not marry. For the next fifteen years, they maintained the proprieties appropriate to their respective stations in life while remaining committed to each other. Then, on 11th February 1929, Johann the Good died. Franz was now the Ruling Prince. He took steps to become the first prince to actually live in his state.

Until then, all Ruling Princes of Liechtenstein had spent most of their time in Vienna, the old Imperial capital, or on their many estates scattered throughout the former Austro-Hungarian Empire in such places as Czechoslovakia. The loss of those properties, at the end of the Second World War when the Eastern European nations fell to the Communists, would considerably reduce the wealth of the family, hence the necessity for later princes to sell valuable art works to keep the state afloat. These territorial losses also affected the peregrinations of the Ruling Family, for until then it was used to moving between its many properties. However, with these now behind the Iron Curtain, they were forced to sink roots in Liechtenstein in a way they had never done throughout the centuries when they were one of the great landowners of the Habsburg Empire.

On the 22nd July 1929, the seventy-six year old Prince Franz I did something no other Liechtenstein monarch had ever done. He married his fifty-four year old, formerly Jewish, paramour in the small parish church in Lainz near the Schönbrunn Palace in Vienna. He promptly took her back to the state of which she was now Ruling Princess, creating a presence which was more visible than any previous Ruling Prince and Princess had possessed. Princess Elsa, as she was affectionately known, fulfilled a full roster of official duties, officiating at ceremonies with and without her husband, undertaking charity work, visiting the poor and the infirm, creating the Princess Elsa Foundation for Hospitals, even founding an organisation for teenagers known as the *Franz und Elsa-Stiftung für die Liechtensteinische Jugend*, which is still operational today. It was obvious to onlookers that Franz I was proud of his wife and intended that she play her royal role to the full.

The rise of the Nazi party in Germany, however, coincided with the reign of Franz I and Elsa. It had an inevitable effect upon Liechtenstein and its Jewish-born Ruling Princess. Following Hitler's appointment to Chancellor in January 1933 by the President of the Weimar Republic, Field Marshal von Hindenburg, there was a gradual increase in pro-Nazi sentiment in both Austria and adjoining Liechtenstein. Although the latter country had no Nazi party, the National Union Party became a repository for Nazi sympathisers who were openly disapproving of their 'local Jewish problem', as they termed the Ruling Princess. Despite this, Prince Franz and Princess Elsa continued to partake of national life, rising above the minority of citizens who disapproved of the Jewish origins of their sovereign's wife.

While Elsa had converted to Catholicism and was therefore no longer technically Jewish, the laws implemented by the Nazis in Germany throttled not only their own Jews but affected Jews throughout Europe as well. Hitler's national boycott of Jewish businesses on the 1st April 1933 was the first step. This was quickly followed on the 7th April by the Law for the Restoration of the Professional Civil Service, banning non-Aryans from the civil service and legal profession. On the 10th

May, the book-burning bonfires, which illuminated all towns and cities as they darkened the mood of the country throughout the Third Reich, became notorious, with all books deemed un-German or un-Aryan being consumed by the 'cleansing' fires of Nazism. This was followed on the 15th September 1935 by the Reichstag enacting the Nuremburg Laws which banned marriage or sexual intercourse between Jews and Aryans. These laws also limited citizenship rights to those who were Aryan; all others being regarded as members of the state without citizenship rights. There were rigid definitions of what constituted Jewishness. Anyone with three or more grandparents, who were originally Jewish, was deemed to be Jewish, irrespective of whether they had converted or even been born Christian. This meant that the Ruling Princess of Liechtenstein was Jewish in the eyes of Nazis, and her marriage to the Ruling Prince fell foul of Nazi ideology. Bravely though, the couple tried to rise above what was happening, when German tanks rolled into Austria on the 12th March 1938, and Nazi Germany annexed Austria in the Anschluss, Franz I retired from active government. This was a wise choice, for, although he did not abdicate, he came as close to doing so as possible, creating a regency and turning over all princely duties to his successor.

This was a bald and successful attempt to deflect Hitler's attention away from Liechtenstein. The heir presumptive was Franz Josef II, the son of his first cousin Prince Aloys and his wife, Archduchess Elisabeth Amalie of Austria. She was a younger half-sister of the Archduke Franz Ferdinand who became Archduke of Austria-Este, then heir to the Austro-Hungarian throne before being assassinated at Sarajevo, making her the first properly royal Ruling Princess of Liechtenstein. The hope was that Hitler, being Austrian himself, would resist the temptation to gobble up Liechtenstein: something which would have been more of a temptation had the Ruling Prince and his Jewish princess remained ensconced on the throne. There was certainly merit to the reasoning, for when King Carol II of Romania refused to give up his Jewish mistress, Elena Lupescu, Hitler had them evicted from their country.

Fortunately for Liechtenstein, matters never came to that pass. On 25th July 1938, less than three months after surrendering power, Prince Franz I died. Princess Elsa went into voluntary exile in neutral Switzerland, where her presence was deemed to be less provocative to the volatile, Jew-hating Führer. She lived in Vitznau on Lake Lucerne, dying there on 28th September 1947. She was the first of the Ruling or Dowager Ruling Princesses not to be buried in the old Liechtenstein burial crypt at Vranov, which by then was in Communist Czechoslovakia, but in the new royal crypt next to Vaduz Cathedral.

Honoured in death as she had been in life by the family she had married into, Elsa's marriage paved the way for the interracial union of her husband's successor's grandson half a century after her death. What also helped to make Prince Maximilian of Liechtenstein's marriage to the Afro-Panamanian Angela Gisela Brown less noteworthy was that his two Habsburg cousins, Franz and Ferdinand, had blazed the trail before him.

Maximilian (1969-), now known professionally as Prince Max since he became CEO of the LGT Group in 2006, is the second son of Prince Hans-Adam II (1945-) and his Ruling Princess, Marie Aglae (1940-). His mother is yet another of the many Kinskys who have married into the family; Hans-Adam's mother, the former Countess Georgina von Wilczek, being another through her mother.

Max's elder brother is the Hereditary Prince of Liechtenstein, Alois (1968-). He has been the ideal first son, setting up his brother to experience the degree of freedom he might otherwise not have enjoyed. After schooling at the Liechtenstein Grammar School in Vaduz, which both brothers attended, Alois went on to follow the military path deemed necessary for the heir to the throne, attending the Royal Military Academy at Sandhurst, and serving in the Coldstream Guards in Hong Kong and London before gaining a Master's degree in Jurisprudence from the University of Salzburg in 1993. That same year he married Sophie, the eldest of the five daughters of the Duke in Bavaria, Prince Max, whose elder, unmarried brother Franz, Duke of Bavaria is regarded by the Jacobites as the rightful King of England, Scotland, and Ireland. Sophie is also the first cousin of the present Duke of Marlborough's half-brother Lord Edward Spencer-Churchill, her mother being the sister of Rosita, Duchess of Marlborough. Although the Bavarian Royal Family is governed by semi-Salic Law, meaning that succession to the great wealth and titles of the Wittelsbachs will pass to the Duke of Bavaria's first cousin, Prince Luitpold, owing to an absence of male heirs, the claim to the British throne is vested in the female line as well. One day, therefore, Sophie, now the Hereditary Princess of Liechtenstein, will possess the Jacobite claim to our Crown. This, of course, is not something she is eager to accentuate. Such claims would only create problems with the British Royal Family, and as ours is the foremost royal family on earth, and all royals and par-royals are eager to eliminate rather than create problems amongst themselves, the question of who rightfully occupies the thrones of England, Scotland and Ireland is avoided at all costs.

Like the British royals, the Bavarians are also descendants of Philippa of Hainault and Madragana of Faro. This means that Prince Alois and Prince Max have married women with African ancestry. The difference, of course, is that the former's wife looks Caucasian, while the latter's looks more African. Princess Angela of Liechtenstein (1958-) was born in Bocas de Toro, Panama, to Javier Francisco Brown and Silvia Maritza Burke. The surnames of her parents suggest that she herself is descended from African slaves who emigrated from the West Indies, mostly Jamaica, to places such as Panama and Costa Rica in search of work in the mid to late nineteenth and early twentieth centuries. Angela moved to New York and studied apparel design at Parsons School of Design in Brooklyn, where she won the prestigious Oscar de la Renta Gold Thimble Award for fashion design. After graduating, she went into business, working as a fashion director for the Coty Award-winning designer Adrienne Vittadini, whose label was inadvertently caught up in a mislabelling incident in 2017 when the Stein Mart G-III Apparel Group confused various Ivanka Trump items with Vittadini's. By this time, Princess Angela had long since left the rag trade to marry her prince and move to his country. Before doing so, however, she had also set up her own fashion line, A. Brown, which she ran for three years. She is the first acknowledged woman of colour to have married dynastically into a reigning European family. Unlike Natalia Pushkina and Sophie von Merenberg, who also married into reigning European families, hers has not been a morganatic marriage. It is a dynastic marriage, one in which the wife takes the rank, style and title of her husband, and any child of the union is in the line of succession.

Eleven years her husband's senior, Angela met Max von und zu Liechtenstein at a party in New York towards the end of the last century. He had recently completed his MBA at the Harvard Business School in Boston, and was working in New York for Chase Capital Partners, the private equity arm of the Chase Manhattan Corporation. When they were sure that their relationship was an enduring one, the prince approached his father for permission to marry. By this time, there were already three heirs to the throne ahead of Max. There was his elder brother with his two sons, Josef Wenzel Maximilian Maria (1995-), and Georg Antonius Constantin Maria (1999), as well as a daughter, Marie-Caroline Elisabeth Immaculata, so Max, who had been the spare at birth, was no longer even that. Hans-Adam II gave his consent, and the couple wed civilly in Vaduz on 21st January 2000, then religiously on the 29th January 2000 at the Church of St. Vincent Ferrer in New York, where Andy Warhol used to attend Mass. A beautiful woman, the new Princess Angela was magnificent in a sleek, white wedding dress of her own creation with a bateau neckline which was a forerunner of Meghan Markle's wedding dress. She also wore the magnificent Kinsky tiara which the bridegroom's sister Tatjana had worn the year before when she married Philipp von Lattorff, thereby conveying the message that the Ruling Family approved of the marriage wholeheartedly. The following year, on the 18th May 2001, the forty-three year old princess gave birth to her only child, Prince Alfons Constantin Maria of Liechtenstein. Like his first cousin and the future monarch, Josef, he was born in London.

Because Max was intended for the family-owned LGT Group, and he needed to gain a wide range of experience before settling down in Liechtenstein. After working for two years for Industrie Kapital, in 2003 he began managing the German office of JP Morgan Partners. This would result in his falling foul of the German tax authorities, who, in 2008, accused him of failing to pay German tax on investment gains while residing in their country. His brother, Hereditary Prince Alois, called the investigation an 'attack' on Liechtenstein, while his father, Prince Hans-Adam II, stated that the Germans 'did not hesitate to commit character assassination on a country and on individual people,' stemming as the investigation did from the German tax authorities purchasing for the princely sum of $6.28m stolen data from a former employee of the

LGT Group.

For a while matters got ugly, as the German, then the American, tax authorities began putting the squeeze on Liechtenstein, with the intention of destroying their banking sector. Matters would ultimately be resolved, but not before the Germans and the Americans accused the Liechtensteiners of being money-launderers and even 'slime'.

Throughout this period, Max remained the CEO of the LGT Group: a position he has held since 2006. He, his wife and his son, who is sixth in the line of succession (the same position as Prince Harry in England), lead quiet but productive lives outside of the public eye. Nevertheless, they are very much respected members of the Establishment. The Liechtenstein Ruling Family, though consisting of some hundred members, is actually a scaled down monarchy. The Ruling Prince and Princess, the Hereditary Prince and Princess, as the heir and his wife are known, and their children are the only ones listed on the country's official website. This means that the other members of the family like Max, Angela and Alfons are, to all intents and purposes, able to pursue private lives without the excessive exposure which other reigning families, such as the British, Belgian, Dutch, Swedish or Danish, have to endure.

Chapter Eight

ANOTHER RULING FAMILY which has welcomed a lady of colour into its midst is the Monégasque. Monaco is the second smallest and most densely populated state in the world. It is only 0.78 square miles, with a population of 38,400, meaning that it has as many people squeezed into it as Liechtenstein has over a much greater land mass. The Grimaldis have been amongst the earliest standard bearers of change in royal and aristocratic circles, pushing the boundaries of convention in a way that no other regnant family has done since Henry VIII sat on the English throne.

Originally an Italian family from Genoa, they have ruled Monaco since 1297 with only two significant interruptions, when Francesco Grimaldi, Il Malizia ('the Malicious'), disguised himself and his band of followers as monks and seized the fortress protecting the Rock of Monaco. Although evicted some years later by the Genoese, the Grimaldis ultimately prevailed when the Genoese and the Crown of Aragon embarked upon a struggle for Corsica. This resulted in the Grimaldis buying Monaco from the Aragonese in 1419, a century before Spain came into existence when Aragon united with Castile. Thereafter, the Grimaldis were the undisputed rulers of Monaco and styled themselves Lords of Monaco.

The first Prince of Monaco was Honoré II (1597-1662). He inherited the territory at the age of 6 when his father was assassinated. His uncle, the 4th Prince of Val di Taro, was intensely pro-Spanish and in 1605 acquiesced in Spain moving troops into what had hitherto been an Italian territory. Honoré and his two sisters were moved to the safety of Milan, while the Council of Monaco tried to limit Spanish influence and retain its independence. To an extent, it was successful, for the Spanish forces of occupation left Monaco in 1614, though that country retained its influence over Monaco until after Honoré came of age and started to play the Spanish off against the French.

He found the French king Louis XIII a willing ally. By 1633, Honoré, who had started styling himself Prince of Monaco, had been recognised as a sovereign prince by the French king , was received at the French Court as the Prince of Monaco and had his sovereign and ruling status further ratified by being styled '*Duc et Pair étranger*'.

Following the Treaty of Péronne (1641), Monaco became a French protectorate, with that country guaranteeing the rights of its sovereign prince and his rights to the French territories of Menton and Roquebrune. Although Honoré lost his extensive Spanish and Italian possessions at the same time, Louis XIII compensated him by endowing him with the marquisate of Les Baux and the duchy of Valentinois. The dukedom had been first created for Cesare Borgia in 1498, then for King Henry II's mistress Diane de Poitiers in 1548. Although French titles no longer have validity in present-day France, those territories linked to the marquisate and dukedom are still claimed by Monaco as living legal entities, along with the many estates in the French province of Dauphine forming a part of them. The sovereign princes of Monaco base their claim on the legal fact that their rights to those territories and titles precede France's change of regime, and therefore supersede the changes the state made when it ceased to be a monarchy and became a republic.

From 1641 until the French Revolution, the status quo between France and Monaco was maintained without interruption or dispute. In 1793, however, revolutionary forces occupied Monaco. Recently, a cache of letters, written by aristocrats the night before their execution, came to light, including a particularly heart-rending farewell to her three children from Princess Joseph of Monaco, the wife of the second son of Prince Honoré III. Born Marie-Thérèse de Choiseul, she was the daughter of the Duc de Stainville and niece of the famous Duc de Choiseul who was Louis XV's Chief Minister. She had hoped to delay her execution by feigning pregnancy, for even the French Revolutionaries shied away from executing pregnant women, but she was nevertheless beheaded on 27th July 1794, the very day of Robespierre's downfall and only a day before his own guillotining. The Reign of Terror then ended as suddenly as it had begun, but it was one day too late for the 27 year old Monégasque princess.

The arrest of the princess was partly due to her mother-in-law, who was one of those colourful characters who decorate the many branches of the Grimaldi family tree. Marie-Catherine de Brignole was known as the most beautiful woman in France. She was also known as the lover of the Prince de Condé, a cousin of King Louis XVI and head of a cadet branch of the French Royal Family. She had been in love with him before her marriage. Forced to marry her mother's former lover, Honoré III of Monaco, she seems to have led a tolerable existence at the Hôtel de Matignon, her husband's magnificent palace in Paris which is now the French Prime Minister's official residence. She produced two sons for her husband, while de Condé continued to pay court to her. Gradually, Honoré III came to realise that his wife and de Condé were actually in love with each other rather than being the harmless swain and the object of innocent courtly devotion then so prevalent in conventional royal and aristocratic circles. This triggered such jealousy on his part that she was confined in Monaco and had literally to abscond from the palace by climbing over a balcony and escaping to France, where she met up with de Condé. Thereafter, in defiance of all decorum, they presented themselves as a couple, with her going to the extreme of moving into the Hôtel de Lassay, an annex of the de Condé family residence, the Palais-Bourbon, until her own palace, the magnificent Hôtel de Monaco, was built.

What made the love affair - for love affair it genuinely was - between Marie-Catherine and Louis Joseph de Bourbon, Prince de Condé, especially noteworthy was that he was a Prince of the Blood. Known at Court as 'Monsieur le Prince', he and Marie-Catherine so scandalised Marie Antoinette, while still Dauphine, that she refused to acknowledge Marie-Catherine's existence at a time when great moment was placed upon whom the Dauphine recognised or snubbed. This did not go down well at all with de Condé, who remonstrated with his cousin, King Louis XV. Since the king was also having trouble getting his headstrong granddaughter-in-law to acknowledge his mistress, the beautiful, lowborn Comtesse du Barry, he put pressure on the Austrian Dauphine who ultimately had to climb down and acknowledge both mistresses.

Ironically, when the Revolution came, de Condé and the Hereditary Prince of Monaco's estranged wife proved to be two of the most loyal supporters of the embattled Louis XVI and Marie Antoinette. Emigrating to Germany as soon as the Bastille fell, by 1791 they were living in Coblenz, with de Condé heading up the Army of the Émigrés which threatened to topple the Revolutionary Government of France. Although this threat would end up uniting the people of France in a wholly unexpected manner, paving the way for the downfall of the monarchy and the arrest of the king and queen, it was conceived as a way of protecting the monarchs against the mob.

The law of unintended consequences would prove how dangerous was the threat of outside intervention, whether from the emigrated members of the Royal Family like de Condé and Louis XVI's brothers the Counts of Provence and Artois, or from other sovereigns like the Duke of Brunswick. By 1793 Louis XVI and Marie Antoinette had lost their heads on the scaffold, and the French Revolutionary Government, rather than collapsing under the strain, had gone from strength to strength.

By 1795, the Reign of Terror was at an end and, with it, the momentum of the Revolution. People longed for peace and stability, which proved impossible to achieve, because Europe, dreading the spread of the Revolutionary Government's ideals, remained at war with it. Meanwhile, the French Government struggled under the weight of war, corruption, and ineptitude. It was during this highly unstable period that Prince Honoré III died, freeing Marie-Catherine to marry de Condé. Their wedding took place three years later, in London, on the 24th October 1798, by which time Napoleon Bonaparte had begun his ascent from feted General to Head of State. Although she would not live to appreciate the significance of the feat she accomplished, Marie-Catherine became the first and only Princess Consort of Monaco to actually be a member of the French Royal Family.

By this time, her son, Honoré IV, had acceded to the throne of Monaco. In reality, it was non-existent, for the state had been absorbed into France and the Crown abolished. He was held as a closely-guarded prisoner in his own country, his health destroyed by imprisonment.

Throughout the Revolutionary, Directory, Consular and Imperial regimes of France, Monaco continued to be a part of France, only reverting to sovereign-nation status with the downfall of Napoleon I in

1814. By then, Honoré IV was so incapacitated after the torments he had had to endure as a prisoner of the French that his brother Joseph had to act as Regent, a role taken over from 1815 by the heir to the throne, his son Honoré V. Although Marie-Catherine did not live to see this, the Prince de Condé did. He returned to France upon the restoration of the Bourbons with his cousin, King Louis XVIII, who created him Grand Master of the Royal Household. He also lived to see his step-son Honoré IV officially reinstated as the sovereign Prince of Monaco at the Congress of Vienna.

For the next hundred years, Monaco's princely family managed to entertain and entrance European Court circles and the newspaper-reading public with conduct that was, to put it mildly, both original and unconventional. Being sovereign yet not really royal, they fell between two stools, in the process taking full advantage of their anomalous status to gain liberties for themselves that ordinary royals and aristocrats dared not claim. They played both sides off against the centre and broke new ground in a way that no other dynasty did.

They also had to wend a wily way through the winding routes of nineteenth century European politics. The Congress of Vienna in 1815 had declared Monaco a protectorate of the kingdom of Sardinia. This destroyed the prosperity of the principality. It also threatened the viability of the state and its very existence, because little Monaco found itself caught up between the power plays of the big powers of France, Sardinia, the Papal States, and Austria, which still ruled large swathes of mainland Italy and the territories adjoining Monaco's.

During the Year of the Revolutions in 1848, when much of Europe, from Italy, Germany, Austria and Hungary to France, was rocked by political unrest, resulting in general destabilisation of the political system and the abdication of the Austrian Emperor, the flight of the French King, and the ultimate restoration of the Napoleonic Empire, the Sardinians showed the Prince of Monaco that their interpretation of protectionism was akin to the Cosa Nostra's. The Sardinians undermined all attempts by the sovereign Prince of Monaco, Florestan I, and the *de facto* ruler of Monaco, his consort Caroline, to provide the citizens of Menton and Roquebrune with a constitution. Instead, the 'protector' encouraged the citizens of those two territories to declare themselves 'free cities', garrisoned Menton, and then arrested, dethroned, and imprisoned Florestan. The Sardinians took over the towns' 'administration' and their king, who was also head of the House of Savoy and its duke, issued a decree declaring both cities an administrative part of the Duchy of Savoy's city of Nice. While the 'free cities' still remained nominally the property of the Prince of Monaco, he derived no benefit from them and lost out on the revenue generated by territories which comprised nine-tenths of his principality's domain.

Although Florestan would subsequently be freed and restored to his throne in 1849, he understandably never forgot nor forgave the treachery of King Charles Albert of Sardinia. However, he seems to have derived some comfort from the fact that, while he was forced to live without access to his 'free cities', Charles Albert had to abdicate following his ignominious defeat by Austria in 1849. That king went into exile after being succeeded by his son, King Victor Emmanuel II, dying a few months later in Portugal, while Florestan himself returned to Monaco and his throne, but still without Menton and Roquebrune.

Prince Florestan I and his consort, the former Marie Caroline Gibert de Lametz, were yet another of those extraordinary couples who proliferated in the Monaco Ruling Family, proving the principle that families, once set on the path of eccentricity, seldom come off it. They hovered somewhere between respectability and eccentricity, having both been actors at the Théâtre de l'Ambigu-Comique on Paris's Boulevard du Temple before acceding to the throne. This, remember, was at time when the acting profession was just beginning its journey from unacceptable to barely respectable, and actors were generally regarded as being barely better than scamps or degenerates.

In *The History of Monaco: Past and Present* (1867), the British historian H. Pemberton observed that Florestan I was 'a man utterly unsuited for the task' of sovereign. Although interested in literature and the theatre, he was one of those artistic types who are otherwise inept. In the Army, he had struggled to cope and only achieved the insignificant rank of corporal with difficulty. This was a rather dubious accomplishment for someone who was a prince, for, under Napoleon I, the *Grande Armée* prized princes as highly as they had been valued under the *Ancien Régime*, and not only those who were created under the new Empire either, but those whose titles originated under the monarchy.

One cannot help but feel that it must have come as something of a relief to Florestan when he was taken prisoner in Russia and treated with all the courtesy due to his rank. Upon his release, he was repatriated to France, where he met the actress who would become the first Princess Caroline of Monaco. His half-sister Amélie d'Aumont had married Caroline's brother Louis-Pierre Mauroy. On the 27th November 1816, he quietly married Caroline Gibert de Lametz in Commercy. Although not of the high nobility, she was a member of an old and established Champagne family, and this would turn out to be financially advantageous for the impecunious, ineffectual but nevertheless charming prince. After their marriage, they bought and restored the Hôtel de Créqui in Paris, living a quiet life of genuine domestic bliss with their two children, a son, Charles Honoré (1818-1889), and a daughter, Florestine Gabrielle Antoinette (1833-1897).

Because their marriage was not extravagantly celebrated, some historians have concluded that Florestan's family disapproved. There is no evidence, however, to support that contention, while there is much to suggest that the family's circumstances were constrained by negative realities at that time. His brother was struggling in the impoverished but newly restored principality where their father was infirm. His mother, born Louise, Duchesse d'Aumont, Duchesse de Mazarin et de La Meilleraye, was twice divorced and living in Paris, the mother of an illegitimate daughter who was already married to the bride's brother, and France itself was in turmoil. Only the year before, it had sent its emperor into exile for the second time in a year, during which its king had been enthroned, exiled, and restored yet again. France itself had been bled dry by the Napoleonic wars. Florestan's family was therefore in as much disarray as the respective countries of his parents, and it is more likely that he and Caroline married quietly because of practical considerations. There is also the fact that large marital celebrations are a modern phenomenon, seldom seen in previous centuries, and certainly not in times of turmoil.

Florestan was a second son who had not been expected to inherit the throne. Though reigning families had recovered a degree of their prestige in the years since the French Revolution, the throne of Monaco was hardly the desirable entity it would become as the century progressed. Indeed, his brother, Honoré V, was a singularly unpopular regent then sovereign, partly because his lifestyle was hermetic, and partly because he was, according to the historian, Professor Victor de la Canorgue, 'extravagant and fond of luxuries for himself, but miserly towards others, even his own family, to whom he gave allowances disproportionate to his means.' Although he had an illegitimate son, Louis Gabriel Oscar Grimaldi, whom he later legitimised, Honoré V remained unmarried, and Florestan therefore became the heir presumptive only when it became apparent that there was no likelihood of his brother marrying. Honoré V died, alone and unlamented, in Paris on the 2nd October 1841, aged 63.

In reality, the problems Honoré V faced as sovereign were those with which Florestan and Caroline would themselves have to contend once they took the throne. Monaco and its ruling family had suffered severe financial hardship as a result of the French Revolution, a state of affairs that was hardly ameliorated under the protection of Sardinia. Irrespective of Professor de la Canorgue's interpretation, it is possible that the bachelor prince's retiring and supposedly miserly ways were nothing more than a struggle to keep his ship of state afloat, while maintaining the dignity required of a sovereign prince as he tried to keep his financial struggles from public view.

Although Florestan I would prove to be as inept a ruler as he had been a corporal, he had chosen wisely when he married his actress from Champagne. Gustave Saige, the French historian who became Archivist of the Prince's Palace in Monaco, asserts in his 1897 opus, *Monaco: Ses Origines et Son Histoire*, that the power behind the throne was Caroline. She was highly intelligent, with superb social skills, and their accession was welcomed by their subjects, who appreciated the fact that their new Prince and his Consort partook of national life in a way their predecessor had not. Caroline also trained the heir, Charles III, to be a capable and effective ruler, so that when their reign soured under the encouragement of King Charles Albert of Sardinia and they attempted to save their throne by handing over power to Charles, he was already a capable ruler.

The Sardinians had been 'administering' Menton and Roquebrune since the Year of the Revolutions in 1848, when much of Europe, from Italy, Germany, Austria and Hungary to France, had been rocked by political unrest. This had resulted, as stated previously, in general destabilisation of the political system as well as the abdication of the Austrian Emperor, the flight of the French King, and the ultimate restoration of the Napoleonic Empire. The Sardinians had taken full advantage of the political instability to undermine all attempts by the Prince of Monaco to provide the citizens of Menton and Roquebrune with a constitution, encouraging them to declare the territories 'free cities' and thereby further impoverishing the principality, presumably with a view to deposing the Grimaldis eventually. Although Menton and Roquebrune remained nominally Monégasque, all benefits accrued to the Duchy and Duke of Savoy, their 'administrators'.

In 1856, Florestan died and was succeeded by his only son, who reigned as Prince Charles III of Monaco (1818-1889). By this time, he had been married for ten years to the rich and well-connected Countess Antoinette de Mérode (1828-1864), daughter of the Belgian plutocrat Count Werner de Mérode. This rather defeats the theory that Charles's mother was somehow beyond the pale, for theirs was a double wedding, shared with her sister Louise, whose daughter would marry King Vittorio Emanuele II of Italy's second son, the Duke of Aosta, and become Queen Consort of Spain. Antoinette's dowry was so sizeable that it not only allowed the new Hereditary Princess of Monaco to acquire the historic Château de Marchais, which had been owned by Charles, Cardinal of Lorraine, brother of Mary Queen of Scot's mother Mary of Guise, and remains in the possession of the Grimaldi family to this day, but it also allowed Charles III to follow the recommendation of his mother and embellish Monaco.

The Dowager Princess Caroline had come up with the brilliant idea of turning Monaco, then unknown to anyone without a connection to the Grimaldis, into a gaming mecca for rich visitors. These would benefit from the mild climate of the Mediterranean while the principality's coffers would swell with the visitors' money. Though it would take some time to surmount the obstacles that at first prevented the concept from achieving the tremendous success it ultimately did, it was Caroline's vision which turned a sleepy, penniless village on a promontory in the Mediterranean into what Monaco has been for the last century and a half. It is equally true that none of it would have been possible without the Mérode dowry.

Caroline got her idea from Bad Homburg, the German town, which became one of the richest and most fashionable spa resorts in Europe, with its healing waters, comfortable hotels, and gambling casino managed by the French brothers, François and Louis Blanc. It was one thing to rip off a good idea, but quite another to implement it successfully. Though Caroline and her son started to realise their dream as soon as he acceded to the throne in 1856, at first, Monaco was more failure than mecca. It faced a host of problems. It was inaccessible by land. There were no roads or railways leading to it. It nestled in a bay surrounded by mountainous territory, the only approach being the Mediterranean Sea. It was also unknown.

Its developers were not up to the task of realising Caroline and Charles's vision of a world-famous resort to which people of consequence would flock, and, after a series of changes of operator, she approached François Blanc, known as the 'Magician of Homburg', whose brother and partner was by this time dead. At first he declined her offer, but Caroline was persistent. Realising that only someone of Blanc's calibre and talents could turn the ailing resort venture from the sow's ear into the silk purse the principality needed it to be, she and Charles III offered him an irresistible package. They would set up a company in which he would have a majority shareholding and a fifty year concession. Capitalised at 15m francs, the Société des Bains de Mer et du Cercle des Étrangers à Monaco (SBM) attracted a host of eminent investors, including the Bishop of Monaco, Charles-Bonaventure-Francois Theuret, and the future Pope Leo XIII, the aristocratic Vincenzo, Cardinal Pecci. In return, Monaco provided Blanc with a venue whose weather permitted year-round visitors, something Bad Homburg, whose season was restricted to the summer alone, did not.

Once committed, Blanc poured his expertise and his money into the principality while making full use of the generous capitalisation of the

SBM. The splendidly Baroque Hôtel de Paris was completed within a year. He wisely insisted that the name of the resort be changed from the unappealing Les Spelugues to something more catchy. After a few false starts, he and his advisors hit upon the memorable and 'sexy' Monte Carlo, Mount Charles in Italian, in honour of the prince. The crucial roads were constructed along with the railway, which was opened in 1868. The newly accessible Monte Carlo then really took off as the mecca Caroline had envisioned.

In the early years of Charles III's reign, while he and his mother were laying the ground for Monte Carlo's success, the new King of Sardinia was also working towards his own elevation. By 1860 Vittorio Emanuele II had realised that he could achieve his ambition of becoming supreme monarch of a unified Italy, if he made concessions to France. His goal was to strip the Neapolitan king, the Austrians and the Pope of their Italian domains. He therefore entered into the Treaty of Turin with the French Emperor, Napoleon III.

This treaty also affected the state of Monaco, bringing about the denouement which had been on the cards since Charles Albert of Sardinia had coveted the towns of Menton and Roquebrune. France and Sardinia proceeded to carve up the principality of Monaco in a mini-version of the way Austria, Prussia and Russia had gobbled up Poland in the previous century. Nice and Savoy having been ceded to France by Sardinia, the latter's army agreed to pull out of Monégasque territory and surrender its claim to protection to France, in return for which France would turn a blind eye while Sardinia seized the Italian territories of the Austrians, the Papal States, and the Kingdom of Naples.

This left the loose end of Monaco's claim to the lost towns affixed to Nice which Sardinia had now turned over to France for 'administration'. In 1861, Napoleon III and Charles III signed the Franco-Monégasque Treaty, whereby France recognised Monaco's sovereignty and independent status as well as the Grimaldi dynasty's right to the throne. In return, France agreed to compensate Charles III to the tune of 4,100,000 francs if he surrendered his claims to Menton and Roquebrune. This treaty formed the basis upon which the principality's future was secured. It now entered its golden days as one of the most glamorous places on earth, a halcyon period which would last until the beginning of the First World War. Caroline would live to see the realisation of her dream, dying in 1879 in the principality which had already become one of the richest and most popular resorts in the world. She was genuinely mourned. Millionaires and royalty, even Queen Victoria, went out of their way to see the realisation of the Dowager Princess of Monaco's vision.

Intermingled with the new fortunes of the family, was misfortune. Charles III's wife Antoinette had died in Monaco aged 35 on 10th February 1864, before the Hôtel de Paris was even completed. Her widower was now blind. According to Dr. Thomas Pickering in *Monaco: Beauty Spot of the Riviera* (1882), 'So far back as 1860, Prince Charles lost his eyesight.' Yet both he and his mother never lost sight of their objective, and it is a testament to their vision that when he died ten years after Caroline, he left his sole child, Albert I (1848-1922), a flourishing state which was rich and known throughout the world.

The new monarch was a combination of his intellectual, unworldly grandfather Florestan, and his practical grandmother and father. Albert I became one of the world's greatest oceanographers, devoting much of his life to the study of the sea and the oceans, and the relationship between living things and their environment. He undertook many exploratory expeditions aboard his four research yachts, studied the polar regions, and founded the world-renowned Oceanographic Museum of Monaco. He also created the Institute for Human Paleontology in Paris, funded several digs investigating the origins of humanity, and was rewarded by having Grimaldi Man named for him after he was found in the Baoussé-Roussé Cave.

A genuine intellectual of scientific bent, Albert was married twice. His mother is supposed to have had hopes of arranging a marriage between him and Princess Mary Adelaide of Cambridge, Queen Victoria's gross-ly-overweight first cousin who subsequently married Prince Franz of Teck and was Queen Mary's mother. Caroline appealed for help in pulling off this ambition to the Emperor Napoleon III, who, together with Empress Eugenie was known to be a good friend of Queen Victoria's. Napoleon III told her that he doubted that the Supreme Governor of the Church of England would allow a marriage between any member of her family and someone whose family's income derived from gambling. He proposed instead that Albert marry his cousin, Lady Mary Victoria Douglas-Hamilton, daughter of the 11th Duke of Hamilton and his wife, Princess Marie of Baden. Princess Marie's parents had been the Grand Duke of Baden and Stéphanie de Beauharnais, a cousin of the Empress Joséphine and the adopted daughter of Napoleon I. As such, the blood of both the old and new dynasties of Europe flowed through Lady Mary's veins. Her close relations included Queen Carola of Saxony, the King of Bavaria, Queen Stephanie of Portugal, King Carol I of Romania, the Empress Consort of Tsar Alexander I of Russia, the last Vasa Queen Consort of Sweden, and King Albert I of the Belgians. Although not quite as prestigious as a union with an English princess, the marriage was nevertheless highly desirable from the Monégasque point of view. The double duke, of Hamilton as well as Brandon, owned a particularly fine art collection, with works by Van Dyck, Canaletto, Lely, Raeburn and Kneller. The Hamiltons had vast land holdings in Scotland that put their future son-in-law's estates into the shade. The Prince's Palace in Monaco did not compare favourably with Hamilton Palace in Lanarkshire or even their secondary residence, Lennoxlove House in East Lothian. However, if the Duke of Hamilton and Brandon agreed to the marriage, his daughter would become a sovereign princess and any grandson through her would become a sovereign prince with his own throne. One, moreover, who would thereafter share a family connection with the throne of France. No one could have imagined that the Bonaparte dynasty would be hounded into exile within eighteen months or that the reigning Grand Duke of Baden would be the first of the German princes to hail King Wilhelm I of Prussia as the new Kaiser of a united Germany at occupied Versailles, while the Emperor Napoleon III remained a prisoner of the Germans.

The marriage was therefore agreed and took place at the Château de Marchais on the 21st September 1869. It was not a success. Mary could abide neither the heat of the Mediterranean nor the confines of Monaco, and seems to have had little more regard for her blue-stocking husband. According to the *grande cocotte* La Belle Otero, who later had an affair with him, Albert suffered from erectile dysfunction. Despite this, he rose to his duty and within ten months of the marriage, Mary had produced a son, Louis Honoré Charles Antoine Grimaldi, born on the 12th May

1870 in Baden-Baden.

Two months later, the Franco-Prussian War broke out and Albert went to war, fighting on the French side. The Hereditary Princess of Monaco found herself in the invidious position of being a member of two families on opposing sides of the war. Determined not to have her life ruined by remaining with a man for whom she had no regard while her mother's relations were on the opposing side, she left him, taking their son with her. The marriage had lasted for less than a year.

It would take another decade for the Catholic Church to annul it, on 3rd January 1880, but Mary did not even wait for her father-in-law Prince Charles III to dissolve it civilly on 28th July. On the 2nd June, she married Count (after 1911 Prince) Tassilo Festetics de Tolna, taking up residence in the immense Baroque Festetics Palace at Keszthely in Hungary. Their descendants include the Agnelli heir Prince Egon von Fürstenberg, who was married to the fashion designer Diane von Fürstenberg, and the 12th Prince of Schwarzenberg, twice Foreign Minister of the Czech Republic and owner of the magnificent Baroque Schwarzenberg Palace in central Vienna. Its gardens, which are closed to the public, must be one of the largest acreages owned privately in a capital city. When I was there, I could not help noting that it is as if Buckingham Palace was owned by a private citizen.

Albert remarried six weeks after his father's death. There is no doubt that Charles III would not have agreed to his son marrying the Dowager Duchess of Richelieu and, without that consent, Albert would have jeopardised his position as heir. Before Court mourning was at an end he took as his bride the 31 year old widow, born Marie Alice Heine in New Orleans, USA. The new Princess Alice was the first consort of a European monarch who had been born Jewish. Although not widely known, her father had been a successful building contractor and property developer in Louisiana, and while the penniless Richelieu family had gratefully opened their arms when Alice's father opened his coffers and refilled theirs with a sizeable dowry, there was no question of Prince Charles III, who no longer needed anyone else's money, doing likewise. In the next century, when another successful, but Roman Catholic, builder's daughter married into the Grimaldi family, John B. Kelly's trade also caused adverse reaction, so it takes no imagination to appreciate how much more undesirable Herr Heine's was. Fortunately, the Dowager Duchess had converted to Catholicism to marry her French duke, so religion was not an obstacle, though her race had been to Charles III.

While Grace Kelly's nationality was not an issue – indeed, it would prove to be the engine driving Princess Grace's worldwide regard to ever-new heights - Alice's German roots were even more problematic than her Jewish ancestry. Monaco's protector France had lost the Franco-Prussian War and anti-German feeling had not subsided in France. If anything, it had increased along with Germany's growing power. Though Alice's father, Michel Heine, had been born in France, he was also the scion of a well-known German-Jewish family. Heinrich Heine, whose lyric poetry had been set to music in the form of Lieder by Schubert and Schumann, was a cousin, and a very well-known one at that. The combination of German with Jewish was fatal to any prospect of Charles III allowing the marriage.

Alice had been widowed at the age of thirty two. Her young son became the 8th and last Duke of Richelieu, which was a prestigious French title, and while her daughter would marry equally well, becoming first Countess then Princess de la Rochefoucauld-Montbel, her many assets held no appeal for Charles III, though they did for Albert I. Despite this, Alice never had children with Albert. There has been the suspicion that it might have been inappropriate for the Monégasque throne to be occupied by a prince who was claimed to be a Jew by Orthodox Jewry, but there is no proof that this was actually the case.

At first, the marriage went well. Alice was as entrepreneurial as the late Princess Caroline. She threw herself into the role of consort, not only fulfilling the conventional charitable and official functions of a sovereign's consort, but seeking out, and fostering, new money-making schemes. Not only did she have a good head for business, but, in keeping with the Heine heritage, she was a highly cultivated woman who understood what a lure culture would be to the principality's visitors. She therefore set about turning Monaco into one of Europe's great cultural centres, upping the game of its opera, ballet, concert and theatre productions by involving the top music directors, conductors, and performers of the day. In 1892, the renowned Raoul Gunsbourg was appointed Director of the Salle Garnier. The following year saw the premiere performance of Hector Berlioz's *The Damnation of Faust*. This set the tone for a series of world-class premieres, including Feodor Chaliapin in Massenet's *Don Quichotte*, Saint Saens's Hélène, Mascagni's *Amica*, and Puccini's *La Rondine*. More ordinary - if such a word can be used - performances included Dame Nellie Melba and Enrico Caruso in *La Bohème* and *Rigoletto*, and Francesco Tamagno in *Otello*. The great Russian impresario Sergei Diaghilev was encouraged to bring his itinerant *Ballets Russes* to Monte Carlo. This kicked off an association which would outlive both Alice and Diaghilev. Every dancer of any consequence would thereafter perform in Monte Carlo. Leonide Massine and George Balanchine were the choreographers. Composers included Stravinsky, Debussy, and Prokofiev, while set designers included Picasso, Kandinsky, Benois and Matisse, with costumes designed by the likes of Leon Bakst and Coco Chanel. In confirmation of the special status Monaco held in the existence of the *Ballets Russes*, after the great man's death in 1929, Diaghilev's company became known as the *Ballet Russe de Monte-Carlo*.

It was Alice's cultural success that would lead to her downfall. In 1894, the English composer Isidore de Lara went to Monte Carlo to stage his opera, *Amy Robsart*, which had been well received at Covent Garden the year before. He and the Ruling Princess hit it off and he was invited to remain in Monaco. As he enhanced the opera scene in his new homeland, he entered into the most productive and successful period of his career. *Moina* was produced there in 1897, followed by *Messaline* two years later, to great acclaim.

During these years, while Alice was building up Monte Carlo's cultural profile and developing an ever-closer working relationship with de Lara, Albert was enjoying being seen in public with the greatest courtesan of the age. Born Agustina del Carmen Otero Iglesias, but known as Caroline or La Belle Otero, she started life in the slums of Spain, working her way up from being a maid to a dancer at the Folies Bergère in Paris, before graduating to the bed of some of the most powerful men of the age. Aside from Albert, her lovers included King Edward VII, the Kings of Serbia and Spain, the Russian Grand Dukes Nicholas and Peter, the Duke of

Westminster and the writer Gabriele D'Annunzio. The men who squired La Belle Otero not only paid handsomely for the privilege – she made a fortune of some $30m by the time she retired during the First World War – but also earned public approbation for their sexual prowess. Although she was an accomplished *grande horizontale* who earned her keep both in and out of bed, Albert's motives in flaunting their relationship have to be suspected. It must have been doubly humiliating for his wife, knowing that he could not function adequately with her, while believing that he was sexually proficient with Otero. And that the whole world could see what was going on. She was not to know that the problems she had with her husband were shared by *la grande horizontale*. She therefore put her foot down and demanded that Otero be banned from Monaco.

It seems to be around this time that Alice and de Lara began an affair. Putting aside the humiliation of Albert's public affair and their own unsatisfactory sex life, he often left Alice alone for extended periods as he explored the seas and poles. There was an air of inevitability about the abandoned, sex-starved and passionate princess falling in love with the attractive and impassioned composer in residence. Also inevitably, word of their affair got back to Albert. One evening, in full view of the audience at the Salle Garnier, he slapped her across the face, exposing himself and Alice to quite unnecessary ridicule. This was the death knell of their marriage, and, on the 30th May 1902, they were legally separated in Monaco. Alice moved back to France, but they never divorced, so that, when he died in Paris twenty years later, she became the Dowager Princess of Monaco.

Without Alice's perspicacity, popularity, and presence, Albert gradually became unpopular. The people of Monaco had not benefited from the wealth of the state because they were excluded by law from employment within the gaming industry. As that was effectively the only game in town, and there were neither farmlands nor industries nor factories in the state, unemployment amongst the native population was high. So too was dissatisfaction as the Monégasques saw outsiders come into the principality to fill jobs they were legally excluded from holding.

To be protected against the evils of the gaming industry was one thing, but to be protected against its fruit another. In March 1910 a delegation demanded that the prince cease being an absolute monarch and grant his subjects a constitution and parliamentary representation; that he terminate the monopoly over the SBM of the Blanc family, in the shape of François' son Camille and his son-in-law Prince Roland Bonaparte; that he replace the French state functionaries with Monégasques; that he separate his financial affairs from the state's; and that he invest his money at home rather than in France. Albert acquiesced to the demands, but the unrest continued as the people demanded an end to French domination of their country's government and economy. It culminated with an angry mob storming the Prince's Palace. While they looted it, Albert escaped with the help of his Praetorian guard, the Compagnie des Carabiniers du Prince, to France, where he remained until the unrest died down and it was safe to return home.

The Monégasque Constitution of 1911 was promulgated on the 5th January. It is still the shortest written constitution in the world. Although the Ruling Prince still held considerable power, he was no longer technically an absolute monarch because he created three branches of government which would advise him. He nevertheless retained the highest executive power, with the power to suspend the constitution, which he did during the First World War.

The French government used the Monégasque constitutional crisis to deprive the lawful heir-in-line to the throne of his rights of succession, employing what Count Louis de Causans, one of its victims, has rightly called 'a sleight of hand'. The problem was that Albert's immediate heir was his son, Louis, a forty one year old bachelor with no legitimate children. Under the house rules, Louis's successor was his first cousin, Prince Wilhelm of Urach, Count of Württemberg and 2nd Duke of Urach.

Albert's sister Florestine had married in 1863 the morganatic Count Friedrich of Württemberg, cousin of the King of Württemberg, following the death of his first wife, the Empress Josephine's granddaughter Théodolinde de Beauharnais, Princess of Leuchtenberg. Four years later he was created Duke of Urach and his son with Florestine became a prince. Two years later, Friedrich died, leaving his son the 2nd Duke a considerable fortune, including Liechtenstein Castle.

At the time, the kingdom of Württemberg was far more important than the principality of Monaco, but Princess Florestine, by then known more formally as the Duchess of Urach, nevertheless ensured that Wilhelm and his younger brother Josef were raised as Francophile princes of Monaco as well as loyal Württembergers, in the knowledge that the throne of Monaco might be theirs one day. They were out of the line of succession to the throne of Württemberg, being morganatic, so their true interest lay in Francophile Monaco rather than Francophone Germany.

By 1910, French paranoia about Germany had reached such heights that all sense of morality, rationality and proportion were willingly sacrificed in pursuit of national self-interest by the French state. Its foreign policy since the loss of Alsace and Lorraine to Germany in 1871 had been to contain German power and regain its lost north-eastern provinces. At the Quai d'Orsay, they feared that a sovereign prince of Monaco with loyalties divided between Germany and Monaco might allow the German navy to create a U-boat base at Monaco, thereby endangering the French naval base at Toulon 150km away. The prospect of the German armed forces topping and tailing France caused such panic in Paris that they refused to countenance the Duke of Urach acceding to the throne of Monaco. They therefore took advantage of the Constitutional Crisis of 1910 to lean heavily on Prince Albert, forcing him to alter the line of succession to exclude his two nephews.

Although it had not hitherto been widely known, Louis, though a bachelor with no legitimate children, was the father of an illegitimate daughter. Charlotte Louise Juliette de Monaco had been born in Algeria in 1898 to Marie Juliette Louvet, the daughter of the prince's laundress. She was a divorced mother of two and a hostess in a Montmartre nightclub when she met Louis through her mother the year before their daughter's birth. At a time when class was of the greatest significance, it says much about the complexities of Louis's personality that he could form a close relationship only with a low-class songstress and washerwoman's daughter, and that, though a relatively young man when securing the succession to the throne became such an important issue, he nevertheless lacked the motivation to father children with what would then have been called a 'suitable' wife, preferring instead to legitimise his sole offspring.

Charlotte had been raised by her mother, but acknowledged in 1900 by her father.

Under pressure from France, on the 5th May 1911, Prince Albert passed an Ordinance decreeing Charlotte a legitimate member of the Grimaldi dynasty and the heiress to her father the Hereditary Prince. This knocked the Duke of Urach and his younger brother Prince Karl out of the line of succession, causing both personal and diplomatic problems for all concerned. Not the least of these was the illegality of the act, for the Monégasque House Law Statutes of 1882 rendered Charlotte's elevation invalid. In an attempt to regularise the irregularity, while the First World War ground on and the prospect of a German prince of Monaco continued to fill the French with ever-mounting horror, Albert was prevailed upon yet again to break his Principality's laws by issuing another Ordinance. On the 30th October 1918, less than a fortnight before the end of the war, Albert gave Louis permission to adopt his daughter. The object of the exercise was to legitimise her legally, but again the act, when it took place in Paris on the 16th May 1919, was invalid. The Monégasque Civil Code (Articles 240 and 243) required the adoptive parent to be at least fifty years old and the adoptive child twenty-one. Although the 1918 Ordinance changed the child's age limit to eighteen, thereby allowing the twenty year old Charlotte to be legally adopted by her father, it did not alter the adoptive father's age requirements. Louis, being 48, fell short by two years, thereby invalidating the adoption.

Nevertheless, Albert bestowed the traditional title of the heir to the throne upon his granddaughter, making her HSH the Duchess of Valentinois. She was married off the following year to the half-Mexican homosexual scion of one of pre-revolutionary France's great noble houses. A descendant of Marie Antoinette's greatest friend – Gabrielle, Duchesse de Polignac who dropped down dead when told of that queen's execution –Count Pierre de Polignac had his surname changed to Grimaldi and was created a Prince of Monaco. He fathered two children with Princess Charlotte, Princess Antoinette Louise Alberte Suzanne (1920-2011), and Prince Rainier Louis Henri Maxence Bertrand (1923-2005) before they took to leading separate lives.

According to his good friend, the British writer James Lees-Milne, Pierre's marriage collapsed under the weight of his homosexuality and Charlotte's promiscuity. They were judicially separated on the 20th March 1930 and divorced in Monaco on the 18th February 1933. In yet another instance of the Ruling Family making exhibitions of themselves when dignity required silence, Louis II was quoted in the press as vowing to 'call out the Monégasque Army if the prince ever set foot in the principality again.' Weeks later, he lifted the banishment and provided Pierre with an annuity of 500,000 francs per annum. Thereafter, Prince Philippe of Monaco, who was judged to be so well bred that you could barely hear him speak, conducted himself with aristocratic exactitude while his ex-wife 'betrayed her washerwoman origins' according to a later Duchesse de la Rochefoucauld.

By then, the Grimaldis were systematically portrayed in the press as little better than tasteless jokes. The legitimisation of Charlotte had made a mockery not only of the law but of the state of Monaco. Much of the prestige that the family had managed to build up in the previous century was lost, along with the true successors to the throne. In royal circles it was felt that only a republican regime like the French could have been naïve enough to think that the Duke of Urach would have put Germany's interests before his own state's. It also meant that the throne would be occupied by the descendants of a washerwoman rather than a king. Since the values of the day were not as egalitarian as they subsequently became towards the close of the twentieth century, this was a difficult stain to wash away. The family was fully aware of the sensitivities of the situation, and Charlotte therefore wisely renounced her rights of succession the day before Rainier's twenty-first birthday on the 30th May, 1944. After he succeeded his grandfather in 1949, she moved to the Château de Marchais, turning it into a rehabilitation centre for former convicts, one of whom she lived with: the notorious former jewel thief René Girier aka René la Canne (René the Cane). Colourful, undoubtedly, but hardly the sort of conduct to uphold the dignity of a ruling house.

Charlotte's father Louis II's reign straddled the troubled period between the end of the First and Second World Wars. By 1919, the world had changed out of all recognition. Many of the royals who had flocked to Monte Carlo, spending vast sums in the hotels and losing even vaster ones at the gaming tables, had been dethroned. It was something of a relief to Louis when the renowned arms dealer and entrepreneur, Sir Basil Zaharoff, rescued the debt-ridden SBM. The Second World War saw Monaco try to preserve its neutrality by adopting a pro-Vichy policy, but even this did not prevent the Italians from occupying it. Following the Italian surrender of 1943, the Germans moved in for a year, pulling out on the 25th August 1944. Monaco was then liberated by the Americans, and the serious business of reconstruction began.

For the principality, as with much of Europe, the period following the Second World War was more trying than after the First. Money was in short supply, austerity everywhere. Although Prince Louis II was still a rich man, his country was not. As it struggled, its 76 year old monarch surprised everyone by marrying an actress from Rheims thirty years his junior in 1946. Ghislaine Marie Françoise Dommanget was neither a great beauty nor a great star, and the marriage hardly added lustre to the tarnished crown. However, she was discreet, staying out of the limelight for the three years she was Princess Consort, and remained in the background, living sedately in France, for the next half century. She died, virtually unknown and unacknowledged, aged 90, in 1991.

Once Rainier succeeded to the throne, in 1949, he began the mammoth task of reconstruction. This was easier said than done. The days of royalty, private trains, and yachts were over. The old elite was broke, the new elite not yet properly nascent. Then Rainier had the good fortune to meet the Greek shipping magnate Aristotle Onassis. He encouraged him to buy up a majority holding of SBM shares, with the understanding that Onassis's shipping empire would benefit while he developed Monaco back into the mecca it had once been. Within a decade, however, it became apparent that the prince and the Greek had different visions for Monaco. Onassis wanted Monaco to remain primarily a gaming resort while Rainier intended to reduce its reliance upon gaming by it becoming a tax haven, commercial and banking centre, an international but more downmarket tourist attraction than hitherto. He also intended to spearhead a massive real estate development scheme by building upwards and outwards, onto land reclaimed from the sea. It was his ambition to flip the proportion of income generated by the gaming industry from 95% to something insignificant. For the next four or so years, the two men were at odds until, in 1966, Rainier, who in reality was almost as powerful as an absolute monarch despite the Constitution, simply approved the creation of 600,000 new shares in SBM which would be permanently held by the state. In one fell swoop, he had reduced the Golden Greek's shareholding from 52% to a third. Although Onassis challenged the act in the Supreme Court of Monaco, it not very surprisingly ruled in favour of its Ruling Prince. He then sold his shareholding to the state for US$9.5m, which in today's money would amount to some $300m.

This epic struggle for control of Monaco's destiny was played out against a welter of publicity, all of which helped to glamorise the country and elevate it beyond its tiny acreage. Onassis and his mistress, the great diva Maria Callas, were arguably one of the five most famous couples in the world. And, after 1956, when Rainier married the Oscar-winning Hollywood star Grace Kelly, so too were the Prince and Princess of Monaco. Grace was justifiably regarded as being one of the most beautiful and glamorous women in the world. She needed to do nothing to attract column inches. Being was enough for Princess Grace. Not, it has to be said, that her definition of being did not include the serious underwater paddling that all graceful swans undertake as they glide through life. I knew her very slightly and we also had a friend in common, the Australian authoress Gwen Robyns, who had written her biography and approached the publisher Jeffrey Simmons, of W.H. Allen, to write mine. Since I was a stripling of twenty five at the time, I thought a biography premature; nor did I want the attention one would bring, but we did remain on cordial terms. Princess Grace used to see her every time she came to England, and even, on occasion, stayed overnight with her.

The fabled Grace had three children with Rainier. All of them have had personal lives that were as convoluted as those of their ancestors'. The eldest child Caroline (1957-), in her quest for true love, made a wildly inappropriate first marriage to the boulevardier Philippe Junot. They were divorced after two years. She then married, while pregnant, the handsome heir to an Italian industrial fortune, Stefano Casiraghi. He was killed in a speed-boat accident aged 30 after six years of marriage and three children. She then proceeded to make a public spectacle of herself as the marriage of her good friend Chantal Hochuli to Ernst August, Prince of Hanover, broke up. Rumours circulated that the marriage was under pressure because Caroline had fallen in love with the head of the House of Hanover, the former ruling dynasty whose last United Kingdom monarch had been Queen Victoria's uncle King William IV. Caroline's very public response to the conjecture about the part she might have played in the collapse of her friend's marriage was to shave her head, generating, in that one act, cascades of media attention questioning her motives. The Hanovers duly divorced and Ernst married Caroline. One daughter and several incidents later, they separated. All of which was yet more fodder for the tabloids.

The youngest child of Rainier and Grace was, if anything, even wilder. Stephanie (1965-) was her mother's heartstring. She could do no wrong, no matter the antics she got up to. Grace herself used to confess that she found it difficult to say no to this favoured child of hers, even when she knew she should be putting her foot down. I remember the seventeen year old Stephanie accompanying her mother to the Red Cross Ball in London, of which I was one of the organisers, shortly before her death. It was obvious who was in charge of that relationship, though, it has to be said, Stephanie was a sweet child. Later on, when she was grown up and I met her in Monaco, I found her to be an equally delightful adult. Nevertheless, it would have taken a brave person to be either her parent or her man. She became a model, a pop singer, and a perfumier, while dating a host of hot 'second generation' names such as the movie star Jean Paul Belmondo's son Paul, Alain Delon's son Anthony, and actors such as Rob Lowe, before settling down with her bodyguard, Daniel Ducruet. They had a son, Louis Robert Paul Ducruet (1992-) and a daughter Pauline Grace Maguy Ducruet (1994-) without benefit of clergy. Neither child was in the line of succession until they married in 1995. They divorced the following year, after which she gave birth to yet another daughter without bothering to marry. Although Stephanie declined to name the father on the child's birth certificate, Camille Marie Kelly Gottlieb (1998-) has confirmed that her father is Jean Raymond Gottlieb, a palace guard, former Paris gendarme and ski instructor, who was Head of Security for the princess.

In sophisticated circles, 'fraternisation with the staff' has always been frowned upon. It puts both employer and employee at a disadvantage, complicates what would otherwise be a straightforward relationship, and is regarded as one of the most inappropriate bases for a personal relationship. But Stephanie was not finished with shocking traditional-ists. In 2001, she moved, with her three children, into the circus caravan of her latest lover, a married elephant trainer named Franco Knie. A year later, she was back in Monaco with her offspring. She had leapt from the elephant trainer's bed to that of another member of the Knie circus, a Portuguese acrobat named Adans Lopez Peres. They were married for a year and two months, the divorce coming through on 24th November 2004.

In upper class circles, marriage has traditionally been a union of more than just man and wife. There was also the question of suitability. This included such elements as family background, social station, fitting in with each other's worlds. Although many of the more worldly criteria which used to motivate unions no longer exist, few families, even nowadays, would grant their members the licence with which the Grimaldis have endowed themselves.

They have been criticised for having a propensity towards 'rough trade'. Whether that is so is not for me to judge, but they do have an earthiness which is pronounced. Even Ernst Hanover is earthy. Alongside this has been an admirable colour-blindness, as exhibited by the present Ruling Prince, Albert II, and his first cousin Christian, Baron de Massy.

Prince Albert II is the father of two natural children of colour, both born while he was a bachelor waiting to inherit the throne. Plainly, the Grimaldis are a family who follow where their sexual attractions lead, so it was almost inevitable, as people of colour joined the mainstream, that they would end up forming relationships with women of colour. By his mid-thirties, Albert was showing just how colour blind as well as class blind he was. With all the women in the world at his athletic grasp to choose from, he managed to pursue a relationship with an American from California named Tamara Jean Rotolo. This was discreet and sexual, and, at a time when the AIDS epidemic ensured that the only people one had unprotected sex with were those one trusted, trusting. In mid-1991, unprotected sex resulted in Albert impregnating Tamara. Their daughter,

Jazmin Grace Grimaldi was born on 4th March, 1992, and registered on her Riverside County birth certificate as Albert's.

I was told that Prince Rainier was so distressed when he found out about the birth of this granddaughter that he ordered his son not to have anything to do with the child. He had spent his whole life trying to live down the déclassé behaviour of his mother and sister. With Princess Grace, he had converted Monaco from being a joke into a world-wide success that people everywhere took seriously. The Grimaldis were now received by all the reigning royals of Europe as fully-paid up members of the club, attending weddings and other royal events with the respect he and Grace had striven so hard to achieve. He saw no reason to have his heir diminish his hard work. Unfortunately, this resulted in Tamara having to sue Albert through the California courts for recognition of their daughter's paternity.

In the short term, Albert's hands were tied by his father. He had no choice but to ignore paternity legally, contesting the lawsuit on the grounds of jurisdiction. As Superior Court Judge Graham Anderson Cribbs put it, there was 'insufficient connection between Albert and the State of California to justify hearing a suit.' Privately, Albert could assist his daughter, but not publicly, at least not until Rainier was dead. Only then could he agree to the DNA test which proved that the child was his. Public acknowledgement came through his lawyer, who announced on the 31st May 2006 that Jazmin Grimaldi was his daughter. He also tendered her an invitation to study and live in Monaco. She is often seen in Monaco nowadays.

The birth of Albert's second illegitimate child of colour took place on the 24th August 2003, when Eric Alexandre Stephane Tossoukpe was born to a flight attendant named Nicole Tossoukpe. The daughter of a merchant in Togo, where she was raised, she worked for Air France. It was while working the cabin that she offered Albert a drink; he asked for her number; she gave it to him, and a relationship lasting several years began. This time, however, it involved protected sex. When Rainier found out about it, he exploded, demanding that Albert end it. According to Nicole, who changed her name on the 10th November 2004 to the French-sounding Coste –her son's name has also been altered to the more

European and regal Alexandre Grimaldi-Coste – Albert impregnated her during a tryst to celebrate her 31st birthday. Notwithstanding his father's wish, Albert continued to visit both mother and child, to whose upkeep he contributed financially. According to Coste, he also promised to acknowledge little Alexandre's paternity if DNA tests confirmed it.

By this time, Rainier was dying. Though the Ruling Prince could console himself with the knowledge that his aims for Monaco had been so successful that gaming now constituted less than 5% of the economy, he was displeased by the direction Albert's private life had taken. It was therefore hardly feasible that Albert, a dutiful if wayward son, would disturb his father's last days with public recognition of a child which was the fruit of a union of which he had disapproved. Rainier died on the 6th April 2005. Coste then played her trump card, displaying a degree of impatience that smacked of insensitivity, considering that Albert had just acceded to the throne. On the grounds that he had not fulfilled his promise, she went public in an interview in Paris Match. As expected, this caused a media storm. Albert declined to comment, using the existence of Court mourning for his father as the reason for his silence. But the furore did have the desired effect of forcing the prince's hand. On the 6th July 2005, his lawyer, Thierry Lacoste, issued a statement on his behalf acknowledging paternity. I am reliably informed by friends who live in Monaco that Alexandre has been incorporated into the extended family. He is often seen in Monaco, where he enjoys a good relationship with his father and step-mother. The young man's two half-brothers and mother, who lives in England, are never seen in fashionable circles.

Neither of Albert's natural children is in the line of succession to the Monégasque throne. Article 10 of the Constitution of Monaco, as amended by Prince Rainier on the 2nd April 2002, states that only direct and legitimate descendants of Monaco's monarch or siblings, who have been married with the monarch's consent, and are citizens of Monaco, may accede to the throne. Article 227 of the Monégasque Civil Code further clarifies the issue. An illegitimate child who is the product of a non-adulterous union is legitimised if the parents marry (with monarchic consent), as happened when Princess Stephanie married Daniel Ducruet, thereby legitimising their two children who had been born out of wedlock.

But if the couple fails to marry, or marries without the sovereign's consent, the children remain barred from the line of succession. A child of an adulterous union cannot be legitimised or included in the line of succession under any circumstances, nor can adopted children accede, although they were able to do so before Rainier's ruling. His mother, of course, was not only adopted and illegitimate but also the product of a relationship which never resulted in marriage, yet she became the Hereditary Princess until she renounced her rights to succession to Rainier. Obviously, he was ensuring that Albert II, when he acceded to the throne, would never be able to pull the sleight of hand which Albert I had done, thereby foisting Charlotte into the line of succession.

By the time Rainier made this ruling, he was only too aware that his days were numbered. A sixty-a-day smoker, he had never got over Grace's death in a car crash in 1982, according to his own children. Though his reign had been nationally successful, his family life was tumultuous. He had turned Monaco into one of the richest per capita countries in the world. He had increased the land mass of his tiny state, retained sovereign power while earning the regard of the people, and seen off the attempt of his sister Antoinette to seize the throne for her son, with herself as the regent. This power play had been concocted with the connivance of her lover (later second husband) Dr. Jean-Charles Rey, President of the National Council (Parliament) of Monaco and their allies in the French Government. It resulted in Antoinette's relations with her brother frosting over, though she and her three children remained in the line of succession. Only when Grace had provided the heir and the spare in the form of Caroline and Albert, did Rainier relax.

Antoinette had been as troublesome personally as his three children would prove to be. Grace played peacemaker, sometimes more successfully than others, with the result that there was no open rupture in the family. Nevertheless, Antoinette blazed a trail of unsuitable lovers and illegitimate children that her nieces and nephew would follow. In the mid-1940s, she became romantically involved with a dashing Monégasque lawyer and international tennis champion named Alexandre-Athenase Noghes. His father Anthony Noghes had founded the world-famous Monaco Grand Prix in 1929, which did so much to put the pocket-sized principality on the map. In 1979, Rainier allowed the last turn of the Monaco circuit to be renamed Virage Noghes in honour of his troublesome sister's first father-in-law.

Antoinette's love life was every bit as convoluted as her mother's had been. Louis II refused to countenance a marriage between his man-eating granddaughter and his tennis-playing subject. This did not deter the head-strong Antoinette, who duly produced three children out of wedlock: Elisabeth-Anne (1947-), Christian Louis (1949-), and Christine (1951-1989). All were surnamed Grimaldi at birth, but after his accession, Rainier created Antoinette Baronne de Massy in her own right on the 15th November 1951, permitting the children to adopt the aristocratic *particule* de Massy. Two and a half weeks later, on the 4th December 1951, Antoinette married Noghes in Genoa with Rainer's consent. This made her children heirs to the throne and created the opening through which she and her ambitious lover sought to depose Rainier.

Because the Grimaldis are a small family, there was a strong incentive to keep the treacherous Antoinette in the fold even after her attempts at seizing power. She was allowed to divorce Noghes in 1954, and remarried Rey in The Hague on the 2nd December 1961. This marriage too ended in divorce in 1974. Her last husband, whom she married in Monaco with the approval of her brother on 28th July 1983, was John Gilpin, the Principal Dancer of the London Festival Ballet and the long-term friend of the renowned dancer/choreographer Sir Anton Dolin. They had met when he danced for the Grand Ballet du Marquis de Cuevas in Monte Carlo, showing yet again how the ballet continued to influence the lives of the Monaco Ruling Family. Six weeks later, he dropped down dead of a heart attack, leaving Antoinette to her increasingly eccentric existence at her residence in Èze, France's perfume capital, with her growing brood of dogs and cats.

If Antoinette's taste in men combined physical appeal with unconventionality, this is a trait she shared with her son as well as her nephew. Albert and his first cousin Christian Louis, Baron de Massy, have shown themselves to be disinterested in class as well as colour. Whomever they have been drawn to, they have pursued, irrespective of worldly considerations that others might have expected would influence them. Indeed, they have both demonstrated in their choices that they are as colour blind as their Habsburg and Liechtenstein cousins. They have also demonstrated that they are most comfortable amongst women whose heritage is black, irrespective of whether those women are black or not. Albert is now married to Charlene Wittstock, the former Olympic swimmer of Zimbabwean-South African stock. While she is white, you only need to scratch the surface of a white citizen of a black country before you come upon the layered, multi-racial culture that is the rich heritage of all citizens of countries of colour. This is as true today as it was during the time of the Empress Josephine, when her West Indian languor was much commented upon. Irrespective of colour, there is a genuine affinity between all the races of black countries. While this sometimes co-exists with discomfiting remnants of the past, it explains why all citizens of countries of colour are nowadays regarded as being members of the black community. White, brown, yellow or black, Zimbabweans, South Africans, Mozambiqueans, Jamaicans, and all the other natives of those countries of colour share a rich racial identity which gives their characters a multi-racial aspect, irrespective of the colour of their skin. With that comes a heritage that is neither black nor white, but uniquely both black and white.

Christian de Massy's fourth and last wife is a lady of colour from Guadeloupe in the French West Indies named Cecile Irene Gelabale (1968-). She was already the mother of Brice Souleyman Gelabale (1987) when they married. He adopted the boy, giving him the surname de Massy. Although Christian de Massy is not actually a member of the Ruling Family of Monaco, patrilineality being the determining factor, because it is so small, anyone with a close blood connection is loosely regarded as being a member. As Christian was also in the line of succession at the time of his marriage, his marriage had to be approved by his uncle, failing which issue of it would not be in the line of succession.

On the 15th January 1997, Cecile de Massy gave birth to a son, Antoine, who would be raised between Miami, Florida, USA, and Monaco. He attended the local College Charles III, named for his ancestor, in Monaco, and lived there while his mother went from strength to strength as an acknowledged member of the extended Ruling Family. She founded the socially desirable and financially successful charitable Ladies Lunch Monaco, became a Vice-President of the Night Associations Monaco, was presented with the insignia of a commander by Albert, was a Vice-President and Honorary Committee Member of the International Academy of Self-Defence and Combat Sports of Monaco, and, following Albert's marriage, she and Princess Charlene attended each other's events, demonstrating public support for each other, as well as private friendship.

Meanwhile, Christian de Massy was appointed Economic Attaché to the Embassy of Monaco in Washington by Albert in 2010, prior to which he was the Monégasque chargé d'affaires for the Caribbean and Latin America. Albert had discovered what the British Royal Family would later learn when Meghan Markle married into it. An attractive, capable, intelligent, personable woman of colour is an excellent addition to a reigning family in this multi-cultural, multi-racial, multi-national world of ours.

Chapter Nine

WITHOUT DOUBT, NO MODERN royal family surpasses the British in terms of prestige. Traditionally, the House of Windsor has been careful to neither buck nor precipitate trends. It breaks new ground when it is safe to do so, when it knows that that is what the people want. Its genius has been to alter its course to accord with the majority of its citizens, while at the same time providing a link to the past and being seen to be guided into the future by moral precepts such as compassion and the good of society as a whole. It has been careful to present itself as representing the entire Nation, even those parts of it that have no time for the monarchy. As the Nation has become more multi-cultural, despite such diversity not been easy to pull off, the Royal Family has nevertheless proven itself adept at doing so.

Time and again, since James II lost his throne in 1688, the British royals have demonstrated excellent adaptive skills. They have edged forward gently while providing a link with the past and appearing to stand stiller than they, in reality, do. This has been especially true in the last fifty or so years. That said, the Royal Family has not functioned in isolation. Each of the other European royal families has had an effect upon the other, and at times, it has been difficult to tell whether the chicken or the egg has come first. For instance, Norway might have been the first country, in 2001, to have a Crown Princess who was a single mother from an ordinary background, but Britain's Princess Alexandra's daughter Marina Ogilvy was the first to marry her 'bit of rough', Paul Mowatt, in 1990, declaring in the newspapers that her parents had suggested an abortion rather than a marriage when she became pregnant. This was potent stuff, as powerful as single motherhood having moved out of the shadows into the light in less than a generation.

Although the freewheeling tendencies of the Grimaldis could be said to have been the ruling world's precursor to the Permissive Society, the reality is that, as the twentieth century progressed to its close, all but the narrowest segments of Western Society had replaced the old, traditional ways with more liberated ones. As the barriers broke down and people in all categories of society mingled in a way they had never hitherto done, each of the European royal and ruling families changed as well. These changes reflected what was happening in Western Society generally, and while one royal family could look at another and say, 'If it's fine for Lilibet/Margarethe/Hans-Adam etc., it's fine for us,' this reassuring perception in reality demonstrated that societal changes had simply worked their way up into royal circles. The concessions being made were therefore not as a result of one royal family breaking ranks and updating its customs courageously, so much as each of them being sensible enough to adapt to changing times so that their family remained reflective of the positive changes taking place more generally in society. As Franz von Habsburg observed when he remarried, the changes being made within royal circles were made so that the families could survive in the modern world.

The last twenty-five years of the twentieth century were undoubtedly a time of tremendous change in society generally. Homosexuality was legalised, miscegenation laws repealed, apartheid anathemised. Peace and love continued to reign alongside birth control, flower power, and a reduction in the colour prejudice that had blighted so much of western life for the previous two centuries. In royal circles, the criteria for marriage loosened up along with the ability of senior royals to be divorced, or to marry in a way that would formerly have been unsuitably, without adverse consequences. For instance, the 64 year old Prince Bertil of Sweden, uncle of King Carl XVI Gustaf of Sweden, Queen Margarethe of Denmark, and Queen Anne-Marie of the Hellenes, was allowed to marry his long-standing mistress, an attractive Welsh commoner named Lilian Craig, aged 61. Geriatric, certainly; romantic surely; but to have had to wait nearly a whole lifetime to marry was poignant, and their ages alone conveyed how positive changes to the criteria for marriage had become. Two years later, in 1978, Princess Margaret became Britain's first senior royal in hundreds of years to be divorced, when Tony Snowdon opportunistically used the revelation of her relationship with the landscape gardener Roddy Llewellyn to force a divorce, enabling Lord Snowdon to marry his long-standing girlfriend, Lucy Lindsay-Hogg.

In fact, in the extended royal family Margaret's divorce was not the first. Her first cousin George, Earl of Harewood, grandson of King George V and son of the late Princess Royal, Princess Mary, had actually been divorced in 1967, but that had had adverse consequences. George Harewood had been ostracised by the Royal Family, especially when it emerged that he had left his blameless first wife of nine years, the Jewish, Austrian-born concert-pianist Maria Donata Nanetta Gustava Erwina Wilhelmine (known as Marion) Stein, for the sister of the world-renowned Australian first horn of the London Symphony Orchestra. They had met by accident in the terminal used by Air France in Milan airport when fog had grounded all flights. He recounted that he had thought himself happily married until he met the Australian horn player Barry Tuckwell's divorced sister Patricia. It was 'not far from love at first sight', but the 7th Earl of Harewood was the father of three young sons: David (1950-), James (1953-), and Jeremy (1955-).

When it proved inconceivable for George and Patricia to live without each other, he asked Marion for a divorce. Marion refused, so he and Patricia 'made a conscious decision to have a child.' After their son Mark was born, George moved three miles away from the Orme Square family home in Bayswater, London, into the six-bedroom house which he had bought for Patricia. The Royal Family cut him dead: 'Not a word,' he said. It was as if he no longer existed. Not even 'a postcard'. His mother 'almost never mentioned' the situation and died without ever meeting Patricia or Mark. It was only following the death of Princess Mary, the Princess Royal and Countess of Harewood that Marion relented. George married Patricia shortly afterwards, on the 31st July 1967, and his ex-wife married Jeremy Thorpe, the leader of the Liberal Party, in 1973.

If the scandal of King George V's namesake grandson and his convoluted private life caused a scandal, and it did, it was nothing compared with what awaited Marion when she became Mrs Jeremy Thorpe. Unbeknownst to her, her new husband had had a lover named Norman Scott (aka Norman Josiffe), some ten years before. No pun intended, but Mr Scott had proven to be a pain in the butt. He had tried and failed over the years to hawk a story to the tabloids revealing his former relationship with Thorpe, while wheedling money, sympathy and everything else he could out of the MP. Thorpe's best man and loyal friend David Holmes then hired Andrew Newton, an airline pilot, to shoot Scott for a fee of a few thousand pounds. Newton lured Scott onto the moors and regrettably decided to shoot first a Great Dane which Scott aka Josiffe was tending, lest the dog try to defend his 'master'. Having killed the unfortunate Rinka, he turned the gun on Scott. It jammed. Scott fled over the moors. Newton failed to give chase, allowing him to escape. Lady Edith Foxwell, a friend of Thorpe's, expressed the view of many of the politician's supporters when she said that it was a pity he had killed the wrong dog.

While Newton was awaiting trial for possessing an unlicensed firearm with intent to endanger life, Scott was tried for the even less elegant, albeit less serious, crime of social security fraud. He used the privilege of the witness box to assert that he was being hounded by the authorities because he had had a sexual relationship with Thorpe some years before. This was rank paranoia, for there was no way Jeremy Thorpe or any other Liberal Party politician was of sufficient national importance for the authorities to spend a decade hounding someone of Scott's ilk, and for social security fraud no less, even if Thorpe and his friends had finally had enough of Scott's bleating and decided to silence him once and for all. Naturally, the press went wild. Mrs Jeremy Thorpe's position as the ex-wife of the Queen's first cousin, and mother of his heir and two spares, fanned the already incendiary story to even greater heights.

Two months later, during Newton's trial, Scott again aimed a fusillade of accusation at Thorpe regarding their sex life together, knowing that the laws of libel do not apply to testimony given in court. This once more allowed the press to quote Scott without fear of being sued for defamation. Newton was found guilty, sentenced to two years in prison, while Thorpe tried to snatch victory from the jaws of defeat with the aid of the *Sunday Times* by answering Scott's allegations under the headline: The Lies of Norman Scott.

It was to no avail. Thorpe's position as leader of the third largest party in the United Kingdom had now become untenable, and he was made to resign the leadership. Marion, however, proved what mettle she had. She stood by her husband with a loyalty and dignity that even his detractors found commendable.

Things went quiet until Newton was released from prison the following year. He then sold a story to the *London Evening News* claiming that he had been paid 'by a leading Liberal' to kill Scott. After a police investigation lasting ten months, Thorpe, Holmes and two associates were charged with incitement to murder. In May of the following year, the six week trial began. Thorpe was defended by George Carman, the leading advocate of the day, who would later represent me in various libel actions. I remember a friend whom he had torn to shreds in the witness box, despite justice and truth being on her side, advising me to hire him to defend me before the other side had a chance to instruct him to prosecute, as 'being cross-examined by George Carman is like being savaged by a rabid dog'. What no one could have prepared me for was that conferences with Carman were like being caught in the vice of a sadist. You could literally see how much he enjoyed tormenting you from the glint in his eye as he tore into you, 'playing devil's advocate' to quote him. It was hardly surprising therefore, that Carman annihilated the Crown witnesses. In his summation, the judge, Sir Joseph Donaldson Cantley, characterised Scott as a fraud, sponger, whiner and parasite, before saying: 'But of course he could still be speaking the truth.' The jury thought otherwise and acquitted all four defendants.

Tragically for Thorpe, the strain of the trial brought on Parkinson's disease, but although the trial destroyed his political career and health, it did not damage his marriage. Marion had been a loyal and public support during the trial, and remained so after it. He and Marion remained devoted to each other, and occasionally one ran across them at parties or concerts. Queen Elizabeth The Queen Mother was especially kind to Thorpe when their paths crossed.

With time, the scandal receded. The Thorpes continued to lead a low-key life accepted by their true friends, but there was no question of public rehabilitation for Jeremy. Although Marion resumed her musical life, she too kept an otherwise low profile. People like Sir Benjamin Britten, who had dropped George Harewood when he had left Marion, continued in her life, while her ex-husband and his wife continued to endure their own brand of regal Siberia. Then, the month before Charles and Diana were married, the Queen brought Lord and Lady Harewood in from the cold. The occasion was the fiftieth anniversary of the English National Opera (ENO), of which George was chairman of the board. Without fanfare or explanation, in the simple act of attending the celebrations, the Queen not only ended George and Patricia Harewood's banishment from royal favour but also confirmed the ENO as being the second most important opera company in the kingdom, after the Royal Opera. Despite this acknowledgement, there was no new cosiness with the Royal Family. As far as they were concerned, that was the extent of the rehabilitation.

Being cast out of the narrower confines of royal life might have been painful for George Harewood, but his banishment had a surprising outcome. It liberated him and the rest of the family in wholly unexpected ways. He had gone on to have an illustrious career in the musical world, while his second son would become the first great-grandson of a British king to become a rock musician and marry a black woman.

The Honourable James Lascelles is on record stating that he was '(b)lessed with musical parents.' He was also blessed with musical parents who were delightful people. He grew up in London and Yorkshire, near Leeds, where Harewood House is situated. Divorce or no divorce, the Harewood children could not have had two more magical settings in which to develop. Off my recollection, Orme Square was a large, comfortably but elegantly furnished house, while Harewood House is commonly regarded as one of the top ten historic houses in the land. Its 1,000 acre park was laid out by Capability Brown, and JMW Turner considered it beautiful enough to paint it in watercolours. The house itself is palatial, originally built to designs by Robert Adam and John Carr for the 1st Lord Harewood in the eighteenth century, and enlarged by Sir Charles Barry, architect of the Houses of Parliament, in the following century.

Some years ago, I was seated at a ball on the right hand of the present Lord Harewood when he was still Viscount Lascelles, the courtesy title used by the heir apparent to the earldom. My cousin Sir Peter Jonas had taken over from his father at the English National Opera, and his mother had also been very responsive when I asked her to see a particularly gifted pianist from Jamaica whom I knew, so our conversation took a less perfunctory path than is typical at such events. I was even able to give him a snippet of information to which he had not hitherto been privy. Although he knew that the ancestor who had built Harewood House was a rich Jamaican and Barbadian plantation owner, he did not realise that the then great trading company of Lascelles de Mercado, founded by the 1st Lord, still existed, and remained a major player in the Caribbean.

Each of the Harewood sons has had an artistic career. David, the present Earl, has been a film and TV producer. Jeremy, the youngest son, played percussion in a band and ultimately became CEO of Chrysalis Music, a music label formed under the aegis of Island Records, founded by yet another Jamaican, Chris Blackwell. They had a series of hits from such artists as Procol Harum and Jethro Tull. In 2012, he became Visiting Professor at Leeds College of Music, in keeping with the musical traditions in his family, his mother having founded the prestigious Leeds International Piano Competition with the legendary piano teacher Fanny Waterman. So there has been a synchronicity about him returning to his Yorkshire roots.

The middle son James has had the most colourful life, both personally and musically. Taught classical piano by Fanny Waterman and the drum by the distinguished percussionist Jimmy Blades, the composer John Taverner also taught him duetting on a full scale size 3 console church organ. In the early 70s he formed his first band, Global Village Trucking Company, playing keyboards while his brother Jeremy played percussion. Three years of non-stop touring resulted in a documentary being aired on the BBC, after which he went into session music, playing various keyboards including Acoustic Piano, Hammond C3, Mini Moog and Fender Rhodes. He recorded and toured with such artists as Joan Armatrading, Frank Zappa, Lee Perry, and L. Shankar, after which he explored other musical cultures in places as disparate as India and Costa Rica. He has been the house composer for the London International School of Music and has ended up teaching, running workshops for disempowered, disaffected youths around the UK in schools and estates, in the process 'giving back' to society some of the tremendous benefits with which he was born.

James Lascelles has been married three times. He first married Frederica Ann Duhrssen in Newport, Maine, USA in 1973. After two children and twelve years, they divorced. He then married Lori 'Shadow' Susan Lee, in Albuquerque, New Mexico, a pretty musician and jewellery designer with a Native American heritage. During a marriage lasting eleven years they had two children, before divorcing. Three years later, he married a Nigerian aristocrat, Joy Elias-Rilwan, an actress, an activist in the fight against AIDS, and mother of four whose uncle, Taslim Olawale Elias, had been Nigeria's Attorney-General and Chief Justice, as well as a Judge then President of the International Court of Justice. A member of the pre-independence Nigerian Constitutional Conference in London, he was one of the architects of Nigeria's post-colonial constitution. The Eliases hold the rank of chieftains amongst the Yorubas of Nigeria, so, while there might have been a colour difference between the new couple there was no class difference.

James's cousin Lilibet gave her consent to the marriage, in keeping with requirements of the Royal Marriages Act of 1772. Being an heir to the British throne, he could not have properly married without the Queen's consent, and she was pleased to give it.

Although their marriage got some attention, it was not a huge story. Presumably part of the reason is that James Lascelles, though a first cousin once removed of the Queen, has functioned so far out of the orbit of the Royal Family that the nearness of his lineal connection was negated by the distance from the royal court that he and the other members of the Harewood family had maintained ever since their father was cast out of royal circles. Nevertheless, the marriage had significance. It was the first union between a grandson of a British Princess Royal and a Sub-Saharan African. Sanctioned by the Queen, it would pave the way for another female of Sub-Saharan ancestry, when her day came.

Another marriage of colour involving the extended Royal Family, which garnered some attention but was allowed to pass without any undue comment, was that of HRH Prince Richard, Duke of Gloucester's daughter Davina (1977-). This was also sanctioned by the Queen, who gave her permission in council for her first cousin's elder daughter to marry Gary Christie Lewis on the 31ˢᵗ July 2004. He is a New Zealand born Maori whose uncle is Witi Ihimaera, the eminent author of *The Whale Rider* which was made into a film of the same name. Gary Lewis was also the first Maori to marry into the British Royal Family, for, while Davina is technically a member of the extended Royal Family, her father is a British prince, the grandson of King George V and son of Prince Henry, Duke of Gloucester, whose brothers were King George VI, the Duke of Windsor, and Prince George, Duke of Kent. You don't get more royal than that.

A day or two before the wedding, I was at Kensington Palace with some friends. The Duke of Gloucester walked into the room with his elder daughter Davina, her fiancé and some of the New Zealand relations. They were obviously giving them a tour of the palace. When she passed to within a foot of me, looking directly at me though I had never met her, I smiled and said 'Congratulations,' the way one would to anyone else in such a situation. Her response was to glower at me and, rather than say 'Thank you,' the way any normal person would, declare in as chippy a manner as any oik could summon up: 'Do you mind. This is private.' I was sorely tempted to point out to her that charm and good manners are beyond the price of rank or rubies, and clearly beyond her, while niggardly behaviour not only lets you down but prevents you from letting in the good intentions of others. Out of deference to her father, who was in the background and oblivious to his daughter's churlishness, I decided to let it pass. But her attitude gave me an unwelcome insight into her disposition, and it came as no surprise that the marriage did not last.

Nevertheless, it began promisingly enough. It took place in the private chapel at Kensington Palace, where the Gloucesters live in the largest of all the flats. Except for the duke and duchess and their two other children, Alexander, Earl of Ulster and Lady Rose Windsor, no other member of the Royal Family was in attendance. It was exclusively for close family and friends, but I can testify to the fact that there was a healthy proportion of the groom's family present. This was a positive sign, for nothing is more ominous than when there is a disparity in rank between a bride and groom and this is matched by a preponderance of representatives from one side of the aisle and under-representation from the other.

The couple had met on holiday in Bali and dated for four years before their wedding. After their 'private occasion' they returned to New Zealand, where Gary continued to work as a carpenter in the property renovation business. They lived so modestly that neighbours in their working class area were surprised to discover that she was not only a Lady, but a royal one at that. However, there was no doubt that the Queen approved of the marriage. In 2005, they were asked to the Queen's reception at Buckingham Palace for New Zealand's national rugby team, the All Blacks, and they also attended the wedding of Davina's cousin Prince William in 2011.

Six years into the marriage, Davina gave birth to a daughter named Senna Kowhai. Twenty-three months later, she produced a son, Tane Mahuta. They became the first boy and girl whose places in the line of succession to the British and Commonwealth thrones were altered following the Succession to the Crown Act 2013, which decreed that girls superseded boys if they had been born first. Senna therefore became 28th and Tane 29th in line to the throne, the only Maoris who stand a chance, no matter how remote, of becoming Queen and King of New Zealand and the United Kingdom of Great Britain and Northern Ireland. Gary and Davina Lewis were divorced in 2018.

The marriage which did more than any other to pave the way for Harry and Meghan was not the Harewood or Gloucester unions, but another which was so aristocratic, the father of the groom such a noted public figure for the last fifty years, the backlash so stinging, that when they wed, Ceawlin, Viscount Weymouth and Emma McQuiston knocked many a boulder out of the path to matrimony for the Sussexes. Had their marriage not taken place first, had what the press called 'the first black Viscountess' not broken the ice, it is likely that Harry and Meghan's coupling would have aroused far more surprise than it did.

Although I do not know Emma and last spoke to Ceawlin when he was a little boy, his father Alexander, Marquis of Bath, is an old chum of mine. I have weekended at Longleat in its heyday and over the decades we have entertained each other and been to so many of the same parties that I have lost track of most of them. Because Alexander and I were both fixtures on the social scene in the seventies, eighties and nineties, I've met many of his wifelets, including the beautiful Tara Moon, Cherri Gilham and Trudy Juggernaut-Sharma. His late brother Lord Valentine Thynne's first wife, Vickie Learmond, has been a chum of mine for nearly fifty years. I've met his wife, the aristocratic Hungarian actress Anna Gaël Gyarmathy, on several occasions, though I cannot say there was a click. She used to live in Paris, supposedly with her lover, at least until he died, while Alexander lived here, where the children, Ceawlin and Lenka, were raised.

Even amongst the aristocracy, used as it is to a variety of arrangements which would raise the eyebrows of people from less sophisticated environments, Alexander and Anna's *modus vivendi* was unique. Nevertheless, I could not help cringing on her behalf when the news was made public that she had asked her son whether he had considered the effect on the family bloodline if he proceeded with marrying Emma. According to an interview Ceawlin then gave to *The Times*, he disinvited her to his wedding. She and Alexander actually attended another wedding on the same day.

The bride's parents and family, however, were out in force. So too was the press, which gobbled up each and every tasty morsel fed to them by parents, son and daughter-in-law. Public sympathy was reserved for the bridal couple, at least insofar as the press was concerned. Anna was deemed to have committed an unpardonable solecism by not welcoming Emma with open arms, thereby establishing the precedent that mixed marriages in elite English circles must be greeted with open enthusiasm, failing which the disapproving parties are to be held up to public contempt and condemnation. There is no longer any room for understanding the values of the past. Those who hold them must be silent or suffer the consequences of being spurned, the way Lady Bath was. She was not only disallowed from attending the wedding, but was also banned from seeing her grandchildren when they were born, and from being a part of such events as christenings. Moreover, this exclusion took place in the full glare of publicity. No one condemned the son for such a draconian take on a viewpoint which had been standard a generation before. The impression was that he was right to protect his children against his mother's old-fashioned attitudes. Giving her a second chance did not seem to enter into the equation. Allowing her to meet, and fall in love with, her grandchildren, was not even viewed as an option, notwithstanding the fact that they all live at Longleat and are therefore in spitting distance of one another. Yet there are countless instances of love overcoming prejudice, as I know from at least one other aristocratic, but less well-known, union where the grandchild of colour has become the old-fashioned grandmother's favourite.

As the Weymouth saga played out in full view of the public, all parents with a public profile and single children were able to take note of the new values prevailing in British society. There could be no tolerance of any intolerance of inclusivity. If you had reservations about a union, you had better keep them to yourself or run the risk of being excluded: permanently. In this post-Christian, secular, politically-correct society of ours, no one argued for such quaint, old-fashioned modes of conduct as forgiveness or second chances. The general tone seemed to be: Anna had shown herself to be lacking, therefore she must be cast out into the wilderness. These were invaluable lessons to take on board, not only for the aristocracy, but for all public figures, the Royal Family included.

What made the Weymouth saga even more poignant was that Ceawlin and Emma had a family connection through marriage. Rather like Prince Florestan I of Monaco and Caroline Gibert de Lametz, Emma's much older (by twenty-four years) half-brother Iain McQuiston was married to Ceawlin's half-aunt, Lady Silvy Thynne (twenty-six years younger than Ceawlin's father). They had therefore known each other for most of her life, but, as in most families, when there is a twelve year age gap, the person you know as a child bears no resemblance to the adult that you then discover you find sexually appealing. So it proved with Ceawlin and Emma, who grew into a strikingly attractive woman.

Emma McQuiston was born on the 19th March 1986 to Suzanna McQuiston, a British divorced mother of two, and to a married Nigerian chartered accountant named Oladipo Jadesimi. He went on to found and chair the Lagos Deep Offshore Logistics base, which supplies support services to offshore gas and oil exploration companies. To say that he ended up making a lot of money is something of an understatement.

Emma was raised by her mother with help from her half-sister Samantha, twenty-one years her senior. Although not from a family of ancient lineage, Suzanna McQuiston was one of the new group of Londoners who had emerged from the seventies onwards, adding lustre to the vibrant social scene consisting of tailors, models, writers and other working-class people made good, who co-existed with the old established order and overlapped with it on occasion. This new elite was often more stylish and invariably more fashionable than the older order. However, they clung to the old-fashioned symbols that confirmed one's station in life in a way that few of the old order did. For instance, while Princess Margaret's son thought nothing of moving to Battersea to live with his family, the new fashionables would not have been caught living out of Chelsea and Kensington. It was therefore only to be expected that the young Emma McQuiston attended chic Queen's Gate School, where previous alumnae included Camilla Shand and the actress Tilda Swinton. She then sat for a degree in art history at University College, London.

Although she and Ceawlin had known each other for most of her life, they really 're-met' as adults when they ran into each other at Soho House in London. She was 25 and he 37. It was then that they saw each other in a new and more personable light.

While Emma's upbringing had been resolutely *haute bourgeois*, with the maintenance of standards typical of the newly established, Ceawlin's had been anything but. In fact, it was a heightened version of *nouveau aristocratique*. I can personally attest to the fact that his father Alexander had a plethora of progressive ideas about everything, child-rearing included. He spent years agitating for the area where Longleat is situated to become the independent state of Wessex. He sent his children to the local state schools. Ceawlin attended Horningsham Primary School and Kingdown Comprehensive School before being released into the relative conventionalism of the wildly unconventional public school, Bedales in Hampshire. Afterwards he attended University College London, where he read economics and philosophy. Tragedy struck when he was twenty-two. On a trip to India with his fiancée Jane Kirby and his business partner Crinian Wilde, the building they were staying in collapsed, killing them and injuring him.

Despite that trauma, Ceawlin had clearly inherited the Midas touch from his Bath grandfather Henry, 6th Marquis, and his father Alexander, 7th Marquis. Both men had managed to turn every venture they were involved with into gold. In keeping with their example, Ceawlin's list of successful enterprises was impressive: Caspian Securities, Sabre Projects, The Lion Trust, Group Menatep, the holding company for Russia's then-largest oil company, Yukos, all convinced Alexander that it would be safe to turn over the fate of his beloved Longleat to Ceawlin. For the last ten years Ceawlin has therefore been chairman of Longleat Enterprises, responsible for the running of the Elizabethan wonder and its 10,000 acre estate as well as other commercial activities, not the least of which is the renowned Safari Park.

Within a year of re-meeting at Soho House, Ceawlin and Emma were contemplating marriage. In many ways, they were ideally suited. The fact that they were already 'family' also helped. There would be none of the surprises that often arise when strangers meet and marry. The last thing on either of their minds was the question of colour. They had so much else going for them that it did not even enter into their reckoning. 'From my perspective – and with hindsight I can see that it was incredibly naïve – I absolutely believed that in the UK we lived in a post-racial society,' Ceawlin said. Emma herself has said that she never experienced any racial prejudice at all growing up.

Both these sentiments strike me as being typical of the inclusivity that characterise much of English upper class life. For instance, the top model Adwoa Aboah's father might be a Ghanaian gentleman named Charles Aboah, but her mother is Camilla Lowther, granddaughter of Viscount Lowther, heir to the Earl of Lonsdale. I remember the late baronet Sir Michael Peto, whose son-in-law was black, telling me while staying at my London house over Ascot week 2002, 'I approve of him wholeheartedly. He's a gentleman and that's what counts. Had he not been, it would've been a different matter. But that would've been true whether he was black or white.'

Ceawlin and Emma's marriage in 2013 got off to an electric start. Between the controversial publicity in the newspapers, the glamorous features in *Hello* and *Vanity Fair*, and a BBC TV documentary which gave an even wider spread to the issues involving the most high-profile bi-racial marriage to have taken place in Britain up to that time, Lord and Lady Weymouth became one of the most identifiable and fashionable couples in the land. The following year she gave birth to their first child, a son and heir, the Honourable John Alexander Ladi Thynn, on the 26th October 2014. Adding to the excitement of the first heir-in-line of colour to a marquisate, and a senior marquisate like Bath moreover, was the fact that Emma had nearly died to produce this much-treasured heir. The consensus in fashionable circles, especially amongst parents and grandparents whose female progeny might one day stand a chance of marrying the baby, was that Longleat House, its Capability Brown park, the estate of several thousand acres, and its world-renowned Safari Park, made the baby a suitable inclusion into just about any family. Of course, the old bugbear of the '*throwback*' was raised occasionally, and I, being Jamaican, was often asked how these things work. I would point out that there was no possibility of a throwback having black skin, with fully fledged Sub-Saharan features to match the skin tones. Throwbacks look like Queen Charlotte. It always entertained me to witness how that simple description allowed the remote and unlikely ambitions of my questioners to flourish. Once they realised that no descendant of theirs would actually look entirely different from them, while those self-same descendants would be living in one of the country's greatest stately homes bearing one of its greatest titles, they were so eager to contemplate a marriage, remote though the possibility was, that one had to laugh. While I could have been cynical and dismissed such reactions as ambition conquering prejudice, I also recognised that the change in attitude the Weymouth marriage had created was so advantageous to all people of colour that one should exult in the change and not denigrate it. After over two hundred years of colour prejudice, British society was finally becoming as accepting of colour as it had once been. Only a fool or a dyed-in-the-wool racist would have failed to delight in this happy occurrence.

If there had been room for doubt that Britain is now what Ceawlin characterised as a 'post-race' society, and that those who do not share that view are so out-of-step with contemporary values that they now function on society's margins, Prince Harry and Meghan Markle's relationship removed it.

They met on a blind date set up by Victoria von Westenholz, daughter of (Frederick Patrick) Piers, Baron von Westenholz, a half-English aristocrat of German origins, born in England in 1943. He went on to represent Britain in Alpine skiing on its 1964 Olympic team before becoming a renowned interior designer and antique dealer as well as close friend of the Prince of Wales. As a result, the three Westenholz children, Frederick Patrick Piers, Violet Marguerite, and Victoria Lilly, grew up with the Wales boys. By the summer of 2016, when Meghan Markle arrived in England on a publicity junket linked to an attendance at Wimbledon on the 4th June, it was no secret in social circles that Prince Harry was eager to meet someone. He had had two relationships which he had hoped would end in marriage, the first to the white Zimbabwean Chelsy Davy, which lasted for five years, and the second with Lady Mary Gaye Curzon's actress/model daughter, Cressida Bonas, which lasted for two years. Neither girl wanted to take on the role of royal duchess, knowing that it entailed being in the limelight more than they found comfortable. Violet von Westenholz, being a good friend of Prince Harry's, will have felt that she was doing him a good turn when she met the actress Meghan Markle in her capacity as a press relations director at Ralph Lauren. The two women became what Harry's mother Diana would have characterised as 'fast friends'.

According to people who have met and liked her, Meghan is extremely personable. She has the gift that many North Americans possess, namely the ability to strike up immediate friendships with people, who are completely captivated by her display of warmth, interest, sincerity, spontaneity, humour, intelligence, and charm. Being good looking, well dressed, and chic, with the alluring balance of confidence overlaid with gentleness that has enchanted many an admirer, she charmed Victoria von Westenholz so entirely that Harry's childhood friend 'set up' a 'blind date', to quote Meghan herself.

There has been speculation that neither Meghan nor Harry knew who the other was. This we can discount; he knew she was an actress in a cable television show named *Suits*, while she knew he was Prince Henry of Wales. Friends from her past have already confirmed that she had a 'thing for' Harry, long before she met him, and at one stage of her development even had photographs of him. In person, he is tall, well built, and exudes masculinity, so there is no reason to doubt that she might well have genuinely found him physically attractive before she even met him. If you have a thing about a stranger before you have met, it is hardly credible that don't recognise him when your dream is given flesh.

Nevertheless, I also know from Baroness Jessica Heydel, who was introduced to Harry under a false name (but of course knew exactly to whom she was speaking) – and was so freaked out by the falsity of the whole situation that she remained tongue-tied, for, as she rightly put it, 'How can you have a real conversation with someone who is pretending to be someone else?' – that Harry liked taking a leaf out of King Henry VIII's book and going incognito, despite the farce and near-tragedy of how that king had ambushed Anne of Cleves while pretending to be someone he was not.

Nonsensical claims to the contrary, Harry and Meghan met on that blind date during the first week of July 2016. The click was immediate. 'We met for a drink, and then I think very quickly into that we said, "Well, what are we doing tomorrow? We should meet again."' The second date proved to be as fruitful as the first. They went to Soho House, where their chum Markus Anderson allocated them an out-of-the-way table so that they could chat to their heart's content while drinking rosé wine. Harry invited Meghan to 'join me in Botswana and we camped out with each other under the stars,' as he put it. Having decided that Meghan was the one 'the very first time we met,' he was thrilled that 'we were really by ourselves, which was crucial to me to make sure that we had a chance to get to know each other.'

For four months, the couple saw as much of each other as they could. The press and public remained unaware of the burgeoning romance, until, on the 31st October 2016, the *Sunday Express* broke the news that Harry's 'happier than he's been for many years' and is 'besotted' with Meghan. That same day, Meghan posted an adorable picture of two bananas spooning, subtly conveying the message that she and an unnamed someone were as close as those two bananas. The following day the *Vancouver Sun* ran a story with Meghan promoting her five-piece collection of spring dresses, all items under $100, for the Canadian chain-store Reitmans. Although she was careful not to mention her boyfriend by name, her profile had surged so exponentially in the previous twenty-four hours that, when she said, 'my cup runneth over and I'm the luckiest girl in the world,' her words needed no translation. In case they did, however, that same day *People* magazine delivered the message to the world that 'Prince Harry is so serious with actress Meghan Markle that an engagement could be in the not-so-distant future, insiders suggest.' The headline stated: 'Prince Harry Has Already Introduced Meghan Markle to Prince Charles…'

Anyone with knowledge of the way the press works will have understood that these stories, appearing as they did in such disparate publications, and coming so hard on the heels of each other, had been planted. Because Meghan was an unknown entity and Harry is renowned for his antipathy to the press, no one knew who was responsible for putting the news out. But it was obvious someone was intent on sharing the joyous couple's coupling with the world.

The backlash came as fast and furious as the pace of the lovers' romance had been. Exactly a week later, Harry felt compelled to issue a statement:

"Since he was young, Prince Harry has been very aware of the warmth that has been extended to him by members of the public. He feels lucky to have so many people supporting him and knows what a fortunate and privileged life he leads.

"He is also aware that there is significant curiosity about his private life. He has never been comfortable with this, but he has tried to develop a thick skin about the level of media interest that comes with it. He has rarely taken formal action on the very regular publication of fictional stories that are written about him and he has worked hard to develop a professional relationship with the media, focused on his work and the issues he cares about.

"But the past week has seen a line crossed. His girlfriend, Meghan Markle, has been subject to a wave of abuse and harassment. Some of this has been very public – the smear on the front page of a newspaper; the racial undertones of comment pieces; and the outright sexism and racism of social media trolls and web article comments. Some of it has been hidden from the public – the nightly battles to keep defamatory stories out of the papers; her mother having to struggle past photographers in order to get to her front door; the attempts of reporters and photographers to gain illegal entry to her home and the calls to police that followed; the substantial bribes offered by papers to her ex-boyfriend; the bombardment of nearly every friend, co-worker, and loved one in her life.

"Prince Harry is worried about Ms Markle's safety and is deeply disappointed that he has not been able to protect her. It is not right that a few months into a relationship with him that Ms Markle should be subjected to such a storm. He knows commentators will say this is 'the price she has to pay' and that 'this is all part of the game'. He strongly disagrees. This is not a game – it is her life and his.

"He has asked for this statement to be issued in the hopes that those in the press who have been driving this story can pause and reflect before any further damage is done. He knows that it is unusual to issue a statement like this, but hopes that fair-minded people will understand why he has felt it necessary to speak publicly."

This statement was a masterstroke. At the very moment that it placed Harry and Meghan in the most positive of lights, garnering them sympathy and empathy from the legions of romantics and admirers who were rooting them on to long-term happiness, it also silenced critics who could thereafter be accused of racism, even if such reservations as they had, had nothing to do with race. Meghan, after all, was a 36 year old actress. She had a past, and quite a colourful one at that. As Ronald Ferguson had rightly observed when his younger-by-a-decade and much-less-worldly daughter Sarah was going out with Prince Andrew and the issue of her ex-boyfriends had been raised, all normal, unmarried girls have pasts after a certain age. And Meghan was not only normal, and unmarried, but she was also a divorcee. And an actress who had successfully made her way to a position of some renown in the jungle of Hollywood, gathering both admirers and detractors in the process. Anyone with any experience of tabloid journalism will therefore have been alert to the danger of all sorts of normal facts emerging which, in the dextrous hands of yellow journalists, could easily be turned into death knells for the burgeoning relationship. But not after that statement was issued, for it placed a very effective muzzle over the mouths of the press, ensuring that thereafter coverage would be positive.

It says much about the attitude of the British media, and the wariness they have felt since they were accused of having played a hand in Diana, Princess of Wales's death, that many of the publications backed off immediately. It also helped that Harry had been a favourite of the press and public for years. People everywhere still remembered the 12 year old boy walking behind his mother's coffin. They cut him slack for having lost his mother so young. They also liked that he had grown into a down-to-earth lad. They accepted, with a mixture of tolerance and compassion, conduct from him that would have seemed intemperate and déclassé in anyone else. They sometimes even gave the impression that his 'one-of-the-lads' conduct was beneficial to the monarchy and indeed the country as a whole, for it demonstrated that he wanted to be perceived as 'one of the people'. Contemporary Britain, it now seemed, had become not only post-race but post-class as well. While people still wanted those they admired to be classy, to use an Americanism that captures the sentiment exactly irrespective of it not being a word condoned in elegant British circles, they also wanted them to be classless.

Nevertheless, after Harry issued his statement, there was speculation that he had gone too far. He was encroaching upon the right of the press to comment when matters are in the public interest. Not only had he laid claim, on his own behalf as well as Meghan's and her mother's, to being treated more circumspectly than the press would normally behave towards a hot-news couple, but he had also deflected attention away from all the other royals, and focused it onto himself and Meghan. His father and step-mother were in the middle of a Middle Eastern tour when his statement and the controversy surrounding it became the news story of the day. As the respected journalist David Jenkins put it in *Tatler*, 'Clarence House can't have been best pleased that its timing knocked their engagements into the back pages.'

For a while, the harbingers were mixed, and it looked as if Harry's statement might rebound upon him, but then William waded in decisively on the 27th November. In so doing, he saved the day. He defeated speculation that he had been unhappy about his brother's decision to so precipitately announce the existence of a girlfriend – something that had never been done before, and therefore set what many at the Palace regarded as a dangerous precedent – by announcing: 'The Duke of Cambridge absolutely understands the situation concerning privacy and supports the need for Prince Harry to support those closest to him.'

Faced with such demonstrable royal support, even those elements of the press who resented the restraints being placed upon their ability to report what they saw as a fair news story, backed off. Harry and Meghan now had the space they wanted. They were also now linked in the public mind as a couple, and a couple whose relationship, though recent, was so serious that Harry was prepared to break new ground to protect and nurture it.

Thereafter, until after the marriage, there was none of the hurly-burly that has characterised the British tabloids when they are reporting on royal or celebrity boy- and/or girlfriends. The press became unprecedentedly respectful, indeed chastened. To a man, they seem to have been backed behind the line Harry's statement indicated he wanted them to toe. More to the point, once it had become apparent that William was supportive of Harry's stance, and that the original statement had been so cleverly drafted that any future criticism, or indeed just ordinary paparazzi attention, could lead to the accusation that the press were unduly invading the couple's privacy or in the alternative being racist, or both, Harry and Meghan's romance was handled with kid gloves.

Who Meghan Markle was now became material. The public quickly learnt that she was bi-racial, with a Caucasian father and an Afro-American mother. Her father Thomas Markle was a retired television lighting director and a director of photography, who had won two Emmy Awards for such shows as *General Hospital* and *Married….With Children*, while her mother Doria Ragland had had a more checkered career. She had started out as a make-up artist on *General Hospital*, where the couple met and, after the marriage failed, had gone on to become a travel agent before filing for bankruptcy in the mid-2000s. She then studied for a Bachelor of Arts in psychology as a mature student, taking a Masters in social work at the University of California in 2011 before working for three years as a social worker at the Didi Hirsch Mental Health Services, in Culver City, California. She resigned in May 2018, right after her daughter married Prince Harry. She also worked as a yoga instructor, an activity her daughter, who is also an avid yoga practitioner, has referred to in speeches.

Both Thomas Markle and Doria Ragland have interesting ancestries. According to Gary Boyd Roberts, Senior Research Scholar Emeritus, New England Historical Genealogical Society, Meghan's father shares colonial ancestors, through his New Hampshire Ellsworth and Merrill great-grandparents, with eight presidents: George W Bush, George H W Bush, Gerald Ford, Richard Nixon, Herbert Hoover, Calvin Coolidge, Chester Arthur, and James Garfield. He also shares ancestors with three former First Ladies: Frances (Mrs Grover) Cleveland, Ellen (Mrs Woodrow) Wilson, and Mamie (Mrs Dwight) Eisenhower; as well as with the writer O. Henry, the fabled advocate Clarence Darrow, Senator Sam Ervin of the Watergate hearings, actors James Dean and Roy Rogers, Senator John Kerry, and former Canadian Prime Minister Lester Pearson. Markle is even descended from royalty. Through the Rev. William Skipper, who emigrated to Boston in 1639, he descends from Elizabeth de la Pole, daughter of Michael de la Pole, 2nd Earl of Suffolk and sister of William de la Pole, 1st Duke of Suffolk, who features prominently in Shakespeare's *Henry VI*, parts 1 and 2.

The de la Poles were one of the great families of the medieval world, descended from King Edward III and his dark-skinned queen, Philippa of Hainault, who feature earlier in this work. Elizabeth de la Pole's daughter Margaret Kerdeston married John de Foix, 1st Earl of Kendal, who in turn married the Infanta Catherine of Navarre, producing a daughter who became Queen Anne of Hungary. Queen Elizabeth the Queen Mother and Diana, Princess of Wales, can also trace their ancestry through Skipper's ancestors Mary Clifford and Sir Philip Wentworth, meaning that Princes William and Harry are descended from Elizabeth de la Pole in a variety of lines, including 4 through King George III and 4 through Diana, Princess of Wales. This means that Harry and Meghan Markle are distantly related in several different bloodlines, most of which are royal, some aristocratic, and a few of colour, which is rather a poke in the eye for the 'one drop' purists. This demonstrates that, while Meghan is undoubtedly the first acknowledged woman of colour to marry into the British Royal Family, she is not the first one who has bloodlines of colour in her ancestry. Through the many royal bloodlines interwoven in their joint ancestry, both Harry and Meghan are descended from people with a dash of colour.

Doria Ragland's ancestry is rather less regal. It was not without its surprises, not only in terms of colour, but also because there was an unexpectedly glamorous connection, albeit a tenuous one. Being Jamaican, I only needed to take one look at Doria's photograph to know that she was not actually black, a description that suggested that her heritage was purely Sub-Saharan African. She was clearly mixed race herself, and so her bloodlines proved when one studied them.

The Ragland family originated in Jonesboro, Georgia, the childhood home of authoress Margaret Mitchell, whose family's experience of plantation life in the South during the days of slavery inspired her great 1936 opus, *Gone with the Wind*. Although the life lived by Meghan's black ancestors was more Hattie Daniel's Mammy than Vivien Leigh's Scarlett O'Hara, a trawl through her family tree revealed that Joseph Betts was categorised as 'coloured', Texie Hendrick 'white', her son Jeremiah Ragland '*mulatto*', his wife Claudie Richie also '*mulatto*', her mother Mattie Turnipseed 'coloured', and Steve Ragland '*mulatto*'. Other ancestors were black, but, having looked at Doria, it was not surprising to see that there was a heavy preponderance of biracialism, indeed an almost equal mixture between that and black. Nor could there be any mistake about who was and was not black, for each of the ancestors was racially categorised in keeping with the custom of their time.

The racial mix of the Ragland ancestors told a story. In the post-Civil War South, people who were categorised as 'white' or 'coloured' were in a more advantageous position than those who were labelled '*negro*'. The upward mobility of Doria Ragland's ancestors corroborate this fact while also illustrating that Meghan's ambitiousness and determination to succeed are qualities inherited from them. According to Sara Jane Overstreet, the local expert who honed her knowledge of the Ragland heritage through the offices of the Genealogical Society of Henry and Clayton Counties, 'The family seem industrious. They're constantly looking for opportunity. Some folks stayed put, but they left.'

Meghan's great-great-grandparents, the abovementioned Jeremiah Ragland and Claudie Ritchie, moved to Chattanooga in Tennessee shortly before the First World War, where he worked as a barber and saloon porter before opening his own tailor shop. She worked as a maid in a shop, which was a step up from being a domestic servant and several steps up from working in the fields. As the Jim Crow era dawned, and with it the violence perpetrated against the blacks, they moved further west just as the Great Depression was beginning to bite. Hollywood was in its infancy, the opportunities there seemed greater, so the Raglands moved again, this time to Los Angeles. The children of the family, Dora and Lillie Ragland, went from attending segregated schools in Tennessee to college in California, with the former ending up as a teacher and the latter the director of an estate agency and sufficiently prominent to appear in Who's Who among African Americans. Their nephew Alvin Ragland, Meghan's grandfather, also graduated from blue- to white-collar status, working in the antiques business. As Meghan herself put it, 'You create the identity you want for yourself, just as my ancestors did when they were given their freedom.'

If the Markles had gone down in the world, from ancestors with royal and aristocratic connections to middle class status, the opposite was true of the Raglands. By Meghan's own account, however, it was her father who gave her the impetus and encouragement to expand her horizons and reach for the sky the way she did. Her parents separated when she was two and divorced when she was six. Enrolled by her father around the time of the separation at the Hollywood Little Red Schoolhouse, the prestigious, private school where many of the Hollywood elite sent their children, she remained there until she was eleven. He then sent her to another prestigious institution, where she continued to mix with the Hollywood elite. This was the renowned Immaculate Heart High School, an all-girls day- and boarding-school where notable alumnae include the actress Mary Tyler Moore, Diane Disney, niece of Walt, and Lucie Arnaz, daughter of Lucille Ball and Desi Arnaz. Graduating from there, her father paid for her to attend yet another prestigious educational institution, Northwestern University in Evanston, Illinois, where she graduated in 2003 with a degree in theatre and international studies.

Upon graduation, Meghan began the long and hard slog to fame. Until the *Sunday Express* broke the story of her relationship with Harry, she was not a household name on either side of the Atlantic. She was undoubtedly a successful jobbing actress by that time, being one of the regular characters in the cable-TV show *Suits* since its inception in 2011. She'd also appeared in a variety of films, such as *Get Him to the Greek* and *Remember Me* (both 2010), *Random Encounters* (2011), *Dysfunctional Friends* (2012), and *When Sparks Fly* (2014), but none of her appearances had made the slightest impact at the box office. Prior to that, the pinnacle of her career had been as one of the briefcase girls in *Deal or No Deal*, a role she got in 2006.

She made no secret of being extremely ambitious, of wanting to make her mark on the world, of being tireless in her pursuit of achieving her goals. No one could accuse her of being faint-hearted, lazy or lacking in persistence. For the first ten years of her acting career, she battered between pillar and post. According to her, calligraphy 'evolved into what was my pseudo-waitressing job when I was auditioning. I didn't wait tables. I did calligraphy for the invitations for, like, Robin Thicke and Paula Patton's wedding.' She claimed that this pastime was 'super-lucrative. Because there are so few people doing it.' Although she 'didn't wait tables', for a while she nevertheless was a hostess in a restaurant.

Her first TV role had been a blink-and-you-miss-her appearance on *General Hospital*, following which she had minor roles in episodes of television shows such as *Without a Trace, Cuts, Love, Inc., 90210, Knight Rider, The League* and *Castle*, so her progress was slow.

According to Meghan, she had made the decision to be 'happy', and happy she remained even in the early days, when she had difficulty getting roles. This she blamed on 'being "ethnically ambiguous", as I was pegged in the industry.' She believed that it 'meant I could audition for virtually any role…. Sadly, it didn't matter: I wasn't black enough for the black roles and I wasn't white enough for the white roles, leaving me somewhere in the middle as the ethnic chameleon who couldn't book a job.'

There might actually have been other factors at play. Both Vanessa Williams and Tyra Banks had had successful careers despite being racially ambiguous. It had not prevented the former from being crowned Miss America when Meghan was only two years old (at a time when race was a bigger deal than it was as Meghan reached maturity), nor had it stopped the latter from becoming one of the most popular models and television presenters when she was past retirement age. Both these women had been bombshells: spectacularly beautiful, with spectacular figures and the height to take them to prominence. Meghan's beauty was more discreet, as was her figure, and she lacked the height they possessed. But she had a personality which would ultimately see her prevail and reach greater stature than any of her peers.

She also had the ability to utilise opportunities when they arose; to create them when they did not; and to tread water happily when she was not making progress. The ability to be happy even when life is not going exactly as you would like is something which attracts others, and Meghan, being also physically attractive, good company, and driven, was attractive to men. From 2004 she had been in a relationship with Trevor Engelson (1976-), who had started out in the film industry as a production assistant before working his way up to being a producer: in fact, he produced *Remember Me*, the 2010 romantic coming-of-age drama one of whose stars is Pierce Brosnan. It was after that movie that he and Meghan formalised their relationship, becoming engaged in 2010 and marrying at Jamaica Inn, one of the world's most elegant hotels, in Ocho Rios, Jamaica on 10th September 2011. She and Trevor can have spared no expense, and their guests cannot have been suffering financially either, for the bridal party took over the entire hotel. The guests were provided with a fun-filled, four-day blast where the wedding ceremony itself was, according to one of the guests, the least of what was happening: 'over in fifteen minutes'.

Meghan is evidently very capable, and micro-managed everything from the timetables and activities such as wheel-barrow races on the beach, to distributing ace ganja spliffs to all the guests in little, specially-made crocus bags that said 'Shh...' This was intended to be trendy and in tune with the Jamaican vibe, except that pot-smoking is a contentious issue in Jamaica, and was a crime punishable by a long prison sentence at the time. She and Trevor are therefore lucky that no one reported them to the authorities, for the whole thing might have ended rather embarrassingly, and indeed very nearly did. Meghan neglected to inform the guests what the special treat was, and one of them reportedly took it back to the United States unwittingly. When they realised that they could have been apprehended by the American authorities, and possibly been charged with smuggling drugs, they were furious. But everyone else seems to have taken the gift at face value and appreciated the 'cool' and 'happening' nature of the event.

Meghan had been commissioned to do *Suits* before the wedding, and right after it she had to report for duty in Toronto, where the series was being filmed. Thereafter, she and her new husband spent several months of the year living on different sides of the American continent, she in eastern Toronto, he on the West Coast of America. Although friends of Trevor say that he went out of his way to travel to Toronto as much as possible to minimise the effects of distance, inevitably being in a long-distance relationship imposed a strain on the marriage. Even so, no one expected Meghan to end the marriage the way she did, by peremptorily posting Trevor the engagement and wedding rings he had given her. According to Andrew Morton, who wrote a biography entitled *Meghan: A Hollywood Princess*, Trevor was so surprised that he refuses even now to make any comment whatsoever about Meghan.

What some people would regard as heartless callousness, others view as commendably dignified and decisive. As Meghan settled into Toronto life, gaining further confidence as her career took off and becoming the celebrity she had always wanted to be, she was making new, more upscale friends. These included Jessica Mulroney, daughter-in-law of former Canadian Prime Minister Brian Mulroney and a stylist who has helped her get her look together, and Serena Williams. She and the now 23 times Grand Slam singles winner were placed on the same team at DIRECTV's New York based Celebrity Beach Bowl in 2014. Being both ultra-competitive, they scored a seven point victory over their opponents, and Meghan, who is an avid networker, with the ability to find things in common with anyone she wishes to charm, would later write on her lifestyle website, *The Tig*, 'We hit it off immediately, taking pictures, laughing through the flag football game we were both players in, and chatting not about tennis or acting, but about all the good old fashioned girly stuff.' By their own account, they also found common ground in being women of colour and how that had textured their lives and experiences.

Meghan pursued the friendship, proudly announcing on her website that Williams 'quickly became a confidante I would text when I was travelling, the friend I would rally around for her tennis matches.' Meghan even showed what a good friend she could be by flying to England to see her friend compete at Wimbledon, which, of course, is where she met Violet von Westenholz.

A powerhouse of directed energy, Meghan's founding of *The Tig* was but one of the many platforms she sought out as she set about making herself into as major a star as she possibly could. She wrote about fashion, beauty, food, and travel. She profiled inspirational women, roping in experts in such disparate fields as diet, make-up, fitness and yoga. The website's audience was primarily fans of *Suits*, but already she was branching out, understanding that charity and activism would provide her with gravitas beyond anything that fashion, style and *Suits* could. She had had her first taste of power, and the approbation it brings, when, as an 11 year old, she had written to Procter & Gamble to complain that an advertisement for their ivory dish soap was sexist. She suggested that they alter the phrase 'women are fighting greasy pots and pans' by substituting 'people' for 'women'. This the company did, and Meghan took great pride in her achievement, informing a UN Women's conference in 2015, 'At the age of 11, I created my small level of impact by standing up for equality.'

Any association with the United Nations was highly illustrious, pitching her beyond being just another somewhat successful actress with ambition to the level of a serious activist, but this was not the only prestigious organisation with which Meghan forged links. She volunteered as a counsellor for the international charity One Young World, and ended up speaking in Dublin in 2014 on the topics of gender equality and modern-day slavery.

She also took advantage of the opportunity to gain herself a new and well-connected agent when their paths crossed at this time. This was Gina Nelthorpe-Cowne of Kruger Cowne Talent Management, whose other clients included Cher, Sir Richard Branson, and Elle Macpherson. Her brother-in-law is also the noted television presenter John Simpson. Before they'd even met, Meghan's ability to trigger an instant connection with whomever she wished to captivate had worked its magic yet again. 'We just clicked. We spoke on the phone and through emails a number of times before actually meeting, but it was an instant connection. You've either got it or you haven't and Meghan is a really warm and genuine person. She just has it.'

When they did finally meet, Meghan's boyfriend Cory Vitiello opened the door to their hotel room and there the actress was, standing in a towelling robe with her hair scraped back. 'We hugged as if we had known each other for ages. She was delightful – warm and personable. And hugely charismatic.' Gina also found Meghan to be 'ferociously intelligent. Even then she was starting to think about her career after *Suits*. She was interested in humanitarian and philanthropic causes – and in animal rights issues too, but her main focus was and I believe still is women's rights. She wanted to be recognised as a humanitarian. She wanted to develop her own causes and the youth summits were perfect for her.' And so began a prestigious two year association for Meghan, who developed a firm friendship with her agent as they spent time together and plotted her upwards trajectory into ever higher levels of accomplishment and renown.

Both clear- and far-sighted, Meghan did not put all her eggs into one basket. She also volunteered for yet another prestigious organisation, the United Services Organizations. This provides entertainment for the US Armed Forces abroad, and she found time to sandwich in tours of Spain and Afghanistan on their behalf between her work and other charity commitments. As people at Buckingham Palace would later learn, Meghan has a formidable work ethic. She aims for greatness, and understands that she can only achieve it through effort and energy.

In the years before they met, while both Harry and Meghan were laying down foundation stones for the edifice that would later on bring them together, he was also discovering the importance of his humanitarian work. He had gained tremendous public respect as a result of his conduct in the Army, especially on his tours of duty to Afghanistan. He had endeared himself to both his Army buddies and the general public by making it obvious that he wanted to be treated as just another one of the lads. And when he left the Army, he put his knowledge of Army life, and the needs of the soldiers, to good use by launching the Invictus Games, an international, adaptive, multi-sport event along the lines of the Olympics, but for wounded, injured, or sick services' personnel and veterans. He also became a patron of the HALO Trust, a charity which removes the debris left behind by war, in particular land mines, thereby doffing his hat to his mother's legacy. He also associated himself with Walking With The Wounded, another charity for injured armed forces personnel, undertaking arduous and dangerous walks on their behalf.

Harry's affinity with people of colour had been pronounced even when he was growing up. I've known of this for many years, because I have friends who are sufficiently close with the Lesotho Royal Family for me to have been asked to lend them my flat in Paris. In circles of colour, especially royal ones, people cannot sing Harry's praises highly enough. No academic, it was obvious while he was at Eton that university life would not be for him. Before going into the Army, he spent his gap year working with disadvantaged youth, in part in Australia and more particularly in Lesotho, which has the second highest incidence in the world of HIV children under the age of 14. While there, he struck up a firm friendship with Prince Seeiso of Lesotho. In 2006, the two princes founded Sentebale (which means 'forget me not'), a charity which seeks to empower vulnerable children to reach their full potential. Harry is also hugely popular in Jamaica and other black countries, where his down-to-earth demeanour and jokey, one-of-the-lads style is much appreciated. In settings such as those, he shines in a way he does not in more rigid and formal environments. There is little doubt that he responds as much to the warmth that is so prevalent amongst black people as they do to his. There is also no doubt that his motivation has been entirely humanitarian. While he may enjoy the emotional rewards approbation brings, no one has ever seriously believed that his decision to do good was a vanity project. His sincerity is unquestionable.

Considering Harry's predilections, it is therefore hardly surprising that he has taken all the girls in whom he had a strong interest to Botswana, which he regards as one of his favourite places on earth. Four went there with him before Meghan. She, however, had the most fruitful impact, and not only because she was the only one who made it clear that they could become an unbreakable unit, but also because she was prepared, indeed enthusiastic, to use his royal status to further their joint interests. That in itself was potent, for both Harry's previous loves had shied away from becoming part of the circus that goes along with being a British senior royal.

Under the African sun, surrounded by the natives and the flora and fauna which are so magical to those who love that part of the world, they discussed their joint interest in humanitarian work. This increased the already pronounced personal attraction they had for each other. Both of them were very aware of the effect their relationship could have, not only upon themselves individually and jointly, but also upon the world at large. They could safely fall in love, knowing that they were not only enhancing each other's lives, but also that their union had the prospect of making the world a better place.

This was truly heady stuff. Giddy as it is to find true love under the romantic stars of an African adventure, it is even headier to discover that, if you join forces with someone else, the power of two can significantly increase the power you have previously possessed as one. When Meghan returned to London, she told Gina Nelthorpe-Cowne that things had very quickly become 'serious and they had started discussing the future.' Meghan then revealed that she and Harry had 'said to each other: "We're going to change the world."'

Within just a few months, it was clear to both Gina and Meghan that Harry was going to propose. The two women were having lunch on the Strand one day when Gina asked her friend and client 'if she knew what she was letting herself in for. I said: "This is serious. This is the end of your normal life, the end of your privacy – everything." Meghan 'just held her hand up and said: "Stop. I don't want to hear any negativity. This is a happy time for us." Shortly afterwards, Meghan 'wrote a lovely email in October, a week before the news about her and Harry became public, saying that she was giving up her career and we had to terminate our contract.' This was the end of their association, but the beginning of a new and exciting phase for Meghan.

As David Jenkins accurately observed, Meghan's confidence, only four months into the relationship, was 'remarkable'. She felt that she was on such firm ground with Harry that she could give up her career. This meant that she was certain that she would be marrying him, that she had moved on from being merely an actress with ambitions to be an activist and humanitarian, to something more profound.

If she was that sure, he must have been as well. This would prove to be the case, but in the meantime such certainty must have been extremely reassuring for a woman who was going to be provided with a greater platform than she could ever have imagined she would earn for herself. It also showed that he too valued what he was getting. Here was a woman whose confidence, intelligence and personality surrounded him with a bubble of love and a degree of certainty which he had lacked since the sudden and premature death of his mother when he was only twelve years old. These were powerful inducements, and what added to her appeal was that she was biracial. She would be an invaluable asset to the British Royal Family as they pursued their joint objectives of representing all the people in the United Kingdom and the multi-racial, multi-national Commonwealth.

As Harry and Meghan's love affair went from strength to strength, they managed to conduct a long-distance relationship with infinitely greater success than she had done with her first husband. They managed to meet up whenever their diaries allowed. As he incorporated her into his life, and those closest to him met her, concerns grew at the Palace that he might be rushing into an inextricable commitment too soon. His brother William and good friend Tom Inskip were two of the people closest to him who suggested taking things at a more relaxed pace. But Harry had been bitten by the love bug good and true and was in no mood to wait. One factor that would have influenced him was Meghan's age. She was in her mid-thirties, three years older than he was. Her biological clock was ticking loudly, and, since they both wanted children, there was indeed an urgency about getting married which might not have been there had she been younger.

The hiatus also gave Meghan, the consummate showwoman, an opportunity to replicate Grace Kelly's Hollywood departure. Prior to marrying Prince Rainier in 1956, she had bowed out of her acting career in *High Society*, a film about a woman whose ex-husband tries to win her back as she prepares to marry another man, the climax of which is of course a magnificent wedding. By giving *Suits* advance warning of her intention to quit, and providing them with knowledge of why she was doing so, Meghan gave the producers of the series the opportunity to create the story line of her character Rachel Zane marrying her long-standing romantic interest. In so doing, there would be two spectacular weddings for Meghan, the first of which would be on television, thereby feeding interest in the second, which would follow in real life. Not for nothing is Meghan known as a true child of Hollywood as well as a bright and resourceful woman who never misses an opportunity to utilise situations advantageously. As Gina put it, she is 'unique in her determination to succeed'.

Art and reality mimicking each other are powerful marketing tools. They have great appeal to anyone in the communications industry, and Meghan had already shown, through her adoption of a variety of platforms, that she understood their efficacy and was adept at exploiting them to enhance her image. Ironically, the unmarried Grace had baulked at having her career used the way MGM did in the run-up to her marriage, but what had seemed tasteless in 1956 was viewed in a different light sixty years later. Commercial exploitation was now regarded as being clever, and no one had the reservations of the late Princess of Monaco, least of all Meghan, who happily went along with the concept of fictional and actual marriages closely coinciding with each other.

As everyone in the communications industry knows, timing is all-important. Meghan and Harry's marriage had to be timed to coincide with the denouement that was Rachel Zane's marriage in *Suits*. While paralegals in television series do not need to be engaged, royal princes do. Exactly a year after the news of Harry and Meghan's relationship became public, they were engaged. Because he was then fifth in line of succession to the throne, and the first six need the monarch's permission to marry, he had to obtain his grandmother's consent. This being forthcoming, on the 27th November Clarence House issued the following statement:

'His Royal Highness The Prince of Wales is delighted to announce the engagement of Prince Harry to Ms Meghan Markle.

'The wedding will take place in Spring 2018. Further details about the wedding will be announced in due course.

'His Royal Highness and Ms Markle became engaged in London earlier this month. Prince Harry has informed Her Majesty The Queen and other close members of his family. Prince Harry has also sought and received the blessing of Ms Markle's parents.

'The couple will live in Nottingham Cottage at Kensington Palace.'

It is not possible to exaggerate the pride that people of colour all over the world felt when they realised that one of their own was now marrying into the world's premier royal family. This was a truly momentous moment. Finally, after two centuries of revilement and a half-century of effort to regain a place of dignity and respect in white society, the grandest white family in the world was welcoming a biracial woman into their midst. It really couldn't get better than this.

As far as the Royal Family was concerned, this was also an opportunity. The Commonwealth has always been important to the Queen, who has been tireless throughout her reign in fulfilling her role as its head in a unifying way. She is not only respected by many of the heads of government; she is actually loved. I have known several Commonwealth heads of government or state over the years, and to a man, they have all sung Elizabeth II's praises. They appreciate the way she has defended the rights and interests of their countries for nearly seventy years. They particularly respect the skilful way she negotiated race relations during the troubled years of apartheid.

Being born in a Commonwealth nation, with many contacts at the highest level of government, not only in Jamaica but also in the Commonwealth Secretariat, I can confirm that the Queen is well-known to be free of colour prejudice. There are many anecdotes about the refreshing way she has put people at their ease, and helped them out of jams both social and political. She is prized for her wisdom, her even-handedness, and the dignity which she has accorded to people of colour long before it became fashionable to do so. 'I'm not surprised the Queen's given her permission,' a former Deputy Secretary of the Commonwealth Secretariat told me, 'I bet she's thrilled this is happening.'

In some ways, Meghan's racial identity was the answer to a royal prayer, especially with regard to who would inherit the headship of the Commonwealth. Because the role is not hereditary, there was some question as to whether the Prince of Wales would ultimately succeed his mother. It was well known in Commonwealth circles that the Queen hoped he would be nominated as her successor. The issue was: would he be regarded as relevant in this day and age by the heads of state and government? Out of the 53 countries that are Commonwealth members, only 16 still retain her as head of state. The other 37 are republics. Of those 16, many of them, Jamaica included, had been debating for some time whether a British head of state was still appropriate. Portia Simpson, the former Jamaican Prime Minister, had been vociferous in her recommendation that the Queen be stood down. Australia had also waxed and waned in its desire to see the Queen replaced with a home grown head of state. Even before Meghan arrived on the scene to turn the tide decisively in favour of retaining links with the British Crown, the visits of 'Kate and William' and 'Harry', as they were called in the popular press, took a lot of the wind out of republican sails. Harry only needed to visit Jamaica and clown around with Usain Bolt, for the populace to appreciate what the anti-monarchist politicians did not: the people like the links with the British Crown, at least as long as the royals interact with them in a relevant way.

The same proved to be true of the republican members of the Commonwealth. The people of those countries also enjoyed the links with the Queen. Over the decades, all but the most rabid anti-monar-chist politicians have come to appreciate the invaluable, indeed unique, role the Queen has played as the Commonwealth's head. She has been an honest-broker in a world where honesty is in short supply. She has been able to counsel, advise, and comfort many a leader who has no one he or she can trust, surrounded as he or she is by those eager to supplant him or her.

It is an acknowledged fact in Commonwealth circles that the whole edifice would have come tumbling down years ago had it not been for the dedication and wisdom of the Queen. But would Prince Charles be a suitable replacement for his mother? Undoubtedly, he has the integrity and benevolence so crucial to the role. There was also the fact that, if a national of any of the Commonwealth countries were selected as its head once the Queen stepped down, he or she might well put his or her national interests above those of the 52 other member states. The Queen, by virtue of being royal, and therefore above politics, does not have a political bias. That alone militated for the next British monarch to be nominated Head of the Commonwealth. But throughout those states, many politicians and intellectuals asked: Is it appropriate for white people, with no links to people of colour, to head an organisation, the majority of whose citizens are people of colour?

Meghan Markle's biracialism provided the resounding answer to that question. Suddenly, the British Royal Family could no longer be perceived as being a white institution. Hereafter, it would be a mixed-race entity with a biracial identity. Little did the public realise that it already had triracial blood flowing through its veins gratis its African and Indian ancestors.

Five months after the announcement of Harry and Meghan's engagement, in April 2018, the Queen told the heads of government and state assembled at Windsor Castle, 'It is my sincere wish that the Commonwealth will continue to offer the stability and continuity for future generations, and will decide that one day the Prince of Wales will carry on the important work started by my father in 1949.' Up to then, the alternative had been to have rotating Commonwealth leaders as a Head of the Commonwealth on an alternate basis. The flaws in that system were evident, for, whether many of the leaders would admit it or not, several of them lived in dread of when the position was held by one of their less ethical number – of which there had been many in the years since Independence. Behind the scenes, the opposition that had previously existed to this appointment disappeared when the leaders were made to understand that there was every likelihood that Meghan and Harry would be appointed to positions of some influence within the organisation. 'Rotating Commonwealth leaders were one thing – and a not altogether desirable one at that,' one former senior-ranking member of the Secretariat told me, 'but a British monarch with children and grandchildren of colour was something else again.' It was therefore no surprise in Commonwealth circles when Charles was appointed the Queen's successor as Head of the Commonwealth, and, following her marriage, Meghan was appointed Vice-President of The Queen's Commonwealth Trust. Harry is its President, while the Queen is its Patron.

The period between the couple's engagement and marriage should have been a trouble-free one. Harry and Meghan had effectively silenced their detractors with that inspired announcement at the time their relationship was made public. People seemed genuinely disposed to the couple. They were discreet, clearly very in love, and seemed an ideal match. Initial impressions of her were as favourable. She was undoubtedly stylish, glamorous, and good looking. She seemed refreshingly contemporary. She appeared to be a woman of substance, gravitas, and intellect. Even better, she functioned well in the limelight while managing to seem to possess an enchanting modesty, which suggested that she was a delightful individual in private. In short, the public and private Meghan both seemed appealing. People all over the country also felt that Harry deserved this crack at happiness, after all he had been through. And of course, people of colour were ecstatic to have a British royal replacing an American president in the pantheon of what could now be achieved by them.

I know, from personal experience as well as a lifetime of observation, that the British press like to build people up then enjoy ripping them down with equal delight. Often there is a cynical element to the inflation of people beyond their merits. The bang is all the greater as the reputation pops. This does not mean to say, however, that there are not times when the press are sincere in their delight in elevating someone who they think deserves the approbation they heap upon him or her. Even cynics like having idols. I believe this was the case with Meghan Markle. There is nothing to suggest that the press wasn't anything less than wholeheartedly honest in its desire to acclaim her. Much of the British press is left-wing, right-on, and woke. The more centrist and conservative elements pride themselves on being humane, on possessing traditional values of decency and fair play, and of being above the judgemental pettiness that characterises the more tabloidesque segments. It is worth remembering that the floodgates, which would soon swamp the pretty scene of a wonderful couple blissfully happy in their own company, were not opened by the press, but by Prince Harry himself.

The scene could not have been better set for controversy, though, on the face of it, it looked as if it had been laid for joyousness. The Royal Family broke its rule of not having anyone who is not an actual member of the family, by including Meghan in the festive celebrations over Christmas 2017. No one, not even a dyed-in-the-wool romantic, likes a good romance better than a Fleet Street editor. And what could be better than the Queen bending her own rules to include the first mixed-race bride of a British prince? This conveyed not only romance, but inclusiveness in a way that resonated with everyone, especially with people of colour. Kate and William, Meghan and Harry only needed to attend church, walking the short distance from the big house at Sandringham in a good-looking, stylish, and beautifully photogenic foursome, for the press all over the world to explode with delight. The Fab Four had been born. Dreams do come true, the message was. Nothing could have been more uplifting.

Two days later, Harry took over as guest editor of the Radio 4 Today programme and showed why advisors over the years have recommended that the royals keep their mouths shut, unless they're smiling for the cameras or the public. Asked about Meghan's first Christmas with his family, he said, 'The family loved having her there. We had an amazing time staying with my brother and sister-in-law and running around with the kids. It's like the family she's never had. It was fantastic having her there. '

Across the Atlantic, Meghan's family could hardly believe what they were hearing. Meghan had had a close and loving family while growing up. Were they being expunged from the picture? They responded with fury. Worse, however, was to come. When it became apparent to them that they would not be invited to the wedding, some responded with even greater fury. Samantha Markle waded in with a few choice descriptions of her 'social-climbing' half-sister, while Thomas Markle wrote an open letter to Harry warning him that he was making the biggest mistake of his life. Their pain and humiliation were painful to watch, and while some people took the view that their comments were inappropriate, others empathised with them.

This exclusion of all members of both her mother and her father's families from the guest list, with the exception of her mother and father, damaged Meghan. When her father had to fall out of leading her up the aisle because he was hospitalised in the United States following a heart attack, it exacerbated an already sparse family representation to even more noteworthy levels. So began the only blight on what would otherwise have been a perfect, and perfectly magical, occasion. Their marriage, on the 19th May 2018, in St. George's Chapel, Windsor Castle, was as splendid an affair as all royal marriages are. It was also unique in that it focussed on the bride's black heritage, with a gospel chorus singing the Ben E. King song *Stand By Me* and the sermon being given by the black presiding bishop and primate of the American Episcopal Church, the Most Reverend Michael Curry. Once more, the Royal Family was openly declaring that it not only approved of the bride's racial heritage, but that it was positively embracing it.

The bride herself looked beautiful in her sleek, Givenchy gown while the groom was handsome in his military uniform. 18 million viewers watched it in the UK; 29 million in the US, and hundreds of millions elsewhere all over the world tuned in. Everyone, but everyone, to whom I spoke in the black community, whether it was in the United Kingdom, the West Indies, North or South America, all agreed that the message conveyed was unmistakably affirmative.

Since then, Meghan has gone on to shine with dazzling brightness. She has also produced the first openly-acknowledged mixed race baby.

Speaking as both a British and a Commonwealth citizen, I only hope she fully appreciates the full extent of what she has taken on, of how she embodies the hopes and dreams of hundreds of millions of people all over the world. She has sought the role of humanitarian. It only remains for her to embody it for the remainder of her life as a member of the British Royal Family. Anything less than that will be to shatter the expectations of the hundreds of millions of people she has chosen to represent.